EDITED BY MAROULA JOANNOU & JUNE PURVIS

THE WOMEN'S SUFFRAGE MOVEMENT

NEW FEMINIST PERSPECTIVES

MANCHESTER UNIVERSITY PRESS
Manchester and New York

Published by Manchester University Press
Oxford Road, Manchester M13 9NR, UK
and Room 400, 175 Fifth Avenue, New York, NY 10010, USA
www.manchesteruniversitypress.co.uk

Distributed exclusively in the USA by
Palgrave, 175 Fifth Avenue, New York NY 10010, USA

Distributed exclusively in Canada by
UBC Press, University of British Columbia, 2029 West Mall,
Vancouver, BC, Canada V6T 1Z2

British Library Cataloguing-in-Publication Data
A catalogue record for this book is available from the British Library

Library of Congress Cataloging-in-Publication Data
A catalog record for this book is available from the Library of Congress

ISBN 13: 978 0 7190 8045 6

First published in hardback 1998 by Manchester University Press
This paperback edition first published 2009

Printed by Lightning Source

We are here not because we are law-breakers: we are here in our effort to become law-makers.

Emmeline Pankhurst on trial, October 1908

TO ALL THE STAFF AND USERS
OF THE FAWCETT LIBRARY,
PAST, PRESENT AND FUTURE

Contents

The contributors

Dr Diane Atkinson is a freelance writer and curator. She has written five books on the suffragettes, including a catalogue of the 1992 exhibition at the Museum of London, *Purple, white and green: suffragettes in London, 1906–1914*. Her most recent are *Suffragettes in pictures* and *Funny girls: cartooning for equality*. She has organised an exhibition of feminist cartooning over the past 130 years for The Fawcett Society and, with Viv Gardner, is currently co-editing the autobiography of the actress, suffragette and birth-control campaigner, Kitty Marion.

Dr Katharine Cockin is the Elizabeth Howe Research Fellow at the Open University. She is a freelance writer, and is currently writing entries for the *New Dictionary of National Biography* and has published the biography, *Edith Craig* (1997). Her study of the Pioneer Players, the subject of her Ph.D. thesis obtained from Leicester University, is to be published in 1998.

Dr Krista Cowman is a lecturer in History and Women's Studies at the University of York. Her research concentrates on women and politics in the Victorian and Edwardian period and she is especially interested in uncovering the relationship between political theories relating to women and their organisational practice at the grass roots. She is the author of *'Mrs Brown is a man and a brother!': women in political organisations on Merseyside 1890–1920* (forthcoming, 1998).

David Doughan has been the Reference Librarian at the Fawcett Library at London Guildhall University since 1977. His publications in the field of women's studies include *Lobbying for liberation* (1980) and, with Denise Sanchez, *Feminist periodicals 1855–1984* (1987).

Dr Claire Eustance was the primary organiser of the 'Seeing through suffrage' conference in April 1996 and is the co-editor, with Angela V. John, of *The men's share? Masculinities, male support and women's suffrage in Britain, 1890–1920* (1997). She is currently editing a new collection of essays on women's suffrage histories and is working on a book on the Women's Freedom League.

Dr Hilary Frances teaches in a secondary school. She has recently completed a Ph.D. at the University of York on the lives and work of four Edwardian suffragists who continued to be active feminists concerned with issues of sexual politics in the inter-war years.

Dr Lesley Hall is the Senior Assistant Archivist at the Contemporary Medical Archives Centre at the Wellcome Institute for the History of Medicine in London. She holds a professional Diploma of Archive Administration and a Ph.D. in the history of medicine from the University of London. Her publications include *Hidden anxieties: male sexuality 1900–1950* (1991), and, with Roy Porter, *The facts of life: the creation of sexual knowledge in Britain 1650–1950* (1995), as well as numerous articles and reviews. She is currently working on a biography of Stella Browne and an edited volume of her writings.

Dr Sandra Stanley Holton is a Senior Research Fellow in the Department of History in the University of Adelaide, South Australia. She is the author of *Feminism and democracy: women's suffrage and reform politics in Britain 1908–1918* (1986) and *Suffrage days: stories from the women's suffrage movement* (1996).

Dr Maroula Joannou is Senior Lecturer in English and co-ordinator of the MA in Women's Studies at Anglia Polytechnic University in Cambridge. She holds a Ph.D. in English from Cambridge University and has published extensively on early twentieth-century women's writing, including *'Ladies, please don't smash these windows': women's writing, feminist consciousness and social change 1918–1938* (1995). She is co-editor with David Margolies, of *Heart of the heartless world: essays in cultural resistance in memory of Margot Heinemann* (1995).

Dr Cheryl Law is a Lecturer in Women's Studies at Birkbeck College, University of London, where she directs the Women's Studies Programme at the Centre for Extra-Mural Studies and teaches on Gender Studies and women's rights courses. She has recently published a book, *Suffrage and power: the women's movement, 1918–1928.*

Dr Leah Leneman is based in the Department of Economic and Social History at the University of Edinburgh. She has recently completed a book on divorce in eighteenth and early nineteenth-century Scotland. Since competing her Ph.D. in 1982, published as *Living in Atholl 1685–1785: a social history of the estates* (1986), she has worked as a freelance writer and researcher. Her books include *A guid cause: the women's suffrage movement in Scotland* (1995) and *In the service of life – the story of Elsie Inglis and the Scottish Women's Hospitals* (1995). *Into the foreground – a century of Scottish women in photographs* (1993) was written for the National Museums of Scotland.

Michelle Myall is a Research Assistant at the School of Social and Historical Studies at the University of Portsmouth, and is working on a project on the suffragette movement in Edwardian Britain. She teaches courses in sociology and Women's Studies and is currently researching her Ph.D. thesis on the militant suffragism of Lady Constance Lytton.

Professor June Purvis is Professor of Sociology at the University of Portsmouth. She has published widely on women's education in the nineteenth century and is the founding and managing editor of the journal *Women's History Review*. She is the co-editor with Mary Maynard of *Researching women's lives from a feminist perspective* (1994) and editor of *Women's history in Britain, 1850–1945* (1995). She is currently researching the suffragette movement in Edwardian England and working on a book about Christabel and Emmeline Pankhurst. She is also editor for a *Women's History Series* with UCL Press.

Dr Claire Tylee is a Senior Lecturer in English Literature at Brunel University. She was an AAUW International Fellow at the Harry Ransom Humanities Research Centre at the University of Austin in Texas in 1989–90 where she worked with Professor Jane Marcus and undertook much of the research for her chapter in this book. She is the author of *The Great War and women's consciousness: images of militarism and womanhood in women's writing 1914–1964* (1990) and of various articles on modernism and literature.

Dr Deborah Tyler-Bennett is a poet who has taught English in the School of Cultural Studies at Sheffield Hallam University. She has published a monograph on Edith Sitwell and critical essays on Djuna Barnes, modernist women's writing, the anthologist Elizabeth Sharp and contemporary poetry. Her poems have been published in *Feminist Review, Writing Women, Scarlet Women, Indelible Ink, Golden Section, Working Titles,* and *Sheffield Thursday.*

Acknowledgements

Maroula Joannou would like to thank her colleagues at Anglia Polytechnic University; Rick Allen, David Booy, Nora Crook, John Gilroy, Rebecca Stott and Nigel Wheale for their support during her editing of this book and Jane Marcus who encouraged her to embark upon the project. The plates used in Diane Atkinson's essay appear by kind permission of the Museum of London and those used for the cover, in the introduction, and in Claire Eustance's essay, are reproduced by kind permission of the James Klugmann Picture Library. The line drawings in Deborah Tyler-Bennett's essay are taken from a set of cards with poems composed by Cicely Hamilton, 'Beware! A Warning to Suffragists', illustrated by M. Lowndes, D. Meeson-Coates and C. Hedley Charlton, published by the Artists' Suffrage League in 1908 and held in the Cambridge University Library. Pam Bowyer compiled the index. The editors and contributors are deeply indebted to the Fawcett Library for the use of much important primary material held in its archives.

MAROULA JOANNOU & JUNE PURVIS

Introduction

The writing of the women's suffrage movement

IN 1934 the English novelist Winifred Holtby provided a summary of the achievements of the women's suffrage movement in *Women in a changing civilisation*. Holtby's observations are unusually perceptive and worth quoting in some detail. For her, the long-term significance of women's struggle lay not just in securing its primary objective – the vote itself – but in the part that the struggle had played in shifting the public perceptions of women, and in chang- ing how women were able to perceive themselves. According to Holtby, the women's suffrage movement had enfranchised women 'from more than their lack of citizenship. It had disproved those theories about their own nature that had hitherto constituted an obstacle to women's advancement.' Moreover, mili- tant political action, such as heckling politicians, window smashing raids, setting fire to pillar boxes, planting bombs in empty buildings, and attacking art trea- sures, had broken down hitherto infrangible taboos: 'It was no longer after 1905 possible perpetually to convince an intelligent girl that women cared nothing for impersonal issues, since women had been ready to jeopardise their lives for them.' It was also no longer possible to convince her that 'women were incap- able of political acumen, since their leaders had shown powers of strategy and action unsurpassed in struggles for reform'. Holtby concluded that 'an emotional earthquake had shattered the intangible yet suffocating prison of decorum. The standard of values which rated women's persons, position, interests and pre- occupations as affairs of minor national importance had been challenged.'[1]

The agitation for women's suffrage is usually dated from John Stuart Mill's campaign to be elected to Westminster in 1865, although the subject had been discussed by feminists for some years before that. Mill made the issue of votes for women part of his election address, and, unusually for the time, three pio- neers of the early women's movement, Barbara Bodichon, Emily Davies and Bessie Rayner Parkes, campaigned actively on his behalf.[2] The following year when a Reform Bill was imminent Barbara Bodichon asked Mill if he would present a petition to parliament in favour of women's suffrage. Mill agreed provided she could get a hundred signatures. Together with Emily Davies, Jessie Boucherett, Rosamond Hill and Elizabeth Garrett, Bodichon formed the first women's suffrage committee collecting 1,500 names for the proposed amendment.[3] Although the amendment to the 1867 Reform Act was not carried, women's suffrage committees and groupings were soon formed with some of the activists becoming national figures in the Victorian women's movement. Of particular importance here are Lydia Becker and Millicent Fawcett, constitutional suffragists who advocated legal means of campaigning such as lobbying MPs and presenting petitions to parliament. There were 'divided counsels' within the movement,[4] but supporters kept in touch with each other, and with the general news, through the *Women's Suffrage Journal*, founded and edited by Becker. This was the first periodical devoted exclusively to women's suffrage, but it ceased to exist when Becker died in 1890. Three years earlier Fawcett's ambition of bringing about closer union and co-operation between the various societies had been achieved by the formation of the National Union of Women's Suffrage Societies (NUWSS). And it was over this organisation, reconstituted in 1907, that she became the dominant figure for more than twenty years.[5]

The peaceful campaigning of the constitutional suffragists is often contrasted with the militant tactics of the suffragettes, a term usually applied to members of the Women's Social and Political Union (WSPU), founded by Emmeline Pankhurst and her eldest daugher Christabel in 1903, and the members of the Women's Freedom League (WFL), founded by Charlotte Despard, Teresa Billington-Greig and others, who broke away from the WSPU in 1907 over disagreements about the devolution of power and democratic control of the organisation.[6] In its early years the WSPU engaged in constitutional, educational work. But as the government refused to yield on women's suffrage, the WSPU adopted, especially after 1912, more aggressive forms of militancy. Such 'unladylike' and often spectacular action received widespread newspaper coverage and is still alive in popular memory, while the patient work of the constitutionalists is little remembered.[7]

The effectiveness of militant tactics in securing votes for women has been a subject of controversy among historians, who have sometimes argued that the more extreme forms of militancy were counter-productive.[8] Nevertheless, a partial victory was won in 1918 under the Representation of the People Act, whereby women over the age of 30 were enfranchised provided that they were householders, the wives of householders, occupiers of property with an annual rent of £5 or more, or graduates of British universities. It was not until 1928 that women could vote on equal terms with men – that is, when they had reached the age of 21.

Were it not for the fact that, as Winifred Holtby reminds us, the importance to women of the sixty-year struggle for the vote resonated far beyond its formal significance, the movement for women's suffrage would merely be one of many little-known episodes in the making of modern Britain. But the ways in which women came together to work for the vote, what that vote came to symbolise and the aspirations of women which it came to represent (many of which, albeit in an updated form, mirror the concerns of women today) have ensured that the women's suffrage movement has remained a topic of continuing interest.

It is widely believed that women's history is a new area of study, but this is far from the case: 'There was a burst of historical scholarship about women in the early twentieth century when a first generation of educated women sought to correct an historical record that had left them out.'[9] The tradition of history-writing by women who were both chroniclers of and participants in the women's movement has a long genealogy going back to the work of Millicent Fawcett, Helen Blackburn, Sylvia Pankhurst, Ethel Snowden, Winifred Holtby, Ray Strachey and others.[10] Of particular importance here are Ray Strachey's *The cause* (1928) and Sylvia Pankhurst's *The suffragette movement* (1931). Written from differing political perspectives, which we may broadly classify as liberal-feminist and socialist-feminist, these seminal works helped to establish the dominant narratives about the women's suffrage movement within which subsequent accounts were often placed.[11]

The feminist historian Ray Strachey had been a member of the NUWSS and an admirer of Fawcett's liberal-feminist approach to women's suffrage. Like Fawcett, she believed that the vote could be won by reason and persuasion. The constitutional wing, she pointed out, 'did not regard their work as an attack upon men, but rather as a reform for the good of all, and the next step in human progress.'[12] Thus, as Kathryn Dodd demonstrates, Strachey uses the political vocabulary of liberalism to position the NUWSS and its leaders as the 'rational' wing of the women's movement, which was responsible for the partial enfranchisement of women in 1918 and their full enfranchisement in 1928. Members of the WSPU, on the other hand, are cast out of 'the making of women's history, because of their reckless activity, their passion for change, their angry propaganda and their autocratic organisation.'[13] The oppositions that Strachey employs to contrast and compare the NUWSS and the WSPU – constitutional/militant, civilised/uncivilised, democratic/autocratic and rational/irrational – helped to establish a framework within which male, liberal historians such as George Dangerfield, Roger Fulford and David Mitchell were later able to construct their influential accounts of the women's suffrage movement.[14] And it was the WSPU that attracted the attention of these historians rather than the NUWSS or any of the other neglected suffragette/ist groupings such as the WFL.

Sylvia Pankhurst, a socialist-feminist to whom social-class inequalities and capitalist exploitation were of paramount importance, frequently disagreed with the woman-centred politics of the two key leaders of the WSPU – her mother Emmeline Pankhurst, and her elder sister Christabel, who both believed that women's interests transcended questions of social class. Furthermore, Sylvia found it painful to observe the close tie between her mother and Christabel, the favoured child, 'the apple of her eye' and deeply resented the influence Christabel had upon her mother.[15] Both her deep socialist political convictions and the critical recollections of her family permeate the account of events which Sylvia offers in *The suffragette movement*. After the Cockermouth by-election in 1906, when Christabel, fearing that heavy reliance on working-class women was a barrier to middle-class women joining its ranks, announced that the WSPU would henceforth oppose all candidates from the Independent Labour Party, which they had previously supported, as well as those candidates representing other political groupings, Sylvia spoke angrily of her sister's 'incipient Toryism'.[16]

The socialist-feminist world-view so powerfully elucidated by Sylvia Pankhurst became the dominant feminist voice in the 'new' women's history-writing that developed in the late 1960s and 1970s.[17] A concern with issues of class led many socialist-feminists to decry the women's suffrage movement as middle class and exclusive. In the changing intellectual context of recent times, in which feminist ideas have come under heavy attack inside and outside the academic world, the old divisions between socialist- and radical-feminists have come to appear irrelevant. But this has not always been the case. Feminist historians in the 1960s and 1970s routinely had to contend with criticism from socialists to the effect that the suffrage movement was a middle-class movement, in which working-class women were absent or had at best had been co-opted and manipulated (like the WSPU's Annie Kenney), but often at the price of severing their lived connections to their roots. Indeed, it was the identification of the cause of women's suffrage with middle-class women, and London-based leaders, especially the suffragettes, that motivated Jill Liddington and Jill Norris to research the 'hidden contribution of working-class Lancashire women to radical politics'.[18]

The process of reappraisal and the rewriting of the history of the suffrage agitation – to which this book is a contribution – got strongly under way in the 1960s and 1970s with Constance Rover's pioneering work.[19] The research of a new generation of feminist scholars, some of which is brought together in this volume, is diverse and reflects a wide range of interests and approaches. But it is frequently characterised by an interest in communities of women, the reclaiming of feminist ideas, a reassessment of the dominant representation of feminist figures, a search for forgotten and neglected women, and the desire to position the women's suffrage movement within the broader context of women's struggles to achieve justice and freedom. It also often ventures beyond this because of the imperative to engage with other categories of analysis, including gender, sexual orientation, religious affiliation, class, race and nationality. As Linda Gordon has put it, the 'documentation and denunciation of women's suppression' which once appeared to be sufficient seems now 'virtually pointless to many historians and readers unless it is integrated with discussions of the resistance, compromises, and ambiguities with which women actually negotiated relations between the sexes. Above all, much of the new women's history contains challenges to determinism.'[20]

The work of feminist historians in this book reflects more general trends within recent feminist history-writing. Some chapters provide important new insights into neglected episodes within suffragette/ist history which enable us to arrive at a more complete picture of the campaign as a whole. Hilary Frances's analysis of the Women's Tax Resistance League, for example, is a study of a remarkable organisation about which very little has been known. Cheryl Law provides new perspectives on the extension of the campaign by women's groups throughout the 1920s, challenging the popular misconception that the struggle effectively ended with the enfranchisement of women over the age of 30 in 1918. Other contributors, Krista Cowman on the United Suffragists and Claire Tylee on male playwrights, shift the focus of attention from exclusively female organisations to the working relationships between men and women that developed during the course of the suffrage campaigns. Four chapters, those by Katharine Cockin, Deborah Tyler-Bennett, Maroula Joannou and Claire Tylee, are concerned with an area that has become increasingly popular among researchers and students; cultural representations. As literary researchers engaged primarily in textual analysis, these four authors sometimes use different methodological approaches which complement that of the in-depth archival work in which most historians have been trained.

Although only two chapters, June Purvis's on Christabel Pankhurst, and Michelle Myall's on Mary Leigh, are primarily concerned with figures in the WSPU this book has a cohesiveness which comes from its overall focus on a span of time that is broadly coterminous with militancy in the first and second decades of the twentieth century, an exception being Sandra Stanley Holton's chapter on the Women's Franchise League. Reassessment of the internal dynamics and the significance of the WSPU has constituted one important strand within the wider feminist project of reappraisal of the last twenty years.

But much interest has focused on what happened away from the metropolis. There are now excellent national, regional and local studies of the suffrage campaigns, including Leah Leneman on Scotland, Rosemary Owens and Cliona Murphy on Ireland, and Kay Cook and Neil Evans on Wales.[21] In this book Leah Leneman argues that a very different account of the movement emerges if the historian moves away from Westminster and the headquarters of the suffrage organisations. Studies of the movement in England concentrating on specific geographical areas, including Claire Eustance's work on the WFL, have usefully illuminated the priorities and perspective of the rank and file away from the centres of power.

Moreover, the suffrage movement had international as well as national dimensions in which the suffragettes/ists took great pride. The Coronation Procession of 1911 contained sizeable contingents of women not only from Ireland, Scotland and Wales, but also from North America, Australia, New Zealand and other parts of the British Empire. There were particularly close connections between English suffragists and their Australian and North American counterparts whose countries had already granted women the vote. Dora Montefiore, a suffragette who had lived for many years in Australia, and who was a member of the WSPU committee, spoke on suffrage platforms in France, Italy, Germany, Holland, Austria, Hungary, Denmark, Sweden, Finland, the Cape, the Transvaal and the United States.

Feminist scholarship of recent years has challenged many of the old assumptions about the women's suffrage movement. The WSPU was never a monolith and often appears to have been hierarchical at its higher but not its lower echelons. Sandra Stanley Holton's work has drawn attention to the fact that many suffragists belonged simultaneously to the militant and constitutionalist sections of the movement. Moreover, Holton has analysed the 'democratic suffragist' tendency that cut across different suffragette/ist groupings and argues not only that the categories of militant and constitutional are unstable, but also that the interpretive frameworks which read the movement in terms of two diametrically opposed sections are of dubious value.[22] As Ann Morley and Liz Stanley put it, 'at the level of individual feminist women and their political actions and allegiances, the organisational divisions and sharp ideological diferences that most accounts of Ewardian feminism have seized upon are, at best, only a small part of the total picture.'[23] The actress Edith Craig, for example, reflected that 'one cannot belong to too many suffrage societies'.[24] But, as Krista Cowman points out in this book, attempts by historians to reclaim the organisational links between suffragists at grass-roots level can lose sight of important differences in policy and tactics between the various suffrage organisations. On a local basis such differences were frequently disregarded and working relationships often were cordial. This is illustrated in Cicely Hamilton and Christopher St John's play *How the vote was won*, in which a provident dressmaker, Madame Christine, divides her assets scrupulously between the NUWSS, the WSPU and the WFL.

Recent feminist research has investigated friendship networks between women and unearthed the strong links that were forged during the campaigns between supporters of various organisations including the WFL, radical elements within the WSPU, and in the Women's International League for Peace and Freedom. In this book Michelle Myall's chapter on the militant suffragette Mary Leigh shows how her actions were often affirmations of friendship. Many of the rank-and-file suffragettes/ists subscribed to what we might now describe as 'alternative' lifestyles and were committed to radical causes including animal rights, children's rights, and vegetarianism.

Socialist currents ran deeply through the twentieth-century suffrage movement. Virtually all the women arrested at the demonstration outside the House of Commons in 1906 – Anne Cobden Sanderson, Emmeline Pethick-Lawrence, Dora Montefiore, Mary Gawthorpe, Irene Fenwick Miller, Minnie Baldock, Teresa Billington-Greig and Annie Kenney – had connections with the labour movement. Although Emmeline and Christabel Pankhurst expediently chose to sever their earlier links with organised labour, other women prominent in the struggle refused to do so. Emmeline Pethick-Lawrence, the WSPU treasurer, had a strong commitment to social democratic ideals. Internationalism inspired Sylvia Pankhurst and many of the working-class supporters of her East London Federation of Suffragettes. Both the WFL, under the leadership of the redoubtable Charlotte Despard, and the NUWSS contained sizeable numbers of socialists and inclined to the left of the British political spectrum. Despard publicly appealed to the Labour Party for support in 1912: 'My years of work on behalf of the ideals of your Party make me earnestly hope that the claim of my sisters, for whom I speak, is at last, through you, to be fulfilled.'[25] In 1912 the NUWSS abandoned its political neutrality and urged its members to vote Labour after a change in policy at the Labour Party conference that year made it the only political party committed to votes for women on the same basis as men.

Middle and late twentieth-century feminist arguments for minimising the significance of votes for women had nineteenth- and early twentieth-century antecedents. Some Victorian and Edwardian radicals argued that the vote would make little difference to women, whose time would be better spent in demanding more far-reaching changes in sexual, familial and domestic relationships between men and women, and in questioning, rather than seeking to work within, patriarchal institutions such as parliament.

In 1911 a disenchanted Teresa Billington-Greig had demanded freedom from 'all shackles of law and custom, from all chains of sentiment and superstition' and decried those who 'fail to see that large areas in which emancipation is needed lie entirely outside the scope of the vote'.[26] Such attitudes often explain the absence of well-known sexual radicals from the suffrage campaigns. Unhappy marriages, punitive divorce laws, the requirements of heterosexual conformity, the double standard which demanded chastity of women but not of men, women's lack of control over childbirth, domestic violence, economic dependency and intellectual infantilisation were reasons why some women were debarred from activism, but why others were converted in the first place. As the heated reception of Christabel Pankhurst's polemic against veneral disease, *The great scourge and how to end it* (1913), illustrates, sexual morality aroused strong passions within suffragette/ist ranks. But Lesley Hall's chapter in this book argues that the division of suffragists into supporters of social purity and sex reform is unhelpful: In looking at the suffragists' considerations of sexual problems, it can be misleading to think in terms of two beleaguered opposing camps, rather than voices opposing contemporary conventional assumptions about sex and gender from a variety of individual and collective positions.'[27]

The interest in social class on the part of many socialist-feminists during the second wave of feminism of the late 1960s onwards was also linked to a dislike of the hierarchical and violent behaviour that was seen to characterise the WSPU but which was considered to be inimical to the women's liberation movement of the 1960s and 1970s, which had a very different ethos. Suspicion of the WSPU was frequently accompanied by a distrust of attempts to read women's history predominantly in terms of changing legislative landmarks and achievements in the public domain. Research into the history of women's social, familial and domestic relationships, about which far too little was known, often appeared a more fruitful line of enquiry. What later hardened into an orthodoxy in some quarters was epitomised in Marion Ramelson's *The petticoat revolution*, which began with a desire to find out what the Pankhursts actually did in order to answer the charge that 'the Pankhursts did a great deal of damage'.[28]

But the revolutionary dimension of the women's suffrage movement, which is often overlooked, is not a retrospective imposition but something of which many women were conscious at the time. This is not, of course, to ignore or to deny the racist and/or eugenicist sentiments that are sometimes to be found in suffragette propaganda – the well-known figure of the proud woman graduate in her university cap and gown juxtaposed to the semi-clad, cringing and stunted figure of 'the male lunatic', which illustrates the suffragettes' claim that particular groups of women were superior to particular groups of men, is one component of a legacy that feminists today will wish to disclaim. Moreover, although radical ideas circulated within the movement, their adoption was partial and selective. Some middle- and upper-class women with Conservative political affiliations who supported the suffragettes had a strong vested interest in opposing other forms of social change. But in a context where inequality was taken for granted as ordained by nature and/or God, the revolutionary implications of the movement that proclaimed women to be at least the equals of men was not lost to many other women at the time. Sylvia Pankhurst referred to a 'movement for liberation' and a 'movement in haste to mend conditions'.[29] Rebecca West suggested that Emmeline Pankhurst, who made pointed analogies between the rebels in the WSPU and those rebelling against British rule in Ireland and parts of the Empire, was the 'last popular leader to act on inspiration derived from the principles of the French Revolution'.[30]

One welcome aspect of the resurgence of interest in women's struggle for the vote is that the enthusiastic reclaiming of this history has not been confined to academics in institutions of higher education. On the contrary, there has been a burgeoning of national and local initiatives, organised both by individuals and by groups, which have been indicative of a strong impulse to challenge history-writing/making as the preserve of the professional historian and to make women's history accessible to all. Among these initiatives have been several interesting oral history and community-based projects, organised 'suffragette walks' through London, the tape-recording of the memoirs of the suffragettes and their descendants, the production of educational study-packs devised for use in primary and secondary schools, and well-received displays of photography and memorabilia at several national museums and art-galleries, including two outstanding exhibitions at the National Portrait Gallery and the Museum of London. The six-part BBC television series, *Shoulder to shoulder* was broadcast to popular acclaim in the early 1970s and was repeated twenty years later, and the restoration of the Pankhurst's home at 62 Nelson Street in Manchester, in the form of a national memorial to the achievement of the suffragettes, has been funded in part by public subscription.

A number of important suffragette/ist novels and autobiographies, such as Hannah Mitchell's *The hard way up* and Elizabeth Robins's *The convert*, have also been reissued by feminist publishing houses.[31] The establishment of the Women's History Network in 1991 has provided an important forum in which women historians could come together and discuss women's suffrage among other issues. In April 1996 a highly successful conference, 'Seeing through suffrage' was organised at Greenwich University by Claire Eustance and others and attracted an attendance of more than 150 people. This conference was a major landmark in the development of research into the women's suffrage movement and by the time it took place the revival of interest in its history was generally acknowledged to have 'come of age'.

The women's pilgrimage, 1913

The women's suffrage movement embodies a deliberate and self-conscious attempt to break the traditional patriarchal mould of British politics, and to discover new, radical and often collective methods of working, which seemed particularly suited to the skills and interests of women The imaginative methods used by the suffragettes to draw public attention to their cause were unrivalled – at least until the advent of the peace movement half a century later – and the impact that these created on the public imagination did much to secure the movement a unique place within British political traditions.

Examples of suffragette/ist creativity, innovation and inventiveness are manifold and may be cited at random. They include the many colourful pageants, processions and demonstrations in which the decorative banners, which will be familiar to readers of Lisa Tickner's superb study of suffragette imagery,[32] were not merely functional but objects of aesthetic interest in their own right. The establishment of a network of suffrage shops and merchandise designed for sale to the public is discussed by Diane Atkinson in chapter 6 of this book. Hundreds of women from all corners of the country converged on London in the 'pilgrimage' organised by the NUWSS in 1913. Others participated in the imaginative overnight occupation of deserted houses on census night in 1911. More examples of suffragette/ist enterprise are the flights over the House of Commons in hot-air balloons undertaken by intrepid members of the WFL (immortalised in the film *Kind hearts and coronets*), the rousing plays written by supporters of the Women Writers' Suffrage League and performed by the Actresses' Franchise League, and the various acts of non-violent civil disobedience employed by the Tax Resistance League, which is discussed by Hilary Frances in chapter 4.

One area where women's creativity was particularly marked was the arts which provided ample opportunities for amateur and professional supporters of the women's cause to put their talents to work in art, music, theatre, prose and poetry. Some of the most stimulating scholarship about the women's suffrage movement in recent years has been in relation to culture, and this is especially true of drama. Poetry has received next to no scholarly attention, a gap that is made good by the inclusion of Deborah Tyler-Bennett's chapter in this collection. Tyler-Bennett analyses the impact of the struggle for the vote on women poets, using the work of Eva Gore-Booth and Sylvia Pankhurst to argue that the 'suffrage poetry' of the twentieth century had its antecedents in the poetry of Victorian writers, such as Isa Craig (Knox), Bessie Rayner Parkes and Adelaide Anne Procter, and that it should be seen to extend the existing debates about women's freedom as opposed to creating new ones.

Fiction and poetry which had hitherto been accessible only to users of the Fawcett Library and other specialised collections has now been made widely available for the first time through the publication of Glenda Norquay's literary anthology, *Votes and voices*.[33] Maroula Joannou's chapter in this book surveys the salient features of suffragette/ist fiction, analysing its relationship to its moment of production, its focus on social class, the double standard of sexual morality, and other recurrent preoccupations. If much of the poetry of World War One, which was to come shortly after the literature of the women's suffrage movement, had an immediacy that was borne out of the conditions that gave birth to it – but which in the eyes of some critics disqualified it from being 'great art' – so the cultural production of the women's suffrage movement had an urgency and insistence that bears witness to the troubled times in which it was conceived, which were not conducive to the recollection of emotion in tranquility.

Suffragette art speaks not of the transcendence of art over politics, which was characteristic of some strains within the modernist movement, nor of the rejection of mass culture, another pronounced modernist tendency, but of the reaffirmation of the traditional interrelatedness of art and society, and of the social function and purpose of art. As Sylvia Pankhurst, a talented painter, sculptor and designer, observed, 'the creation of a Michael Angelo [sic] would have ranked low in the eyes of the WSPU members beside a term served in Holloway'.[34] Political activism constituted a diversion from their work for many gifted women artists: the composer Ethel Smyth interrupted her music to dedicate two years of her life to the struggle, and the illustrator of children's books, Marion Dunlop Wallace, was the first woman in prison to go on hunger strike. But it also often informed, enriched and inspired that work. The notion that the art, writing or music of the suffrage era was disfigured by its feminist politics must depend in part on a formalist valorisation of style over content and in part on the abstraction of art from the history of the social relations in which it participates.

Two strands run through otherwise disparate cultural initiatives. The first is the breakdown of the usual divisions between popular and high art in music, art, fiction, poetry and drama. Suffragist plays were performed both on the prestigious West End stage and across the country in small, amateur venues; Holloway jingles took their place in suffragette literature alongside poetry with more lofty aspirations. The second is the conviction, widely shared at the time, that artists and intellectuals had a key role to play in bringing about cultural change, and that cultural change in itself was in the long term no less significant than political change in helping to reshape the possibilities of what might be understood by being fully human. Apart from the galaxy of women writers who are discussed by Deborah Tyler-Bennett, Maroula Joannou and Katharine Cockin in this book, the intellectual luminaries who lent their name to the suffragette/ist cause included Thomas Hardy, George Meredith, George Bernard Shaw and John Galsworthy. They were all writers whose work intimates a strong awareness of the sexual and social predicaments of women – Tess, Diana, Vivie and Irene in *Tess of the D'Urbervilles* (1891), *Diana of the crossways* (1885), *Mrs Warren's profession* (1898) and *The Forsyte saga* (1922) – and whose support for 'the cause' was linked to the hope that votes for women might redress the imbalance of power between the sexes.

The special relationship between Edwardian actresses, whose very struggles to establish their presence on the stage constituted a challenge to Victorian ideas about feminine decorum, and the women's suffrage movement has long been recognised. In 1908 Israel Zangwill observed in *Votes for Women* that 'in real life a suffragist will not always make an Actress; but it is a cheering fact that an actress is nearly always a suffragist.'[35] A number of feminist studies have helped to chart the map of early twentieth-century suffrage and theatre including Julie Holledge's *Innocent flowers* and Sheila Stowell's *A stage of their own*. Carole Hayman and Dale Spender's *How the vote was won and other suffragette plays* and *Sketches from the Actresses' Franchise League*, edited by Viv Gardiner, have made drama accessible to a new generation of readers and there are now several good biographies of actresses in the suffrage movement including Lis Whitelaw's study of Cicely Hamilton and Angela John's life of Elizabeth Robins.[36]

In chapter 9 Katharine Cockin addresses questions about the relationship between individual genius and collaborative work in drama, avoiding those works which she argues have now achieved canonical status to concentrate on forgotten plays associated with the Actresses' Franchise League. John Austin's *How one woman did it* introduces the notion of cross-dressing to question the idea of gender stability, and two other texts – Margaret Wynne Nevinson's *In the workhouse* and Edith Lyttleton's *The thumbscrew* are concerned with issues of class, the representation of women as workers, and the economic foundation of women's oppression. In chapter 10 Claire Tylee foregrounds the importance of men in the struggle, and the role played by such stalwart supporters of women suffrage as Harley Granville Barker, George Bernard Shaw and Henry Woodd Nevinson, who were intent on renegotiating ideas about masculinity, as well as lending their support to women in the theatre. She also draws attention to the rank-and-file members of the Men's League for Women's Suffrage, some of whom faced imprisonment for acts of civil disobedience.

The picture of the women's suffrage movement that emerges from this book is one of great richness, complexity and diversity. It is hardly recognisable as the picture with which historians were familiar twenty years ago, and must call into question the familiar accounts of suffragette/ist activity to be found in many well-known mainstream histories. But although the work of feminist historians has told us much about how gendered identity was lived in specific times and places, much more work remains to be done. The final chapter in this book is contributed by David Doughan, the Reference Librarian of the Fawcett Library, the national research archive for women's history, who provides a check-list of resources which we hope will be of use to those readers of this book who wish to pursue their interest in suffrage beyond it.

NOTES

1 Winifred Holtby, *Women and a changing civilization* (London, John Lane, 1934), pp. 52–3.

2 See Jane Lewis (ed.), *Before the vote was won: arguments for and against women's suffrage 1864–1896* (London, Routledge and Kegan Paul, 1987), p. 1.

3 Ray Strachey, *The cause: a short history of the women's movement in Great Britain* (London, G. Bell and Sons, 1928), p. 105.

4 Helen Blackburn, *Women's suffrage: a record of the women's suffrage movement in the British Isles with biographical sketches of Miss Becker* (London, Williams and Norgate, 1902), p. 181.

5 David Rubinstein, *A different world for women: the life of Millicent Garrett Fawcett* (Hemel Hempstead, Harvester/Wheatsheaf, 1991), pp. 136–7.

6 We shall follow the usual convention of referring to the non-militants as suffragists and the militants as suffragettes, although, as Sandra Stanley Holton has pointed out in *Feminism and democracy: women's suffrage and reform politics in Britain 1900–1918* (Cambridge, Cambridge University Press, 1986), p. 4, the constitutional/militant distinction is not straightforward.

7 For an excellent account of women's suffrage activity in the nineteenth century see Sandra Stanley Holton, *Suffrage days: stories from the women's suffrage movement* (London, Routledge, 1996).

8 See Arthur Marwick, *Women at war 1914–1918* (London, Fontana, 1977), p. 25; Andrew Rosen, *Rise up women! The militant campaign of the women's Social and Political Union 1903–1914* (London, Routledge and Kegan Paul, 1974), p. 243; Robert Ensor, *England 1870–1914* (Oxford, Oxford University Press, 1936), p. 388, David Morgan: *Suffragists and Liberals: the politics of women's suffrage in Britain* (Oxford, Blackwell, 1975), p. 160; Brian Harrison, *Separate spheres: the opposition to women's suffrage* (London, Croom Helm, 1978), p. 196.

9 Linda Gordon, 'What is women's history?', in Juliet Gardner (ed.), *What is history today?* (Basingstoke, Macmillan, 1988), pp. 91–3.

10 Millicent Garrett Fawcett, *Women's suffrage: a short history of a great movement* (London: T. C. and E. C. Jack, 1912); Helen Blackburn, *Women's suffrage*; E. Sylvia Pankhurst, *The suffragette movement: an intimate account of persons and ideals* (London, Longman, 1931); E. Sylvia Pankhurst, *The history of the women's suffrage movement 1905–1910* (London, Gay and Hancock, 1911); Ethel Snowden, *The feminist movement* (London and Glasgow, Collins, 1913).

11 See June Purvis, 'A pair ... of infernal queens'? A reassessment of the dominant representations of Emmeline and Christabel Pankhurst, first wave feminists in Edwardian Britain', *Women's History Review*, 5, 2, 1996, pp. 259–80.

12 Strachey, *The cause*, p. 307.

13 Katharine Dodd, 'Cultural politics and women's historical writing: the case of Ray Strachey's *The cause*', *Women's Studies International Forum*, 13, 1/2, 1990, pp. 127–39: 134. See also Laura Mayhall, 'Creating the "suffragette spirit": British feminism and the historical imagination', *Women's History Review*, 4, 3, 1995, pp. 319–44.

14 George Dangerfield, *The strange death of Liberal England* (London, Paladin, 1970); Roger Fulford, *Votes for women* (London, Faber and Faber, 1957), David Mitchell, *The fighting Pankhursts: a study in tenacity* (London, Jonathan Cape, 1967).

15 Pankhurst, *The suffragette movement*, p. 267.

16 *Ibid.*, p. 211.

17 See June Purvis, 'From "women worthies" to poststructuralism? Debate and controversy in women's history in Britain', in June Purvis (ed.), *Women's history, Britain 1850–1945* (London, UCL Press, 1995), pp. 1–22.

18 Jill Liddington and Jill Norris, *One hand tied behind us: the rise of the women's suffrage movement* (London, Virago, 1978).

19 Constance Rover, *Women's suffrage and party politics in Britain, 1866–1914* (London, Routledge and Kegan Paul, 1967).

20 Gordon, 'What is women's history?', p. 86.
21 Leah Leneman, *A guid cause: the women's suffrage movement in Scotland* (Aberdeen, Aberdeen University Press, 1984); Rosemary Cullen Owens, *Smashing times: a history of the Irish women's suffrage movement 1889–1922* (Dublin, Attic Press, 1984); Cliona Murphy, *The women's suffrage movement and Irish society in the early twentieth-century* (Hemel Hempstead, Harvester/Wheatsheaf, 1989); Kay Cook and Neil Evans, '"The petty antics of the bell-ringing boisterous band": the women's suffrage movement in Wales 1890–1918', in Angela John (ed.), *Our mothers' land: chapters in Welsh women's history 1830–1939* (Cardiff, University of Wales Press, 1991), pp. 159–89.
22 Holton, *Feminism and democracy,* p. 4.
23 Ann Morley with Liz Stanley, *The life and death of Emily Wilding Davison: a biographical detective story* (London, Women's Press, 1988), p. 183.
24 Quoted by Katherine Cockin in chapter 9 of this book, p. 139.
25 *The Vote,* 12 February1910, p. 185.
26 Teresa Billington-Greig, *The militant suffragette movement – emancipation in a hurry* (London, F. Palmer, 1911), pp. 2 and 173.
27 See chapter 13 of this book, p. 190.
28 Marion Ramelson, *The petticoat rebellion: a century of struggle for women's rights* (London, Lawrence and Wishart, 1967), p. 11.
29 Pankhurst, *The suffragette movement,* p. 226.
30 Quoted in Brian Harrison, *Peaceable kingdom: stability and change in modern Britain* (Oxford, Clarenden Press, 1982), p. 37.
31 Hannah Mitchell, *The hard way up: the autobiography of Hannah Mitchell: suffragette and rebel,* ed. Geoffrey Mitchell (London, Faber and Faber, 1968; Virago reprint, 1977); Elizabeth Robins, *The convert* (London, Virago reprint, 1980).
32 Lisa Tickner, *The spectacle of women: imagery of the suffrage campaign 1907–1914* (London, Chatto and Windus, 1987).
33 Glenda Norquay, *Voices and votes: a literary anthology of the women's suffrage campaign* (Manchester, Manchester University Press, 1995).
34 Pankhurst, *The suffragette movement,* p. 284.
35 *Votes for Women,* 5 December 1913, p. 142.
36 Julie Holledge, *Innocent flowers: women in the Edwardian theatre* (London, Virago, 1981); Sheila Stowell, *A stage of their own: feminist playwrights of the suffrage era* (Manchester, Manchester University Press, 1992); Carole Hayman and Dale Spender (eds), *How the vote was won and other suffrage plays* (London, Methuen, 1985); Viv Gardiner (ed.), *Sketches from the Actresses' Franchise League* (Nottingham, Nottingham Play Texts, 1985); Lis Whitelaw, *The life and rebellious times of Cicely Hamilton* (London, Women's Press, 1990); Angela John, *Elizabeth Robins: staging a life* (London, Routledge, 1995).

1

Now you see it, now you don't: the Women's Franchise League and its place in contending narratives of the women's suffrage movement

THE Women's Franchise League was active for almost a decade from its for- mation in 1889. It attracted the support of figures like Elizabeth Wolsten- holme Elmy, Emmeline and Richard Pankhurst, Ursula and Jacob Bright, as well as Elizabeth Cady Stanton, one of the pioneers of the women's rights movement in the United States, together with her daughter Harriot Stanton Blatch. It also made a number of assertive and effective interventions in the British campaigns for the vote during its relatively short life. Yet its appearances in the history of the suffrage movement have been surprisingly erratic and various. It is quite absent, for example, in those accounts that represent the early 'official' suffrag- ist chronicles – those by Helen Blackburn, Bertha Mason, Millicent Fawcett. These tell a story of the winning of the vote as the slow, steady march of progress through respectable and conventional pressure group politics.[1] They form a nar- rative that emphasises unanimity and continuity at the expense of acknowledg- ing fully the episodes of conflict and rupture that also marked the history of the movement from its earliest days.

Sylvia Pankhurst's towering *The suffragette movement*, published in 1931, provides an alternative narrative, and like the 'official' histories was shaped by the internal politics of the suffrage movement itself. Her story plays down the achievements of the nineteenth-century movement, and celebrates the emer- gence of a new 'militant' temper among suffragists in the early years of the twentieth century. The spectacular and shocking phenomenon of suffrage mili- tancy, not patient, dogged political pressure, is credited with securing the parlia- mentary franchise for women. Sylvia Pankhurst's 'alternative' interpretation, in contrast to the 'official' histories, renders the formation of the Women's Fran- chise League an event of great significance during the nineteenth-century cam- paigns.[2] She describes its beginnings chiefly as the achievement of her father and mother, Richard and Emmeline Pankhurst. It appears as the precursor of the Women's Social and Political Union (WSPU, formed by her mother in 1903), and hence of twentieth-century militancy.[3] Such an originating role is suggested also in the autobiography of Harriot Stanton Blatch, for a few years a close colleague of Emmeline Pankhurst within the Women's Franchise League, and one of those credited with taking militancy back to the United States when she returned there to live in the early 1900s.[4]

A third narrative emerged in the 1930s in George Dangerfield's *The strange death of liberal England*. This was one which, in the main, followed Sylvia Pankhurst in seeing militancy as an abrupt and sudden eruption into the staid, liberal politics of women's rights. But it gave her story a new twist, rejecting her account of suffrage militancy as the creation of heroic individuals intent on changing the course of history.[5] Instead, suffrage militancy is analysed in terms of social and individual pathology. It becomes the symptom of the breakdown of an old political order, and of some women's retreat into a lesbian world free of men, in the decade or so before the First World War.[6] There is no appreciation of the value to women of female community and solidarity. Equally, there is little place for consideration of the nineteenth-century suffrage movement as itself a site of contest, or as offering a radical challenge to the existing sexual order and an autonomous political dynamic. So, once again, the Women's Franchise League disappears from view.

Most recent interpretation of the suffrage movement might be termed 'revisionist' narrative. This, to a degree, extends the 'official' narrative in offering a fresh account of the suffrage movement in which the central role of the Pankhursts is displaced or modified. Instead, this story explores a range of various and previously neglected aspects of the twentieth-century movement: the role of working-class women, the work of the constitutional wing of the movement organised by the National Union of Women's Suffrage Societies, the relationship between the suffrage and labour and socialist movements, the sexual politics of suffragism, and the cultural work of artists in providing alternative representations of women created during the campaign for the vote.[7] Though it appears to escape the thrall of the Pankhurst family, this revisionist history accepts, albeit it implicitly, an understanding of the twentieth-century suffrage movement as something quite new and of itself.[8]

David Rubinstein has recently put forward a significant challenge to this tendency to view the suffrage movement as composed of two distinct periods. In his history of the women's movement in Britain in the 1890s, he presents a picture of a varied, lively, vigorous decade for women's politics, not a time of fragmentation and dormancy when the enfeebled nineteenth-century movement came to an end, and women awaited some new impetus to political action. Indeed, he identifies a range of continuities between the nineteenth- and twentieth-century movements. Significantly, he is also the first among the current generation of historians to have explored to any degree the history of the Women's Franchise League, though he does not accord it the importance suggested by both Sylvia Pankhurst and Harriot Stanton Blatch.[9] *Before the suffragettes* offers, then, a significant refinement of the revisionist narrative, one which not only looks beyond the role of the Pankhurst family, but which recognises the variety and complexity contained within the suffrage movement, and acknowledges more fully than ever before some of the continuities between the nineteenth- and twentieth-century stages of the campaigns.[10]

The more extensive exploration of the history of the Women's Franchise League undertaken here is offered as a further refining of the revisionist narrative.[11] It questions both some of the absences and silences in the 'official' histories, as well as the adequacy and accuracy of Sylvia Pankhurst's account of alternative, dissident currents within the suffrage movement. It pushes even further back than the 1890s in its search for continuities, and locates the origins of the Women's Franchise League in a Radical–Liberal current that continually contended with more moderate approaches for the leadership of the suffrage movement in the nineteenth century. It argues that some of the political legacies that shaped twentieth-century suffrage militancy are to be found, variously, in the abolitionist movement, and in the middle-class Radicalism of the 1860s–90s.

The divisions that occasioned the formation of the Women's Franchise League in 1889 reached right back to the beginnings of an organised, national movement for women's suffrage in the latter half of the 1860s. The first suffrage committees were formed when John Stuart Mill agreed to present a petition on this issue to the House of Commons in 1865, and immediately the question arose: how to formulate the demand for votes for women? Some feared a claim in terms of sexual equality would appear too radical, and preferred to make it only on behalf of those women who held enough property to satisfy the existing qualifications for men. Such women might assert their 'independence', a concept on which long-standing radical claims to the franchise were generally founded. But this way of conceiving the citizenship claims of women raised the issue of whether wives ought to be expressly excluded from the demand. The civil status of a married woman was that of 'femme covert', that is to say her legal personality was subsumed under that of her husband. This doctrine of coverture also meant that married women were generally unable to own real property, the main qualification for the franchise. So in both these ways, married women might be defined as dependent persons with no rightful claim to the vote.[12]

John Stuart Mill advised formulating the demand simply in terms of the principle of sexual equality, and this strategy was gradually accepted as a compromise between those who wished expressly to exclude married women, and those who opposed such exclusion as compounding the wrongs of married women. Given the doctrine of coverture, few, if any, married women would, in practice, have qualified if the vote were extended to females on equal terms with males. But such a formulation at least offered no reinforcement of the disabilities of wives. Mill's stature, and the growing dominance of Radical–Liberals within the suffrage societies, ensured that this compromise held for some years. The first women's suffrage bill was drafted on equal-rights lines by a Manchester lawyer and Radical, Richard Pankhurst, and introduced in the House of Commons by another Manchester Radical–Liberal, Jacob Bright, in 1870.[13]

Manchester became the centre of a circle of Radical–Liberal suffragists that included Elizabeth Wolstenholme Elmy, Ursula Bright, wife of Jacob Bright, and Josephine Butler, then living in Liverpool. Beyond the north-west they found further support in Radical parliamentary circles in the metropolis, especially around Clementia and P. A. Taylor, MP. Their London home provided the social centre for the growing number of Radical–Liberal Members of Parliament who gained election in the 1860s. The women of the Bright kinship network included Ursula Bright, Priscilla Bright McLaren (sister of John and Jacob Bright), Anna Maria and Mary Priestman, and their sister Margaret Tanner (sisters-in-law to John Bright by his first marriage), and Helen Priestman Bright Clark (eldest daughter of John Bright, and hence niece to both Bright and Priestman sisters).[14] Members of this Radical–Liberal suffrage network initiated a separate campaign to bring an end to the doctrine of coverture, when Elizabeth Wolstenholme Elmy established the Married Women's Property Committee in Manchester in 1867. They also helped promote a campaign for repeal of the Contagious Diseases Acts, legislation which undermined the civil rights of women identified by the authorities as prostitutes, by requiring their medical supervision and treatment on pain of imprisonment, with hard labour for non-compliance. This campaign was prompted by Elizabeth Wolstenholme Elmy, led by Josephine Butler and managed on a day-to-day basis by Mary Priestman and Margaret Tanner, with the active support of all the Bright circle of suffragists. Subsequently, these same networks were at the forefront of other committees and associations directed to securing full civil rights and equality before the law for women, perhaps most notably the Vigilance Association for the Defence of Personal Rights.[15]

From 1873 on, however, the equal-rights formulation of the demand came under repeated challenge. After the death of John Stuart Mill, and following the election of a Conservative government, there was fresh pressure to reformulate the demand so as expressly to exclude married women. This was achieved through the 'Forsyth proviso' within subsequent women's suffrage measures. This addition won the support of the secretary of the National Society for Women's Suffrage, Lydia Becker. Radical–Liberal opponents saw it simply as reducing the claim to a 'spinsters' suffrage bill'. They continued to uphold the equal-rights formulation, and movement policy went to and fro on this issue over the next decade or so, as Radical–Liberal suffragists like Ursula and Jacob Bright regained and then lost once more the leadership of the movement.[16]

The party-political tensions among suffragists intensified with the failure to secure a women's suffrage amendment to the Liberal government's 1884 Reform

Act, with the subsequent split within the Liberal Party over Irish home rule, and with the prospect now of a lengthy period of Conservative government. Women Liberals attempted to change the rules of the National Society for Women's Suffrage so as to make it possible for the growing number of branches of the Women's Liberal Federation to affiliate to the suffrage body. This was resisted by the Liberal Unionists and Conservatives among the suffrage leadership, and suffragists now divided between membership of the confusingly named Central National Society for Women's Suffrage (more conveniently referred to by the address of its office, as 'the Parliament Street Society') and the Central Committee of the National Society for Women's Suffrage (or 'the Great College Street Society').

The split was not simply over partisan affiliations, however. The Great College Street Society was headed by Lydia Becker and Millicent Fawcett, who now withdrew altogether their support for compromise formulations of the suffrage demand. The Great College Street Society held firmly to a formulation of the demand that *explicitly excluded* married women.[17] The Parliament Street Society, however, contained an uneasy mix of Gladstonian Liberals and ultraist Radicals, a mix that proved unsustainable, for its supporters were divided over formulations of the demand. Its policies attempted to recognise the breadth of opinion within it by offering support both for compromise, sexual-equality measures of women's suffrage, and those which excluded married women. But the disappointments and divisions of the previous few years had produced a new intransigence among ultraist-Radical suffragists. They were no longer content to support the compromise formulation of the demand in terms of equal rights, and now insisted on a formulation of the demand that *expressly included* married women. At the first annual meeting of the Parliament Street Society, Richard Pankhurst attempted, unsuccessfully, to secure a compromise whereby this body would at least withdraw its support from deliberately exclusivist measures of women's suffrage.[18]

These were the circumstances that led, the following year, to the formation of the Women's Franchise League. It was founded by three women. Its first secretary was Elizabeth Wolstenholme Elmy, a long-time member of Radical–Liberal suffragist circles in the north-west of England.[19] The first chair of its Council was Harriet McIlquham, who had established the right of married women to be elected Poor Law Guardians, and to vote at parish meetings, thus proving 'in her own person, that marriage is no legal bar to the enjoyment and exercise of electorate and elective rights, at any rate in matters parochial'.[20] The third of this group was Alice Scatcherd, another of the most energetic of Radical–Liberal suffragists in the north of England, active both in the Manchester Society for Women's Suffrage, and in the early unionisation of women textile workers in the Leeds area.[21] She remained the treasurer of the Women's Franchise League throughout its existence, and helped launch it with a personal subscription of £50 a year.[22] Other early recruits to the League included Radical–Liberal suffragists such as Jane Cobden (subsequently, Unwin), Emilie Venturi, Florence Fenwick Miller, Clementia and P. A. Taylor and Josephine and George Butler, as well as Emmeline and Richard Pankhurst.[23]

The correspondence of Elizabeth Wolstenholme Elmy shows that plans for the new society were in hand early in 1889. Such evidence gainsays Sylvia Pankhurst's account, which sets the founding of the League at an impromptu gathering around Emmeline Pankhurst's bed, after her confinement some months later. At the League's inaugural meeting Richard Pankhurst himself recognised Elizabeth Wolstenholme Elmy, Harriet McIlquham and Alice Scatcherd as the founders of the new society.[24] Harriot Stanton Blatch, an American-born founding member of the League, for her part linked its formation to the intervention in the British movement some six years before of her mother Elizabeth Cady Stanton, a foremost suffragist in the United States.[25] During a visit to Britain in 1882–83, Elizabeth Cady Stanton had joined Ursula Bright in urging a reformulation of the demand so as expressly to include married women. And it is the case that she also became a corresponding member of the new League.[26] However, contrary to the recollections of Harriot Stanton Blatch, Ursula and Jacob Bright initially held aloof from the new society, for reasons that remain unclear.[27] It was only in the late summer of 1890 that Ursula Bright moved into a dominant position in the leadership of the League, having joined it a few months beforehand. Of her own part, and that of her friend Emmeline Pankhurst at this time, Harriot Stanton Blatch recalled: 'Mrs Pankhurst and I, burdened as we were by young children and domestic cares, were the admiring neophytes of the circle.'[28] It is the case, however, that Emmeline Pankhurst and, to a lesser extent, Harriot Stanton Blatch subsequently became the principal aides to Ursula Bright in the leadership she now provided for the League in London, while Alice Scatcherd continued to organise League activities in the north on a largely autonomous basis.

The accounts of the formation of the Women's Franchise League provided by Sylvia Pankhurst and Harriot Stanton Blatch are both somewhat distorted – no doubt quite unconsciously – by the partiality of family memory. The League's origins in long-standing tensions among the founders of the suffrage movement may only be glimpsed in these accounts. Each also fails to locate Emmeline Pankhurst and Harriot Stanton Blatch within a wider current of Radical suffragism, to which they were, at this time, a new generation of recruits. Such distortion is evident in Harriot Stanton Blatch's neglect of any acknowledgement of Elizabeth Wolstenholme Elmy's role in the League. It is evident also in the altogether misleading and erroneous account of the expulsion of Elizabeth Wolstenholme Elmy from the League to be found in Sylvia Pankhurst's account of these events.

Elizabeth Wolstenholme Elmy had evidently been made uneasy by the recruitment of Ursula and Jacob Bright to the leadership of the League sometime early in 1890.[29] She believed it had been engineered by Richard and Emmeline Pankhurst as part of a plan to re-establish the political career of Sir Charles Dilke, a mutual friend of both the Brights and the Pankhursts whose reputation had been destroyed by the salacious revelations surrounding a divorce case in 1886. His supporters sought a new political role for him, by promoting a combination of women's rights issues with the emerging desire for the independent representation of labour in parliament. Elizabeth Wolstenholme Elmy had always believed it wisest to keep the suffrage issue clear of the divided loyalties that might result from such exterior goals, and was also personally contemptuous of Charles Dilke. Now she began to encounter opposition from within the League to her position as its secretary, opposition which claimed she was unbusiness-like in her management of its activities. She herself felt that such criticism had been worked up by Florence Fenwick Miller with the aim of replacing her in the paid position as secretary of the League.[30] Florence Fenwick Miller (1854–1935) was of working-class origins and had made a career for herself in the women's movement over the previous decade or so. Like Elizabeth Wolstenholme Elmy, she depended upon it for her living.[31]

Elizabeth Wolstenholme Elmy, for her part, felt that much of the blame for some of the less-than-successful undertakings of the League lay with its committee, which she claimed had given her 'minimal help' and support. Perhaps more significantly, she had increasingly found herself at cross purposes with Alice Scatcherd. As a joint founder of the League, she appears especially to have resented the demands which the wealthier Alice Scatcherd, in an honorary role as treasurer, made upon her time as the League's paid secretary. Elizabeth Wolstenholme Elmy complained that both she and her assistant, Romola Tynte, had experienced 'brutal' treatment from their employers, though she excluded Ursula Bright from any responsibility for this. Romola Tynte had apparently been 'worked and worried' into a dangerous illness from which she was still recovering in October 1890, while Elizabeth Wolstenholme Elmy recorded that she too had been 'really ill' as a result of these strains. During this period an anonymous and slanderous leaflet, purporting to provide a history of her life, had been circulated among League supporters. She knew nothing of it at the time, but later learned that she was there reported 'as greedy and self-seeking, whereas I was sacrificing everything, time, money, health and strength, life itself for the cause I believed in'.[32]

After resigning as secretary of the League, Elizabeth Wolstenholme Elmy stayed with Harriot Stanton Blatch and Elizabeth Cady Stanton in preparation for a special executive committee meeting which she hoped would resolve her differences with its leadership. But when the committee refused to reinstate her as secretary, she resigned from the League altogether. The position subsequently remained an honorary one, and was held at various times by Emmeline Pankhurst, Harriot Stanton Blatch and, most continuously, by Ursula Bright.

Harriet McIlquham also resigned from the League within a few months of these events, and a year or so later helped Elizabeth Wolstenholme Elmy form another body with very similar aims and outlook to the League, the Women's Emancipation Union.[33]

Sylvia Pankhurst's account of these events is misleading in terms of the timing that it suggests, and it seems most probable that she confused them with a subsequent dispute that arose within the Women's Franchise League over a demonstration in support of a women's suffrage bill introduced by Sir Albert Rollit in 1892. Certainly, Elizabeth Wolstenholme Elmy, by this time expelled from the League's leadership, supported this measure, while Ursula Bright, the Pankhursts and others did not. But Sylvia Pankhurst's account also built on this erroneous timing to suggest that Elizabeth Wolstenholme Elmy's departure from the League came about because she had retreated from her support for including married women in the suffrage demand. Elmy never made any such retreat, either in 1890, when she was ousted as secretary of the League, or in 1892 when Sylvia Pankhurst situates these events. She continued to prefer the ultraist formulation of the demand that *expressly included* married women. But, unlike many of her former colleagues in the League, she was prepared to lend support to compromises such as Rollit's bill that did *not expressly exclude* them.[34]

What distinguished the Women's Franchise League from all other suffrage societies, then, was the ultraist nature of its programme, an ultraism matched by its campaign methods, policies and tactics. This outlook became increasingly marked after the departure of Elizabeth Wolstenholme Elmy, but it was evident right from the formation of the Women's Franchise League. Nor was such an approach seen as anything new. An early manifesto declared, for example: 'This League has been founded by some of the oldest and most devoted of the friends of justice to women, partly because of their profound dissatisfaction with the conduct of the existing Women's Suffrage Societies.' It went on to explain that the promoters of the League believed 'that the time has now come for the demand by women, and on behalf of women, of that full civil and political equality with men, which is the only fitting goal of progress'. A second manifesto issued a few months later went further and claimed: 'The formation of the League has been rendered imperative by the falling away of existent organisations from the first principle of the movement, and by their introduction or sanctioning of restrictive and even aggressive alterations to the original measure.' The extensive range of its goals was also emphasised: 'The practical work before the League is great; its province being to seek the removal of every disability imposed upon women by a privileged sex ascendancy, whether enforced by law or social custom.'[35]

The League distinguished itself from the other societies at this point by its refusal to support either of the women's suffrage measures then before parliament. William Woodall's bill, it explained, excluded married women, 'and in the most insulting terms' (that is, by express reference to the doctrine of coverture). Walter McLaren's bill, as even its supporters admitted, would also fail to enfranchise married women, though it did not expressly set out so to do.[36] In consequence, the League found it necessary to pursue its ultraist approach to women's rights by drafting its own women's franchise measure. The Women's Disabilities Removal Bill was brought before the House of Commons in 1889 and 1890 by Richard Haldane, the young Radical Member of Parliament who was eventually to hold cabinet posts first in Liberal, and then later in Labour governments. It incorporated three provisions: that in all legislation relating to local and parliamentary franchises, 'words importing the masculine gender shall be deemed to include women'; 'that no woman shall be subject to legal incapacity from voting in such elections by reasons of coverture'; and that 'No person shall be disqualified from being elected or appointed to, or from filling or holding, any office or position, merely by reason that such person is a woman, or being a woman, is under coverture.'[37] Speaking in support of this bill at a public meeting, Richard Haldane explained that its intention was 'to influence the country, and he was sure they would never influence the country if they had so little courage of their opinions as the promoters of Mr Woodall's bill'. In this he reflected the ultraist belief in the education of public opinion as the main role of the reformer.[38] This was a perspective on reform agitation first expounded to significant effect by William Lloyd Garrison, one of the leaders of the anti-slavery movement in the United States, who had also greatly influenced many of the pioneers of the women's-rights movement both there and in Britain.[39]

At the inaugural meeting to establish the new society, William Lloyd Garrison, the younger, drew a direct comparison between the ultraism of the League, and that of the 'immediatists' among abolitionists in the United States in the 1830–60s. While division within a reform movement was to be avoided as far as possible, he insisted: 'Where the variance is on principles, cohesion is, of course, impossible.' He upheld his father's distinction between the role of the reformer and the role of the politician, describing the function of the former in these terms:

> A reformer sees an evil that is to be uprooted; he contemplates nothing short of its total abolition, which he desires with earnestness. No matter whether people will bear or whether they will forbear, in season and out of season it is for him to urge the iniquity of the wrong and ask for its immediate rectification. The enemy, always alert and shrewd, is most dangerous when urging delay on ground of policy.

In his view, one of the greatest obstacles that had faced the abolitionists was support from those who urged moderation and gradualism: 'The reformer who uses the political methods is necessarily confined to present possibilities and the count of votes', and in this way threatened the full realisation of the ultimate goal. The Garrisonian approach, in contrast, sprang from a conviction that 'uncompromising advocacy would mould legislation more powerfully than

temporising and wire-pulling to accomplish partial Acts'. This was an approach
to reform, then, that rejected the compromise and the pragmatic manoeuvring
of parliamentary and party politics, that insisted on the need to hold steadfastly
to the fundamental principle at issue and that refused absolutely any modification of, or gradualist approach to, the ultimate reform goal.[40]

Another speaker on this occasion was also from the United States. Harriot
Stanton Blatch had married an Englishman in 1882, and lived in Britain at this
time. She and her mother Elizabeth Cady Stanton had found themselves most
in sympathy with the Radical–Liberal current within the British movement. Her
mother's links with the Bright circle went back to 1840, and the World Anti-Slavery Convention in London.[41] Harriot Stanton Blatch explained how, with the formation of the Women's Franchise League, she at last felt there was a suffrage
society in Britain in which she was at home, recalling her first impressions of the
British movement seven years before: 'I cannot tell you what a feeling it gave me
to come among the men and women here and find you talking upon such narrow lines.' Like William Lloyd Garrison, the younger, she expressed the conviction that only an out-and-out approach to the issue would bring success, and
she too drew attention to the lessons learned in the anti-slavery campaigns. After
endorsing 'the educating effect of a broad basis to any movement', she commented:

> You are clearly behind us as to general freedom. Women in the United States have
> far more liberty that women here, and I lay it exactly to the door of your Women's
> Suffrage Movement, which has been so narrow. We have had a great education in
> America by the Anti-slavery movement (hear, hear), and by the Women's Suffrage
> Movement. They have been placed upon the broad basis of the brotherhood of all
> mankind (Applause).

She insisted: 'if we pray for grit, for the determination to show others that we
mean business, the vote will come, and in very quick order.'[42]

The Women's Franchise League stood resolutely for no more compromise,
no more watering down of the object of the vote for *all* women, and rejected not
only the sex qualification, but also the doctrine of coverture. It also made clear
that it did not limit this outlook to the question of the vote, but sought to address
all civil disabilities of women arising from their sex. Alice Scatcherd, who also
spoke to the inaugural meeting, declared:

> We are really here to claim for the first time full and absolute and complete
> freedom for women. I, for one, am perfectly tired of joining societies which fight
> only for a little bit, a little shred of freedom. It is a waste of power and a waste of
> organisation when we form societies to obtain just a little shred of justice for
> women. We are here this afternoon to say that we have nailed our flag to the mast,
> and to announce that our desire is to obtain full and equal justice for women with
> men.

Alice Scatcherd then declared that 'revolt has set in' among women, and more particularly, a revolt against 'complete self-effacement ... the complete abnegation of self' so sedulously taught to women by those who upheld the *status quo*.[43] The ultraism of the Women's Franchise League was evident, then, not simply in the stance it took towards women's suffrage, but in the expansive nature of the programme of reform that it set itself to pursue.

After the expulsion of Elizabeth Wolstenholme Elmy, Emmeline Pankhurst, the Countess Schach, Harriot Stanton Blatch and Ursula Bright each served for some period as honorary secretary to the League, but eventually this role came to fall almost entirely to Ursula Bright. Alice Scatcherd continued to organise the work of the League in the north. Remaining records of the League's activities suggest that it never wavered in conceiving of itself principally as the voice of Radical suffragism, committed to a more advanced programme than the more moderate societies, deliberately linking itself to the international women's movement, most especially to the movement in the United States, and pursuing new sources of support for the demand in the emerging labour and socialist movements. It did this principally by providing speakers on women's suffrage for radical clubs, progressive clubs and branches of the Women's Cooperative Guild.[44] But with the growing dominance of Ursula Bright it became increasingly an organisation of Gladstonian women Liberals, and the Women's Liberal Federation became a main focus for many of its activities.[45]

The League has left few records.[46] The details provided of its finances in the only surviving minute book suggest that Alice Scatcherd and, to a lesser extent, Ursula Bright remained its financial mainstays.[47] A generous reading would suppose that it only ever attracted at most a membership of a few hundred. Nor does the central executive appear to have kept in very close touch with those local branches that were established, largely in the suburbs of London and in the region of Leeds. Indeed, the work of the League in the Leeds area seems to have run virtually autonomously under the direction of Alice Scatcherd, while individual members of the executive on several occasions undertook activities in the name of the League for which they only subsequently sought its endorsement.[48] But such indices cannot provide a proper measure of the success or significance of the League.

Radical agitation was what gave the League both its identity, and its rationale. It acted as the conscience of Radical suffragism, constantly keeping this perspective before audiences both within the women's movement and within popular politics, though without seeking to become a mass movement in itself. Florence Fenwick Miller asserted that its programme was 'different from the objects of any society that has hitherto existed' in its search for the complete civil equality of men and women, and explained its choice of name in these terms:

> We have been asked why a Franchise League works for anything else but the Suf-
> frage. That query is based on a misconception of the word 'Franchise'. The Par-
> liamentary Suffrage is only a portion of Franchise, which, of course, as you are all
> as well aware as myself, means simply freedom; and the object of the Women's
> Franchise League is nothing less than to obtain freedom for half the human race.[49]

She justified this search for women's freedom on three grounds: to achieve self-
development; to release the 'moral power', intelligence and 'public spirit' of
women and 'the impetus which women could bring to the world's improvement';
and, most challengingly, to 'avoid for women the sufferings of slavery', insisting
that 'the condition under which the women of this country lived ... was simply
slavery', until recent reforms they had secured for themselves. And she grounded
this claim, ultimately, on the operation of coverture: '[W]hen I speak of the
enslaved position of English women I speak of the position of those – the
immense bulk of the adult women of the country – who were married.'[50]

  Under coverture, she argued, married women were denied both a separate
legal identity from their husband's, and possession of their own persons, rendering them merely the chattels of men: 'There was no protection from the law
for women except it was invoked by the men who owned them, while it was the
most cruel fact in many a woman's lot that in her master she found her sternest
enemy, her most heartless oppressor.' This wrong was compounded by the sham
of legal requirements on husbands as the 'bread-winner' of the family: 'I fancy
that there was a little more obligation on a master to support his own slave than
there was – aye, and practically than there now is – upon a husband to support
his wife and family.' Family law also still robbed women of rights over their children, even after a husband's death, and once again she made an analogy with
the condition of slave mothers on the plantation, as portrayed in *Uncle Tom's
Cabin*:

> The woes and flight of the mulatto mother invented by Mrs Stowe's genius set all
> England weeping; but English and Scotch mothers too – refined women, adoring
> mothers like you and me – have seen their children torn from their embrace, or
> have fled secretly and lived in desolate concealment with their little ones.

As so often, even Radical equal-rights proponents like Florence Fenwick Miller
might reveal, by such references, a presumption of their own greater sensibility
and civilisation and hence, implicitly, their greater oppression when compared
with slave women. It was its particular emphasis on such wrongs, however, that
led the League to extend its programme beyond the claim to the suffrage, and
simultaneously to promote bills to equalise the laws of divorce and to secure the
rights of wives in cases of intestacy.[51]

  But, above all, it was the husband's right to sexual service from a wife that
Florence Fenwick Miller saw as rendering married women 'absolutely a slave,
with no free-will in herself'. These were rights that the courts had upheld as

recently as two years prior to the formation of the League. It was in such terms that Florence Fenwick Miller explained the opposition of the League to those whom she accused of exploiting twenty years of women's-rights campaigning 'for the benefit of the unmarried women' (that is, in the limited formulation of the demand embodied in both the Woodall and McLaren bills). Though she acknowledged the enormous contribution that single women had, and continued to make, to society, she insisted: 'It is a preposterous notion to make celibacy an additional test of the right to vote in the case of women'. She insisted that such a limitation would be ridiculed were it suggested for men. She also insisted that the League was not claiming the suffrage 'for wives as such', but rather 'for every woman'. What was objected to was the exclusion of any one class of women from the demand.[52]

The analogy between the position of women in Britain and slavery was a theme that was to recur often in League pronouncements. At a debate on 'Women and Politics' at the St Pancras Reform Club, a male speaker on behalf of the League explained its position in these terms:

> There is a sacred duty of self-assertion as well as one of self-denial. Human beings who tamely submit to be trampled on put a premium on tyranny and injustice, and encourage the wrong-doing by their own self-abasement. Men and women owe it to their common humanity to carry themselves erect, and not to throw themselves under the wheels of the car of any social or political Juggernaut. The willing slave is only one degree less contemptible than the willing despot.[53]

It was this large perspective and broad programme that Ursula Bright again chose to emphasise when describing the work of the League to an international audience at the World Congress of Representative Women, organised during the Chicago World Fair of 1893. The programme that she outlined there combined an extensive range of goals: equal political rights and duties; equal educational opportunities; equal wages for equal work; equal access to paid, honorary or elected public office; equality under family law; equality in the rights and liabilities of contract.[54] Ursula Bright further sought to establish the radical credentials of the League by emphasising its links with the labour movement: 'The leaders of the working men are almost to a man on our side.'[55]

Links with labour and socialist groups were clearly central to the approach to suffrage campaigning for a number of the League's leadership. Alice Scatcherd continued her long association with the organisation of working-class women in the Leeds area, now extending her interests beyond trade-unionism to the recently established Women's Cooperative Guild. Harriot Stanton Blatch became in these years a member of the Fabian Society. Emmeline and Richard Pankhurst were drifting away from Radical–Liberal circles towards socialism, and were among the earliest members of the Independent Labour Party in 1894. At the League's inaugural meeting Alice Scatcherd had argued:

> There are only two great questions presently before the public. These are the
> labour question and the women's question. And when we come to consider these
> questions really they are united; for it is largely on the economic condition of
> woman that her freedom in the future will depend.

Here she was giving expression to a new perspective on women's rights that
proved especially influential in the work of the League, one linked to a fresh Radical formulation of women's claim to citizenship.[56]

This new perspective emerged in Radical suffragist argument in the early
1880s, and based claims to citizenship on the labour of women. At the same
time, it adopted a broad definition of labour, so as to include every kind of
women's work – in reproduction and sexual labour, as well as the workplace; in
unpaid as well as in paid labour. May Dilke put forward just such an understanding of women's claim to citizenship in these years, to counter the militaristic account that was so often used as an argument against votes for women.
She argued, for example, that women in childbirth put their lives at risk equally
with men called on to do battle, insisting that the maintenance of society rested
not on warfare but on labour in all its forms. Though it was the case that much
of women's labour went unpaid, it was 'quite as fundamental a part of civilised
life as the paid labour of men'. Moreover, she argued, women were also increasingly entering the paid work-force, and therefore needed their own voice in the
making of laws which controlled the labour market.[57]

Harriot Stanton Blatch characterised such understandings of the citizenship claims of women as an 'economic' approach, one that attended especially
to the need of working women for the vote. As such, it appealed particularly
strongly to Radical suffragists, and clearly informed much of the work of the
Women's Franchise League.[58] This new 'economic' perspective within the
women's movement sometimes also linked women's rights to a critique of social
relations in general under capitalism, and emphasised the need to unite industrial women workers with middle-class women in the campaign for the vote. Here
again Fabians like Harriot Stanton Blatch were an especially important
influence. She later recalled how she had explained her involvement in campaigns for women's rights to fellow Fabians, Beatrice and Sidney Webb, in these
terms: 'Women are the source of the race. Its supreme moulders. To do that work
efficiently, they must be politically and economically independent beyond all call.
Free they cannot be under capitalism: the capitalistic system and feminism are
at war.'[59]

Hence, the League might on occasion look for support from the campaign
for the eight-hour day, for example. And increasingly even Ursula Bright, who
retained some reservations about the newly formed Independent Labour Party,
emphasised the value of working-class support.[60] An appeal for such backing
was central, for example, to perhaps the most notorious episode in the League's
history. This was occasioned by the organisation by the other suffrage societies

in 1892 of a public meeting in support of Sir Albert Rollit's women's suffrage bill. Though this bill did not expressly exclude women under coverture, it was so drafted as effectively to leave them out. All the other suffrage societies, including Elizabeth Wolstenholme Elmy and the Women's Emancipation Union, were prepared to back the bill, and felt that if the League were unable to offer support, it ought not, at least publicly, to oppose any such compromise. The League thought otherwise, however, and through its socialist members issued a call to the working class to attend the demonstration in order to oppose such a measure of 'class legislation'. On the evening of the demonstration, according to Elizabeth Wolstenholme Elmy, some members of the League arrived early at the St James Hall to leaflet it with a denunciation of the Rollit bill. They were only prevented from taking over the platform by the forceful resistance of her husband, Ben Elmy. During the meeting, members of the League supposedly rushed the platform, and overturned the reporters' table. Sensationalised accounts appeared in the press, and division and tension ensued within both the Women's Franchise League and the Women's Emancipation Union.[61]

Ursula Bright's increasing reliance on labour movement support grew out of her growing disillusion with erstwhile Radical supporters in parliament, most especially with Sir Charles Dilke. He proved less than steadfast in his support for the Local Government Act of 1894, an advance that Ursula Bright saw, not altogether fairly, as principally the achievement of the Women's Franchise League. This measure finally established the right of married women with the necessary qualifications to vote in local government elections. In establishing in principle the right of women under coverture to the franchise, this act paved the way for the reunification of the suffrage movement behind a simple equal-rights formulation of the demand – there was no longer any case to be made for the exclusion of married women from that demand.[62]

Now, the League hoped Sir Charles Dilke would include women in the Registration Bill that he planned to introduce after the passage of the Local Government Act. But in the event Ursula Bright could only confess her despair to Emmeline Pankhurst, recording 'the awful difficulty of getting all our friends up to scratch at the right moment ... First one then another jibs till I get so disgusted, I only lose heart.' Dilke himself continually equivocated, and ultimately retreated from his earlier commitment to include women in his bill. She hoped Emmeline Pankhurst might be able to advise her on how best to mobilise new political forces behind a demonstration to demand the inclusion of women: 'Think for me what can be done for this meeting. If we could only get the working men to move in a body to the hall with banners and music!' But by this stage, and almost certainly for the first time in her career as a suffragist, Ursula Bright found herself attempting to moderate the ardour of her colleagues in the League's leadership. She was especially worried at the 'irreconcilable attitude' of Alice Scatcherd, who was urging suffragist MPs to vote against the Dilke Bill if the women's suffrage amendments failed. Ursula Bright considered such intransigence unwise, and sought the help of Emmeline Pankhurst. Regarding parliamentary supporters, she urged; 'We must consider their party sympathies'. She counselled her friend, 'Be wise as a serpent and as gentle as a dove.' The Pankhursts evidently shared her view of the matter, pressing Manchester suffragists not to follow Alice Scatcherd's direction, and there is some evidence of growing tensions between members of the League leadership as they each became increasingly involved in party-political and sectarian divisions external to the League.[63]

For her part, Ursula Bright understood the impatience of Alice Scatcherd as a consequence of the long, wearying, experience of the older generation, who had 'borne the brunt of these widows and spinsters'. She also confided that some of her old colleague's abrasiveness was a consequence of her time of life which 'makes her irritable and weary at times'. Ursula Bright maintained that she remained nonetheless 'a very fine woman and a most valuable worker'. She herself was under considerable strain in these years. Jacob Bright was seriously ill with the disease that eventually took his life in 1899, and much of her energies were devoted to his care. In 1898 Emmeline Pankhurst suffered the sudden and personally devastating death of her husband Richard, and she retired from political life for some years. Alice Scatcherd appears to have been keeping the Women's Franchise League alive almost single-handedly by 1897, after the Parliament Street and Great College Street Societies reunited in the National Union of Women's Suffrage Societies. Sometime thereafter, the League faded away.[64]

To explore the Women's Franchise League in greater detail is to tell a more complex story than is possible within existing narratives. It requires recognition of certain continuities so long obscured in accounts of the suffrage movement. The story of the League provides evidence, on the one hand, of a vigorous and continuous radical current, the fortunes of which waxed and waned throughout the nineteenth-century campaigns, but which formed the outlook of some of the most tenacious and assertive of suffragists. It was a current that also provided the apprenticeship of a second generation of suffragists, among whom were Emmeline Pankhurst and Harriot Stanton Blatch, the earliest promoters of the 'militant' approach to the twentieth-century campaigns in their respective countries. The Women's Franchise League matched, and in some respects possibly surpassed, the militancy of the WSPU in a number of ways: in its pugnacious opposition to alternative approaches to women's enfranchisement; in the breadth of its analysis of women's oppression; in the political alliances it sought with the socialist and labour movements; in its sometimes unconventional modes of protest. Nor was it formed simply, as Sylvia Pankhurst's account would have it, around the figures of her parents. It was the product of a far broader Radical suffragist current of long standing. If Richard Pankhurst had helped create and sustain that current, the Women's Franchise League, in its turn, helped form the intransigence and assertiveness on which Emmeline Pankhurst founded suffrage militancy in the early 1900s.

NOTES

1 H. Blackburn, 'Great Britain. Efforts for the parliamentary franchise', in E. C. Stanton, S. B. Anthony and M. J. Gage (eds), *History of woman suffrage*, 6 vols, 1881–1922 (New York, Source Books, 1970 reprint), 4, pp. 1012–25; *Women's suffrage: a record of the women's suffrage movement* (London, Williams and Norgate, 1902); B. Mason, *A history of the women's suffrage movement* (London, Sherratt and Hughes, 1912); M. G. Fawcett, *Women's suffrage: a short history of a great movement* (London, T. C. and E. C. Jack, 1912), which names no nineteenth-century suffrage society, and so avoids discussion of the issues that divided suffragists in the early period. This 'official' narrative also structures R. Strachey, *The cause: a short history of the women's movement in Great Britain* (London, Virago repr., 1978) though she does make reference on p. 276 to an unnamed committee of 'extremists', led by Ursula Bright and Emmeline Pankhurst, with headquarters in the north of England. Ray Strachey associates this body with the 'internal troubles' of the suffrage movement in 1883, following fresh attempts then to exclude married women from the demand. It is unclear whether she had the League in mind, though this was, of course, only formed some six years later and with a different initial leadership. R. Strachey, *Millicent Garrett Fawcett* (London, John Murray, 1935) also follows its subject's lead in ignoring all divisions among nineteenth-century suffragists, except for 'the party question' dividing the movement from the late 1880s, p. 92. The earliest histories were written prior to the formation of the League, and similarly skirted any discussion of the divisions that subsequently led to its formation, see C. A. Biggs, 'Great Britain', in Stanton *et al.*, *History of woman suffrage*, 3, pp. 834–94; M. G. Fawcett, 'England', in T. Stanton (ed.), *The woman question in Europe* (New York and London, G. P. Putnam and Sons, 1884), pp. 1–29.
2 E. S. Pankhurst, *The suffragette movement: an intimate account of persons and ideals* (London, Virago, 1977 reprint), esp. pp. 95–7, but note the neglect in her earlier history, *The suffragette* (London, Emmeline Pankhurst, 1911), put together in the heat of campaigning, principally as an apologia for militant methods and a celebration of militant martyrdom, and before the 'alternative', Pankhurstian narrative had been fully formed.
3 There are now a number of stimulating explorations of how the history of the twentieth-century British suffrage movement has been formed, and more especially that of the militant wing of the movement, see J. Marcus (ed.), Introduction, *The Pankhursts and women's suffrage* (London, Routledge and Kegan Paul, 1987); K. Dodd, 'The politics of form in Sylvia Pankhurst's writings', in her edited collection, *A Sylvia Pankhurst reader* (Manchester, Manchester University Press, 1993), pp. 1–30, and also, K. Dodd, 'Cultural politics and women's historical writing: the case of Ray Strachey's *The cause*', *Women's Studies International Forum*, 13, 1990, pp. 127–39; H. Kean, 'Searching for the past in present defeat: the construction of historical and political identity in British feminism in the 1920s and 30s', *Women's History Review*, 3, 1994, pp. 57–80; L. E. N. Mayhall, 'Creating the "suffragette spirit": British feminism and the historical imagination', *Women's History Review*, 4, 1995, pp. 319–44.
4 H. S. Blatch and A. Lutz, *Challenging years: the memoirs of Harriot Stanton Blatch* (New York, G. P. Putnam, 1940), esp. p. 73, refers to Harriot Stanton Blatch's involvement, alongside Ursula Bright and Emmeline Pankhurst in 'The Equal Franchise Committee' in these years. I have been unable to find documentary evidence of any such body, though see n. 1 and Strachey's reference to a committee of 'extremists' in 1883. Possibly the Women's Franchise League was built on foundations laid by some short-lived body six years before.

5 G. Dangerfield, *The strange death of liberal England* (London, Paladin repr., 1975). For a
   more extended discussion of the Romantic feminism that informed militancy, see S. S.
   Holton, "'In sorrowful wrath'. The Romantic feminism of Emmeline Pankhurst and suffrage
   militancy', in H. L. Smith (ed.), *British feminism in the twentieth century* (Aldershot, Edward
   Elgar, 1990), pp. 7–24.
6 Variations of this 'pathological' interpretation may be found in R. Fulford, *Votes for women*
   (London, Faber and Faber, 1957); S. Hynes, *The Edwardian turn of mind* (Princeton, Princeton University Press, 1968), esp. pp. 200–8; A. Rosen, *Rise up women! The militant cam-
   paign of the Women's Social and Political Union 1903–14* (London, Routledge and Kegan
   Paul, 1974); D. Mitchell, *Queen Christabel: the biography of Christabel Pankhurst* (London,
   Macdonald and Janes, 1977); S. Romero, *E. Sylvia Pankhurst: portrait of a radical* (New
   Haven, Yale University Press, 1987). For recent challenges to some of these interpretations,
   see E. Sarah, 'Christabel Pankhurst: reclaiming her power (1880–1958)', in D. Spender (ed.),
   Feminist theorists: three centuries of women's intellectual traditions (London, Women's
   Press, 1983), pp. 256–84; R. Pankhurst, 'Sylvia Pankhurst in perspective. Some comments
   on Patricia Romero's *E. Sylvia Pankhurst: portrait of a radical, Women's Studies International Forum*, 11, 1988, pp. 245–62; I. Bullock and R. Pankhurst (eds.), *Sylvia Pankhurst:
   from artist to anti-fascist* (London, Macmillan, 1994).
7 See J. Liddington and J. Norris, *One hand tied behind us: the rise of the women's suffrage
   movement* (London, Virago, 1978); L. P. Hume, *The National Union of Women's Suffrage
   Societies, 1897–1814* (New York, Garland Press, 1982); S. S. Holton, *Feminism and democracy: women's suffrage and reform politics in Britain 1900–1918* (Cambridge, Cambridge
   University Press, 1986); L. Tickner, *The spectacle of women: imagery of the suffrage campaign 1907–14* (London, Chatto and Windus, 1987).
8 A notable exception is C. Rover, *Women's suffrage and party politics in Britain, 1866–1914*
   (London, Routledge and Kegan Paul, 1967), whose focus ensures a sense of continuity in
   suffrage politics. See also S. K. Kent, *Sex and suffrage in Britain, 1860–1914* (Princeton,
   Princeton University Press, 1987). Here, a focus on the sexual politics of the campaign for
   the vote allows a recognition of some of the continuities within the movement over the
   course of its history, though undoubtedly at the cost of neglecting tensions and conflicts
   among suffragists concerning sexual issues. For a corrective, see L. Bland, *Banishing the
   beast. English feminism and sexual morality, 1885–1914* (London, Penguin, 1995).
9 D. Rubinstein, *Before the suffragettes. Women's emancipation in the 1890s* (Brighton, Harvester, 1986).
10 P. Hollis, *Ladies elect: women in English local government* (Oxford, Clarendon Press, 1987)
    serves to support a similar line of interpretation, though it does not expressly set out so to
    do.
11 I pursue this re-interpretation elsewhere in S. S. Holton, 'Women and the vote', in J. Purvis
    (ed.), *Women's history: Britain, 1850–1945* (London, UCL Press, 1995), pp. 277–306, and
    in *Suffrage days: stories from the women's suffrage movement* (London, Routledge, 1996).
12 I review this question in more detail in Holton, 'Women and the vote', and *Suffrage days*,
    esp. chs. 1, 2, 3, 4.
13 For a more extended discussion of some of the activities of these Radical–Liberal suffrag-
    ists, see Holton, *Suffrage days*, pp. 27–33, 44–7, 56–8, 81–9.
14 For more on this circle, see S. S. Holton, 'From anti-slavery to suffrage militancy', in C. Daley
    and M. Nolan (eds.), *Suffrage and beyond: international feminist perspectives* (Auckland,
    Auckland University Press, 1994), pp. 213–33.
15 A detailed analysis of these campaigns is to be found in M. L. Shanley, *Marriage, feminism
    and the law in Victorian England* (London, I. B. Tauris, 1989), and see also Bland, *Banish-
    ing the beast*, ch. 4.
16 For a more detailed account, see Holton, *Suffrage days*, chs. 2 and 3.
17 L. Becker's editorial in *Women's Suffrage Journal*, 20, 1889, p. 48, when describing the
    NSWS split, argued that the married women's claim for the vote was an 'uncalled for and
    gratuitous obstruction' to the demand for women's suffrage, while she designated her oppo-

nents in the Parliament Street Society as the 'left-wing' and 'extreme section' of the movement.

18 Anon., 'The women's suffrage crisis', *The Personal Rights Journal*, April 1889, pp. 26–7.

19 The career of Elizabeth Wolstenholme Elmy is discussed in more detail in S. S. Holton, 'Free love and Victorian feminism. The divers matrimonials of Elizabeth Wolstenholme and Ben Elmy', *Victorian Studies*, 37, 1994, pp. 199–222, and *Suffrage days*, chs. 1, 2 and *passim*. See also the brief portraits in E. Ethelmer (pseudonym of her husband, Ben Elmy), 'A woman emancipator: a biographical sketch', *Westminster Review*, 145, 1894, pp. 424–8; E. S. Pankhurst, *Suffragette movement*, pp. 30–4; and the discussion of some of the bodies with which Wolstenholme Elmy was involved in Shanley, *Marriage, feminism and the law*.

20 These details of her history are recorded in anon., 'Women's Franchise League', *Personal Rights Journal*, 95, December 1889, p. 93. For a more extended discussion of the role of such women as Guardians in this period, see Hollis, *Ladies elect*, pp. 195–299, and esp. pp. 206–7 for McIlquham's role.

21 Alice Scatcherd's career is followed in more detail in Holton, *Suffrage days*, pp. 35–6, 62–8, 79–82, 100–3, and see also the brief portrait in E. S. Pankhurst, *Suffragette movement*, p. 97.

22 Anon., 'Women's Franchise League'.

23 See the list of officers provided in 'Women's Franchise League', *Objects*, (n. p., Women's Franchise League, December 1889), which includes many more names from Radical–Liberal networks, especially those in the north.

24 Richard Pankhurst's speech, reported in Women's Franchise League, *Report of proceedings at the inaugural meeting, London July 25th 1889* (London, Hansard Publishing Union, [1889]), and compare S. Pankhurst, *Suffragette movement*, p. 95.

25 T. Stanton and H. S. Blatch (eds), *Elizabeth Cady Stanton, as revealed in her letters, diary and reminiscences*, 2 vols (New York and London, Harper and Bros, 1922), 1, p. 208, n. 4.

26 Elizabeth Cady Stanton's endorsement of the League and involvement in its business in 1890 is evident also in Programme for the Women's Franchise League international conference, 16–17 July 1890, proof copy in Harriet McIlquham papers, Fawcett Library, London. This conference was apparently conceived as a successor to a similar event in Paris the previous year, and to the first international suffrage convention in Washington in 1888. I have found little remaining evidence as to the role of British suffragists at the European events, but see anon, 'International congresses upon the rights and works of woman', *Personal Rights Journal*, March 1890, pp. 29–30. Elizabeth Cady Stanton was also in this period exchanging ideas on methods of agitation with Alice Scatcherd, with whom Harriot Stanton Blatch was working closely in the Women's Liberal Federation as well as in the Women's Franchise League, see fragment of A. Scatcherd to E. C. Stanton, enclosed with E. C. Stanton to A. Clark, 20 October 1890, Box 75, Millfield Papers, Clark Archive, C and J Clarks, Ltd., Street, Somerset (henceforth, MP). I examine these transatlantic links, and the importance of Garrisonian abolitionist immediatism to the outlook of the new League, in Holton, '"To educate women into rebellion". Elizabeth Cady Stanton and the creation of a transatlantic network of radical suffragists', *American Historical Review*, 99, 1994, pp. 1113–36.

27 See the Appendix to the Women's Franchise League, Report of proceedings, pp. 30–1, where Ursula and Jacob Bright are notable by their absence, both from the proceedings and from the council elected there, which otherwise contain the names of all the long-established members of Radical-suffragist circles, as well as a younger generation, among whom were Emmeline Pankhurst and Harriot Stanton Blatch. See also E. W. Elmy to H. McIlquham, 9 May 1889, 5 June 1890, and her reminiscences of this period in *ibid.*, 19 Sept 1904, 27 Sept 1904, in Elizabeth Wolstenholme Elmy Papers, British Library, Add. MS, 47449–4756 (henceforth, EWEP), vols 1 and 6, respectively.

28 Blatch and Lutz, *Challenging years*, p. 73.

29 Their names do not appear in the list of League officers printed in December 1889 in Women's Franchise League, *Objects*, but had been added by the end of February 1890, see the list of officers of the League in Mrs. F. F. Miller, *On the programme of the Women's*

Franchise League: an address delivered at the National Liberal Club, Feb. 25th, 1890 (London, Hansard Publishing Union, 1890).

30 E. W. Elmy to H. McIlquham, 26 May 1890, 5 June 1890, 27 October 1906, EWEP, vol. 1 and vol. 7 respectively. In return, her opponents saw Elizabeth Wolstenholme Elmy as less than straight-dealing in continuing to receive and issue receipts for new subscriptions to the League for some time after her resignation. See Women's Franchise League, minute book of the executive committee 1890–6, 15 September 1890 (henceforth, WFLMB), North-western University Library, Special Collections, with my thanks to Russell Maylone for making this available to me on microfilm.

31 Florence Fenwick Miller has been surprisingly neglected in studies of the nineteenth-century women's movement, but see Hollis, *Ladies elect*, pp. 90–110; R. T. Van Arsdel, 'Florence Fenwick Miller 1854–1935: a life of many choices', unpub. manuscript held at the Fawcett Library, the London Guildhall University.

32 E. W. Elmy to H. McIlquham, 9 October 1890, 29 October 1890, EWEP, vol. 1.

33 For more detail on this organisation see Rubinstein, *Before the suffragettes*, pp. 144–5; Holton, *Suffrage days*, esp. pp. 82–8, 102–5.

34 E. S. Pankhurst, *Suffragette movement*, p. 96, where the behaviour ascribed to Elizabeth Wolstenholme Elmy almost certainly recalls, in fact, a dispute between another member of the League, Mary Cozens, and the League's leadership, over arrangements for a demon-stration in Hyde Park in 1892 in support of Rollit's bill, see WFLMB, 10 March, 2 May 1892, and Mary Cozens to Ursula Bright, 1 April [1892], E. Sylvia Pankhurst Archive, International Institute of Social History, Amsterdam (henceforth ESPA), 135.

35 Women's Franchise League, *Provisional executive committee and objects* (n. p., Women's Franchise League, May 1889); Women's Franchise League, *Objects*. Almost certainly Elmy was responsible for the actual drafting of this statement.

36 Women's Franchise League, *Provisional executive committee.*

37 Women's Franchise League, *Objects.*

38 Anon., Women's Franchise League, pp. 93–4. See also Women's Franchise League, *Report of meeting in support of the Women's Disabilities Removal Bill, Abridged from report in The Scotsman, of Nov. 8th, 1889* (London, Hansard Publishing Union, c.1889).

39 For an extended discussion of the role of Garrisonian ultraists in the women's movement in the United States, see N. Hewitt, *Women's activism and social change: Rochester, New York* (Ithaca, Cornell University Press, 1984); L. D. Ginzberg, *Women and the work of benevo-lence: morality, politics, and class in nineteenth-century United States* (New Haven, Yale University Press, 1990), with my thanks to Paul Bourke for this reference. On the links between women abolitionists and the women's rights movement in Britain, see C. Midgley, *Women against slavery: the British campaigns, 1780–1870* (London, Routledge, 1992).

40 William Lloyd Garrison, the younger, reported in Women's Franchise League, *Report of Pro-ceedings*. The Garrisonian wing of the anti-slavery movement had found its sympathisers in Britain in the 1840s among the same circles that subsequently articulated the Radical-Liberal perspective on women's suffrage. For a more extended discussion, see Holton, 'From anti-slavery to suffrage militancy', and '"To educate women"'.

41 K. K. Sklar, 'Women who speak for an entire nation: American and British women compared at the world anti-slavery convention, London 1840', *Pacific History Review*, 59, 1990, pp. 453–99, compares the significance of this event for women's politics in each country.

42 Harriot Stanton Blatch, reported in Women's Franchise League, *Report of proceedings.*

43 Alice Scatcherd, reported in *ibid.*

44 WFLMB, 23 April and 29 May 1891; also 24 November 1890; 2 January 1891; 2 February 1891; 18 March 1891; 4 December 1891; 25 April 1893; 18 May 1893; 16 March 1894; 9 June 1894.

45 For example, WFLMB, 15 September 1890; 2 February 1891; 3 February 1892; 18 May 1892; 9 June 1894. Lilias Ashworth Hallett recorded some attempt to re-unite the League with the remaining, and largely Gladstonian, members of the Parliament Street Society in the spring of 1891, and reported Eva McLaren's account of proceedings at a joint confer-

ence when 'Dr Pankhurst showed signs of his intention to boss the whole business', leading the Parliament Street Society to decline a merger, L. A. Hallett to M. G. Fawcett, May 1891, Manchester Public Library Archives (henceforth, MPLA), M50/2/1/141.

46 The only minute book I have so far been able to trace is that cited in n. 30. There is a minute book in the Sylvia Pankhurst Archive, ESPA 322, which was originally ascribed to the Women's Franchise League, but this ascription was mistaken. The people involved in the committee whose activities are recorded there suggest that it is probably the minute book of the Parliament Street Society, more formally known as the Central National Society for Women's Suffrage. I have not been able to trace any of the League's annual reports, and Elizabeth Wolstenholme Elmy's correspondence suggests that aspects of the first annual report, prepared by her, did not satisfy at least some of the committee. The other pamphlets and leaflets cited in these notes are held either at the Fawcett Library, the London Guild-hall University, or in the Archives of the Manchester Public Library, and I thank each for locating these and providing copies for me.

47 WFLMB, 2 February 1891; 18 March 1891 (which suggests that its income for the previous year was a little over £350; 4 May 1891; 11 November 1891; [12 April] 1894, and see also E. W. Elmy to H. McIlquham, 27 October 1889, EWEP, vol. 1.

48 WFLMB, 15 September 1890; 2 February 1891; 18 March 1891; 23 April 1893. In keeping with its tendency to weak and unhierarchical organisation, the role of chair of the executive meetings rotated around its members, whose attendance could also be very irregular.

49 Miller, Women's Franchise League, p. 1.

50 Ibid., pp. 3, 4.

51 Ibid., pp. 7, 8, 15.

52 Ibid., pp. 11, 13, and see Personal Rights Journal, March 1890, pp. 28–9, for an account of the debate which followed this paper at the National Liberal Club.

53 J. H. Levy, quoted in a report of the debate, 'The enfranchisement of women', Personal Rights Journal, December 1890, p. 112. Florence Fenwick Miller reiterated this view to the international conference of women in 1894, see F. F. Miller, 'Work of the Franchise League', in M. W. Sewell (ed.), The World Congress of Representative Women (Chicago, Rand McNally, 1894), pp. 420–4.

54 Mrs J. Bright, 'Origins and objects of the Women's Franchise League of Great Britain and Ireland', in ibid., pp. 415–20, esp. pp. 416, 418. Ursula Bright did not herself attend the Congress, and her paper was read for her by Jane Cobden Unwin, as a representative of the League.

55 Ibid, pp. 416, 417, 420.

56 Women's Franchise League, Report of proceedings, p. 22.

57 M. Dilke, The Nineteenth Century, 26, 1889, pp. 97–103.

58 This perspective is evident also in R. Haldane, 'Some economic aspects of women's suffrage', Contemporary Review, 58, 1890, pp. 830–8.

59 Recalled in Blatch and Lutz, Challenging years, p. 79. See also E. C. Stanton, S. B. Anthony and M. J. Gage (eds), History of woman suffrage, 6 vols, 1881–1992 (New York, Source Books, 1970 reprint): S. B. Anthony and I. H. Harper (eds), vol. 4, pp. 310–11 which gives the text of part of her paper, 'Women and the economic factor', delivered to the National-American Convention in Washington in 1898, and compare also D. Kirkby, Alice Henry. The power of pen and voice. The life of an Australian–American labour reformer (Cambridge, Cambridge University Press, 1991), which also examines the international exchange of ideas among suffragists, most especially through the Women's Trade Union League, and which characterises these new ideas as 'industrial feminism'.

60 E. S. Pankhurst, Suffragette movement, p. 119, records that Ursula Bright offered to join the Pankhursts in leaving the Liberal Party for the ILP, but was dissuaded by Emmeline Pankhurst, who felt it was likely to lead to the loss of many of Ursula Bright's oldest friends.

61 See E. W. Elmy to H. McIlquham, 18 May 1892, vol. 6, EWEP, and compare with E. S. Pankhurst, Suffragette movement, p. 96. The episode is also discussed in Rubinstein, Before the suffragettes, pp. 144–5; Holton, Suffrage days, pp. 85–6.

62 For a more extended discussion of this measure, see Holton, *Suffrage days*, esp. pp. 87–8.

63 U. Bright to E. Pankhurst, 30 May, 1 June, 26 June, 10 July 1894, ESPA, 325.

64 Alice Scatcherd appears not to have been at all supportive of the campaign among the tex-
    tile workers, promoted by the secretary of the Manchester branch of the NUWSS, Esther
    Roper, around the turn of the century, in which Christabel Pankhurst gained her early
    experience of suffrage campaigning. Possibly this reflected tensions in this period within the
    influential Manchester society, in which Alice Scatcherd had long been a prominent figure,
    and from which Emmeline Pankhurst also appears to have become alienated. Certainly,
    Priscilla Bright McLaren blamed this uncharacteristic hostility towards an initiative among
    working-class women to Alice Scatcherd's earlier being 'spoiled' by joining the Women's
    Franchise League, see Priscilla Bright McLaren to Esther Roper, 11 July 1901, MPLA
    M50/1/2/84. Alice Scatcherd died in 1906, just as the WSPU was becoming a national pres-
    ence. Elizabeth Wolstenholme Elmy was among its earliest and most earnest promoters,
    also becoming a member of the ILP in these years. Ursula Bright was increasingly drawn
    away from political life, especially after the death of her husband, and following her conver-
    sion to theosophy. By 1908 her own ill-health confined her to a wheelchair. Nonetheless,
    she, too, consistently offered the WSPU her public endorsement.

2

A truly national movement: the view from outside London

WE are so accustomed to thinking of the metropolis as dominating every aspect of our lives, from politics to the media, that we forget it has not always been so. Earlier in the century a very much smaller percentage of the population lived in the south-east; there was far more local democracy and far less centrality of political life; and every city and region had a thriving local newspaper that helped to shape opinion as much as, or more than, the nationals. All this was even more true of Scotland and Wales than of England.

This is not to deny that London, as the home of parliament, represented the 'centre', which is why the Women's Social and Political Union (WSPU), led by Emmeline and Christabel Pankhurst, moved there from Manchester, and why headquarters of all the other suffrage organisations were also based there. But those at the centre see things from a very specific, metropolitan viewpoint, which may not be shared by residents in other parts of the country.

Historians have recently begun to look at how the history of the women's suffrage movement in Britain was shaped in the years after the vote was won, and to question whether there are alternative histories which have been ignored or dismissed by those who did the shaping.[1] The only way to find out is to go back to the original source material, and, by asking new questions, try and discern what has been distorted or missed. One approach is to move right away from the 'centre', away from Westminster and the suffrage organisations' headquarters, to elsewhere in Britain, to view what was going on in both urban and rural areas away from London. My own work on Scotland, combined with studies of particular cities and regions of England, and preliminary studies of Wales, may provide a different perspective on the movement.

Before attempting any kind of 'alternative' history, let us rehearse, albeit in a very simplistic way, the 'orthodox' history, as taught in schools.[2] The women's suffrage movement properly began, it is generally agreed, in 1867, when John Stuart Mill's women's franchise amendment to the Second Reform Act was thrown out of parliament. Three local societies – in London, Manchester and Edinburgh, subsequently followed by Bristol and Birmingham – were formed and joined together to campaign for propertied women to be granted the vote. A recent publication described the Victorian campaign as 'tiny',[3] and those involved in the Edwardian movement emphasised the futility of the earlier campaign tactics. From 1906 onwards 'militancy' ensured public awareness of the issue, though not everyone agreed with the Pankhurst style of leadership, and in 1907 a second militant organisation, the Women's Freedom League (WFL), was formed (though it hardly features at all in any histories of the movement).[4] The movement for women's suffrage was very middle class in composition. In contrast to the suffragettes, the law-abiding suffragists carried on campaigning in traditional ways, while their membership numbers grew and grew. Eventually they disowned the militants as being counter-productive to the cause. Militancy, meanwhile, having failed in its milder manifestations to get women the vote, became increasingly violent (especially after 1912), escalating from window-smashing to home-made bombs and arson. In retaliation, the government passed the infamous Cat and Mouse Act in April 1913, and when that failed to have an effect, had hunger-striking women forcibly fed. Violence and schism alienated many of the early, brighter, supporters of the WSPU, leaving only an extreme rump to carry on the fight. Deadlock was averted by the outbreak of the First World War, after which the government granted women – or, at any rate, some women – the vote.

Oversimplified the above may be, but it is a recognisable picture, so let us look at how accurate a representation it appears to be when we move away from London, the 'centre'.

It is true that the London National Society for Women's Suffrage grew out of a committee temporarily formed in May 1866 to present a petition to parliament, but the assertion that the societies that formed in Edinburgh and Manchester (and, a little later, in Birmingham and Bristol) were 'local' until they joined together as the Central Committee of the National Society for Women's Suffrage[5] is not. As they said themselves at the time, they were 'parts of one National Society – united yet independent'.[6]

The most obvious tactic at the time seemed to be the collection of petitions in order to reveal the strength of public feeling on the matter. Between 1867 and 1876 some two million signatures were collected in Scotland alone, where there was, of course, a much smaller population than in England.[7] A movement that can collect millions of signatures is hardly 'tiny'. It is also worth recalling that the key figure in the movement from the 1860s until her death in 1890 was the editor of the *Women's Suffrage Journal*, Lydia Becker, who operated from Manchester, not London. By the early 1870s there were committees of the National Society in towns and cities all over Scotland, as far north as Orkney and Shetland and as far south as Dumfries and Ayr, and in many English towns, including Liverpool and Birkenhead.[8] The Scottish press was certainly on the side of suffragism in those earlier days. An editorial in the *Scotsman* of 13 November 1868 concluded:

> In this country the highest political rights are held by that one of the female sex who wears the honoured name of Queen Victoria, and these political rights have seldom been so well exercised in the history of the world ... A vote at a Parliamentary election is about the lowest of all political rights. It is within the reach of every man who has property qualification a grade or two removed from beggary, although he can neither read nor write, and although he be as ignorant of political questions as a horse. And yet that small common political right is denied to women, however rich and however intelligent, and that too in a country in which the legislative performance of M.P.'s and of noble Lords are of no effect until they have received the royal assent of a woman.

One difficulty in charting the course of the Victorian movement is that it was not a single-issue campaign. Women in the 1860s had a host of disabilities to overcome: they were denied higher education or entry to the professions, they could not vote for councillors, magistrates or members of school boards – let alone stand for them – and if they were married their husbands had an absolute right over all their property. Activists were therefore campaigning on many fronts, and progress was faster on some than on others.

That the activists were almost entirely middle class is undeniable; it was they who had time to spare. However, there was at least one speaker in the Victorian movement who stressed her working-class background, and she deserves to be remembered. Jessie Craigen, the daughter of an Italian actress and a Scottish sailor, addressed innumerable meetings – many of them out of doors and to working-class audiences – throughout Scotland and the north of England during the early 1870s. She had no paid employment in the movement, but collected minimum expenses to keep her going.[9] Her emphasis was on the 'unity of womanhood'. Without denying the 'barriers of caste, creed and education', she believed that those divisions 'are not deep or high ... they do not separate the hearts of womanhood that beat in unity'.[10]

The president of the Edinburgh society was Priscilla Bright McLaren. She was the third wife of the radical MP, Duncan McLaren, whose household was a centre for the women's movement (McLaren's daughter Agnes, by his second marriage, campaigned for the vote as well as for women's entry into medical schools, and eventually qualified as a doctor). She was also the sister of anti-Corn Law campaigner John Bright, and champion of women's suffrage in the House of Commons, Jacob Bright, which indicates something of the links and networks the movement had in the British Isles. Another key household in Edinburgh was that of the Stevenson sisters, with the unmarried ones, Flora, Louisa and Eliza, being prominent in every aspect of the women's movement.[11]

The death of Lydia Becker in 1890 signalled the end of the *Women's Suf-*

frage Journal, but it did not signal the end of the women's suffrage movement. By the 1890s women had achieved many of the other goals for which they had been campaigning, as a result of which they were more highly educated and active than ever, but the parliamentary franchise was still denied them. Activity was particularly marked in the Lancashire cotton towns, where two middle-class suffragists, Esther Roper and Eva Gore-Booth, galvanised the factory women – the highest paid and most well-organised of any working-class women at the time – into campaigning for the vote.[12]

At the other end of the spectrum a new recruit to the cause was Lady Frances Balfour, a daughter of the Duke of Argyll, who campaigned for some twenty-five years for the franchise.[13] With the aristocracy a solid, immoveable bastion of conservatism and the *status quo*, Lady Frances's position was in many ways as awkward and difficult as that of any working-class woman.

Lady Frances was present in the House of Commons in 1897 when a suffrage bill passed its second reading by 230 votes to 159. When they heard the numbers and a majority of 71 'we were left without words, "incredible" one woman said in my ear, then I was shaking hands with a dozen also being kissed, and I saw 2 sobbing! ... No one had dreamt of such a success.'[14] This was a private member's bill that did not proceed further, but it shows that the cause was anything but moribund at the end of the nineteenth century. Indeed, it was in 1897 that the National Union of Women's Suffrage Societies (NUWSS) was formed when seventeen societies joined together under the leadership of Millicent Fawcett. And there was an upsurge of activity in the opening years of the new century. A Glasgow and West of Scotland Association for Women's Suffrage was formed in 1902, and a new national magazine, the *Women's Suffrage Record*, was launched at about the same time. The Pankhursts' WSPU did not arise out of a vacuum but out of a movement that was burgeoning in many parts of the country.

The publicity-grabbing tactics of the WSPU, particularly the disturbance in the women's gallery of the House of Commons in April 1906, made headlines in newspapers all over Britain and 'votes for women' a subject for discussion everywhere. The WSPU headquarters had moved from Manchester to London, but though the emphasis in most histories is on the demonstrations in the capital, at the time the Pankhursts were well aware of the need to carry with them the whole country, and not just the metropolis. Together with other key figures in the early stages, such as Charlotte Despard and Teresa Billington-Greig, they travelled the length and breadth of the country, rousing enthusiasm.

The effect they had on existing suffrage societies can be traced in the minutes of the Glasgow and West of Scotland Association.[15] Some of the founder members were inspired by Teresa Billington-Greig and tried to persuade their committee to invite her as a speaker, but a core group would have no truck with any kind of militancy, and the dissatisfied members eventually left and joined the WSPU instead. They included Janie Allan, who was thereafter one of the wealthiest supporters of the WSPU, and Mary Phillips, their paid organiser who also left to join the WSPU as a paid organiser.[16]

The arrival of the WSPU must have made a similar impact on many other established, non-militant ('constitutional') suffrage societies. One writer commented that 'whether the WSPU's action horrified or excited the Manchester constitionalists, it definitely forced them to become more active and adopt new tactics'.[17] This was not true everywhere: the Glasgow and West of Scotland Association, once rid of its dissidents, continued to function much as before, though naturally there were many more members and many more activities as time went on. However, in general the statement is valid, and because of this it was possible, at least in the early stages, to belong to more than one organisation. An early defection in the other direction was that of Helen Fraser, who had been inspired by Teresa Billington-Greig to devote her life to the movement, and who was the first WSPU organiser for Scotland. She was so shocked when stones were thrown that she threw in her lot with the constitutionalists. In turn, she brought in some of the new methods of campaigning, such as tours of the country in a horse-drawn caravan to deliver open-air speeches, something which would never have been contemplated before the advent of the WSPU.[18]

Of course, there were many parts of Britain that in 1906 did not have any kind of functioning suffrage organisation. This was true of Wales, where the first such organisation was established in Llandudno (a town with a large English middle class) in January 1907. Although the WSPU sent speakers to Wales at an early stage, including Emmeline Pankhurst herself in 1906, most of the new societies being set up in both the north and south were constitutional and affiliated with the NUWSS. Wales was solidly Liberal in its political leanings, so the WSPU's slogan of 'Keep the Liberals Out' did not go down well, and WSPU speakers faced hostility.[19]

Scotland was also a Liberal stronghold of Britain, but the labour movement was well established there, particularly in Glasgow, where a new weekly socialist journal was established in 1907. The *Forward* was a lively paper, and its editor, Tom Johnston, strongly supported the suffrage movement and carried a column by Mary Phillips. While the Pankhursts might have increasingly distanced themselves from their early associations with the Independent Labour Party, in Scotland the connection remained strong. In autumn 1907 the *Forward* gave individuals on both sides of the rift between the WSPU and the breakaway organisation that subsequently became known as the Women's Freedom League the opportunity to air their viewpoints.[20]

As so many of the Scottish WSPU members had been inspired to join by Teresa Billington-Greig (who married Frederick Greig in 1907 and thereafter made her home in Scotland) rather than the Pankhursts, it is not really sur-

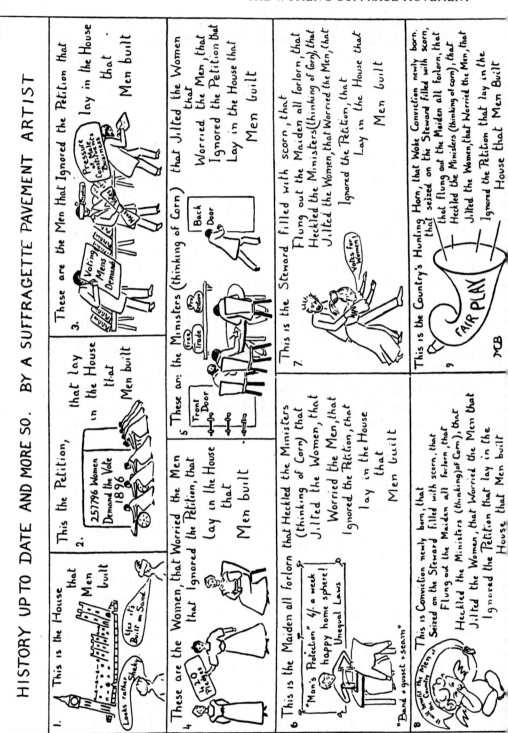

prising that they should have left the WSPU for the WFL. The WFL maintained a strong presence in Scotland throughout the campaigning years, though the WSPU branches remained intact, and many individuals, like Mary Phillips and Janie Allan, remained loyal to the Pankhursts.

The WFL was the most active of the suffrage organisations in south Wales, and had strong support in mid-Wales as well.[21] The NUWSS also had many societies in Wales, but the WFL certainly attracted more adherents than the WSPU there. The likeliest explanation appears to be that Welsh women who were attracted to militancy but unwilling to abandon their Liberal principles found a home in the militant society that did not pursue anti-Liberal tactics.

Traditional histories of the movement tend to present an either/or situation: an activist was either a law-abiding suffragist or a militant suffragette. This view has been presented by women who had themselves been totally committed to one side or the other, for example, in *The Cause*, written by Ray Strachey, secretary to the NUWSS leader Millicent Fawcett, or in Sylvia Pankhurst's *The Suffragette Movement*.[22] However, when Ann Morley and Liz Stanley attempted to trace the life of Emily Wilding Davison they came to the conclusion that that was 'no convincing evidence of any complete local divide between NUWSS, WFL and WSPU women at any stage. In spite of formal pronouncements by leaders, many women from different organisations supported a wide range of militant activity and worked closely together at a local level over various issues.'[23] And, indeed, as soon as one moves away from the centre, this becomes very evident.

To give just a few examples: in November 1908 there was a mass meeting held in Portsmouth, described as 'one of the largest political or semi-political gatherings that had ever taken place there'. On the platform were representatives of local branches of both the NUWSS and the WSPU. In February 1909, when Christabel Pankhurst visited Liverpool for the first time, her hostess was Mrs Allan Bright, a leading member of the local constitutional society. As late as June 1912, militants and non-militants joined together in Manchester to organise a large demonstration in Platt Fields. In that same year the Edinburgh constitutional society (which was much less rigid and conventional than the Glasgow one) sold tickets and provided stewards for WFL meetings. The very mention of the WFL shows how mistaken the idea of rigid demarcation lines really is. Claire Eustance found that WFL branches in Portsmouth and Brighton co-operated with local branches of the NUWSS and the WSPU, and also with men's societies for women's suffrage, and this certainly happened in other parts of the country as well.[24]

Consideration of the WFL also raises the question, 'What *was* militancy?', discussed by Claire Eustance in chapter 3. In January 1906 Flora Drummond (from Arran, but already a leading member of the WSPU central committee)

Cartoon (facing) by an anonymous supporter of the Women's Suffrage League attended a meeting in Glasgow with a woman companion, addressed by the Prime Minister. Knowing that heckling was a feature of Scottish political meetings, both women expected courteous replies when they raised the question of votes for women; instead they were unceremoniously thrown out of the hall. Women soon came to realise that, as far as men were concerned, interrupting a political meeting was acceptable only when done by them; when attempted by women it put them beyond the pale: 'The woman who faces the crowd', wrote Bella Brand in the *Dundee Advertiser*, 'and stands up in a meeting to utter her protest against the subjection of women to men defies convention and throws aside that much-prized virtue – respectability. She gives up friendships that she values; often she renounces all her past life.'[25]

No doubt this was one reason why in the early years Scottish women would take part in demonstrations – and even go to prison – in London, rather than on their home ground, where they would be recognised by members of the local community. The first Scottish WSPU 'demonstrations', involving women hiding on rooftops of halls (in hopes of sneaking into political meetings), and attempting to force their way into halls where meetings were taking place, were in Glasgow and Dundee in 1909, and in neither city were the ringleaders local.[26]

Did the movement, therefore, emanate entirely from London? The answer, of course, is 'no', and particularly clear proof is provided by the letters pages of a Dundee newspaper. In 1908 Winston Churchill fought – and won – the seat for Dundee, so from then onwards the central committee of the WSPU took a close interest in the city. But before that happened – in the closing months of 1907 – a very lively debate on the whole issue of women's right to the vote took place in the *Dundee Advertiser*. It arose within Dundee itself, so it is clear that the strength of the movement in the city came from its citizens, not from outsiders.[27]

And, while Scottish women might at first have hesitated to make a public spectacle of themselves on home ground, in common with England and Wales they were busy forming themselves into suffrage societies affiliated to the NUWSS. Even in Shetland – as far as one can get from London and still be in the Britain – such a society was formed in 1909. The minutes show that while the members lacked confidence in their abilities as public speakers, they knew themselves to be a part of a great movement that linked women the length and breadth of the land.[28]

After the failure of the conciliation bills and the 'torpedoing' of Asquith's reform bill, there was a new mood of desperation.[29] Scottish militants no longer shrank from taking part in demonstrations on home ground, or from expressing their feelings publicly. Instead of being a matter of shame, it was now one of pride to be branded a militant suffragette. Naturally, the Scottish press, while expressing shock and horror, took every advantage of the situation.

In Andrew Rosen's history of the WSPU he paints the organisation in the final months of its existence as a 'rump', with virtually all of the best minds having at various stages deserted.[30] There is no denying that many names that appeared regularly in the WSPU paper *Votes for Women* in the early years were absent in the latter ones, but the traffic was by no means only one way. Dr Alice Ker (who qualified in 1879), for example, was a niece of those pioneers of women's rights campaigning in Edinburgh, the Stevenson sisters. She went to live in Birkenhead in 1888 after marrying her cousin Edward Ker, a shipping merchant in Liverpool, and continued practising as a doctor. In the 1890s she became involved in the local suffrage campaign, and after her husband's death in 1907 she became more deeply involved. But it was only in 1912, with the scrapping of the second conciliation bill, that she switched her allegiance entirely to the WSPU and was imprisoned in Holloway after taking part in the massive window-breaking action in London in March of that year. She was not a young woman, and had two teenage daughters, so to undergo such an ordeal was no easy option, and she continued to work for the organisation after her release in spite of the fact that none of her friends in the NUWSS followed her.[31] The discovery of such a woman seriously challenges Rosen's contention that the finest minds had abandoned the WSPU when militancy became extreme.

Similarly, in Scotland, Arabella Scott, a university graduate and teacher, spoke at open-air meetings under the auspices of the WFL from 1909 onwards, but clearly decided that non-violent militancy was getting nowhere, for in April 1913 she was convicted of attempting to set fire to a stand at Kelso racecourse. Fanny Parker, a niece of Lord Kitchener and graduate of Newnham College, Cambridge, was involved in the Scottish Universities Women's Suffrage Union from 1909 until 1911, but from 1912 onwards she was a WSPU organiser, and in July 1914 she was caught trying to blow up the cottage where Robert Burns was born in Alloway. Both women ended up being forcibly fed in Perth prison.[32] Again, such a course of events contradicts Rosen's version of what happened, and can only be seen if one moves away from the centre and looks at the movement elsewhere.

Reactions to the radical change of policy by the NUWSS in the final years of campaigning are interesting to note at local level. Having operated as an entirely non-partisan organisation for most of its existence, the National Union also lost confidence in the two main political parties to deliver the franchise to women, but as the Labour Party had a manifesto commitment to introduce votes for women, an election fighting fund (EFF) was set up to campaign for Labour candidates. How would such a policy go down in Liberal-dominated Scotland and Wales? In Scotland, even within the constitutional wing of the movement there were women in sympathy with the labour movement, and they, of course, wholeheartedly supported the policy. Some pragmatists who did not support Labour for any other reason appreciated that the party offered the best hope of getting the vote. But in Glasgow support for the Liberals was so strong that the Association there voted their chairman onto the Scottish Federation EFF committee in order to monitor the situation, which led to ructions between that body and the national committee. Meanwhile, the South Wales Federation, inevitably, was rigidly opposed to the whole idea of the EFF, and did its best to sabotage the policy, though national organisers there worked with Labour supporters.[33]

That the Edwardian women's suffrage movement in Britain was dominated by middle-class women is undeniable. They had the time, the means and the educational background to become organisers, speakers and committee members. Nobody doubts that there must have been a working-class component to the movement; the difficulty is in tracing it. The existence of a large body of women factory workers, in whose welfare the suffrage societies took a great interest, did not necessarily mean that those women would themselves become involved. Sarah Peacock was unable to find any evidence of working-class women in the dress trade in Portsmouth playing any part in the movement in that town. The Lancashire cotton towns were different, according to Liddington and Norris, for there the factory women were highly organised and motivated. However, Catherine Leech, who wrote a thesis on Manchester before Liddington and Norris published their book, found that the leaders there were middle class and that one of the few exceptions, Sarah Reddish, who had started out as a textile worker, was, by the time of the campaign, a Poor Law Guardian and a member of Bolton Education Committee. And Terry Jane Berry, who studied Oldham in the light of Liddington and Norris's book, found, to her surprise, that the movement there, right in the centre of the cotton factory area, was very upper middle class in nature.[34] Thus, even in a part of Britain which seemed to Liddington and Norris to be dominated by a strong working-class presence, that presence seems more elusive when looked for more closely.

In October 1907 the *Dundee Courier* noted a large representation by the Jute and Flax Workers' Union amongst the hundreds of women who travelled from that city to Edinburgh for a suffrage procession. And the Dundee representative on the WFL national executive committee called her branch 'entirely working class', though we know that many branch members were teachers, so, without doubting that there were also working-class members, there seems to have been some fudging between 'working' and 'working class'.[35]

When the names of working-class women emerge from the mist, unless they either fought their way up to middle-class status, like Sarah Reddish, became national figures, like Annie Kenney,[36] or wrote an autobiography, like Hannah Mitchell,[37] it is through sheer historical accident. A Dunfermline factory worker, Jenny McCallum (a WFL member) was arrested in a 1908 disturbance outside the House of Commons and imprisoned for a month in Holloway. Her name does not appear in any suffrage literature of the period, and her brief involvement is known only because in 1968 a reporter on the *Dunfermline Press* unearthed the story.[38] The name of Jessie Stephen, who joined the WSPU at the age of 16 in 1909, does not appear in any contemporary sources either, though she took part in the pillar-box campaign in Glasgow; dressed as she was in the muslin apron, black dress and cap and cuffs of a domestic servant, no one suspected her of dropping acid into letter boxes. Jessie Stephen later went to London where she worked for the East London Federation of Suffragettes, the breakaway socialist- and-working-class-oriented organisation founded by Sylvia Pankhurst. She was an active socialist, pacifist and trade-unionist throughout her life; that is why she came to be interviewed in the 1970s, which in turn is why we now know about her.[39] She insisted that the picture of the movement as solely middle class was a 'distortion', and that there was 'a tremendous number of working-class women'.[40] Alas, all but a handful remain in the shadows, but the more local investigation that is undertaken, the greater the chance of discovering more – the latest being a key figure in the WFL in Wolverhampton, Emma Sproson.[41]

Was the women's suffrage movement in any way different in Scotland and Wales? The obvious response to that question is: different from what? Nancy Bonney looked closely at one English county, Essex, and found that certain towns, such as Clacton, Rayleigh and Chelmsford, were centres of WSPU activity, while Colchester was noteworthy for its constitutional campaigning, and Saffron Walden was disappointing from every point of view. No one apparently attempted arson in Essex: 'non payment of taxes and the chalking of pavements seemed to be the limit of militant action'.[42] If there was so much variation within one county, and such a vast difference in the level of activity between counties of England, comparisons between England and Scotland or Wales become rather meaningless.

However, there are clear differences between Scotland and Wales. Scotland, as was noted earlier, had a strong women's rights organisation in place at the time the WSPU was formed, so though militancy may have imported, there was no sense, as there appears to have been in Wales, of a group of upper-middle-class English women trying to thrust the new campaign down alien throats. (The Welsh did have one 'indigenous' suffrage organisation – the Cymric Suffrage Union – but it was in London.[43]) The movement clearly grew much more quickly in Scotland than in Wales, but when it came to the final phase of violent militancy, there were many attacks of arson and home-made bombs in both countries, some at least carried out by local women who were imprisoned – and, in Scotland, forcibly fed – as a result. In this way, at least, Scotland and Wales were arguably more 'typical' than Essex.

Both Scotland and Wales were targeted from the beginning of the WSPU's campaign because they were the Liberal strongholds of Britain. But Lloyd George was a national hero in Wales, so to attack him, as the WSPU naturally did, was to attack a Welsh icon. In Scotland, by contrast, Asquith and Churchill

48 THE WOMEN'S SUFFRAGE MOVEMENT

were Englishmen who had chosen to stand for Scottish seats simply because they were 'safe'; to attack such men was in no way to attack a Scottish idol.[44]

When the NUWSS journal, the *Common Cause*, headed a front-page drawing on the 15 June 1911 issue 'The March of England's Women', Scottish members were understandably irate. However, they, and the Welsh, possessed what has been called 'concentric loyalty': they were at the same time proud to be either Scottish or Welsh and proud to be British. (In this, of course, they were quite different from the Irish, who, on the whole, did not wish to remain British, and for whom the story of the suffrage movement really was different.) The WSPU utilised the colourful cultural stereotypes of both countries. When Mary Phillips was released from jail in 1908 the WSPU put on a grand show, with women decked in tartan, the skirl of bagpipes and a wagonette covered with purple heath and giant thistles. Mary was 'very proud of the Scottish welcome', when they all sang 'Scots Wha Hae wi' Wallace Bled'. Similarly, the red dragon of Wales, and Welsh national costumes, were prominent in suffrage processions.[45]

Has this chapter seriously challenged the potted 'history' presented at its beginning? It has certainly challenged aspects of it, but, more important, it has revealed how much there still remains to be learned about the women's suffrage movement in Britain. The movement was altogether more complex than older histories would have us suppose, and there is plenty of scope for further discoveries by moving away from the centre and into other parts of the country where women fought for the right to vote.

NOTES

I gratefully acknowledge the financial support of the ESRC for my research into the women's suffrage movement in Scotland. Graham Sutton's comments on an earlier draft of this paper improved the final version.

1 L. E. Nym Mayhall, 'Creating the "suffragette spirit": British feminism and the historical imagination', *Women's History Review*, 4, 1995, pp. 319–44.
2 See, for example, R. Fulford, *Votes for women – the story of a struggle* (London, Faber and Faber, 1957), Andrew Rosen, *Rise up women! The militant campaign of the Women's Social and Political Union 1903–14* (London, Routledge and Kegan Paul, 1974); M. Pugh, *Votes for women in Britain 1867–1928* (London, Historical Association, 1994), and Diane Atkinson *Votes for women* (Cambridge, Cambridge University Press, 1988).
3 Atkinson, *Votes for women*, p. 10.
4 The Pankhursts defined 'militancy' as 'demanding', rather than 'asking for' the franchise. Initially 'militancy' consisted mainly of interrupting political meetings and of demonstrations outside the Houses of Parliament.
5 Pugh, *Votes for women in Britain*, pp. 9–10.
6 Letter from Clementina Black to Lydia Becker, 8 August 1867, Manchester City Library archives, M50/1/2/27.
7 E. King, *The Scottish women's suffrage movement* (Glasgow, People's Palace Museum, 1978), p. 10.
8 I traced the formation of Scottish committees and societies from the *Women's Suffrage*

Journal, as did M. van Helmond for her *Votes for women – the events on Merseyside 1870–1928* (National Museums and Galleries on Merseyside, 1992), pp. 15–16. It would be easy to do the same for other parts of England from the same source, but I do not know of anyone who has undertaken this.

9   L. Leneman, *A guid cause: the women's suffrage movement in Scotland* (2nd edn, Edinburgh, Mercat Press, 1995), pp. 22–7 and 257. Sandra Holton recently discovered much more about this unusual woman: see S. S. Holton, 'Silk dresses and lavender kid gloves: the wayward career of Jessie Craigen, working suffragist', *Women's History Review*, 5, 1996, pp. 129–49.

10   S. S. Holton, *Feminism and democracy: women's suffrage and reform politics in Britain 1900–1918* (Cambridge, Cambridge University Press, 1986), p. 27.

11   Leneman, *A guid cause*, pp. 264, and 271–2; Fulford, *Votes for women*, p. 83.

12   J. Liddington and J. Norris, *One hand tied behind us: the rise of the women's suffrage movement* (London, Virago, 1978); Gifford Lewis, *Eva Gore-Booth and Esther Roper, a biography* (London, Pandora Press, 1988).

13   Leneman, *A guid cause*, p. 33.

14   Quoted in *ibid.*, p. 36.

15   The minutes are in the Department of Rare Books and Manuscripts, Mitchell Library, Glasgow.

16   Leneman, *A guid cause*, pp. 44 and 50.

17   C. E. Leech, 'The feminist movement in Manchester 1903–1914' (unpublished MA dissertation, University of Manchester, 1971), p. 23.

18   Leneman, *A guid cause*, pp. 63–6.

19   K. Cook and N. Evans, '"The petty antics of the bell-ringing boisterous band": the women's suffrage movement in Wales 1890–1918', in A. V. John (ed.), *Our mothers' land: chapters in Welsh women's history 1830–1939* (Cardiff, University of Wales Press, 1991), pp. 159–188:167–9.

20   Leneman, *A guid cause*, pp. 43 and 51.

21   L. Dee and K. Keineg, 'The Swansea suffragettes', in *Women in Wales: a documentary of our recent history*, vol. 1 (Cardiff, Womanwide Press, 1987), p. 68; C. Eustance, 'Daring to be free' (unpublished Ph.D. thesis, University of York, 1993), pp. 104–5.

22   R. Strachey, *The cause: a short history of the women's movement in Great Britain* (London, G. Bell and Sons, 1928, reprinted Virago, 1978); E. Sylvia Pankhurst, *The suffragette movement: an intimate account of persons and ideals* (London, Longmans, Green, 1931).

23   A. Morley with L. Stanley, *The life and death of Emily Wilding Davison* (London, Women's Press, 1988), p. 152. See also K. Cowman, 'Engendering citizenship' (unpublished Ph.D. thesis, University of York, 1994).

24   S. Peacock, *Votes for women: the women's fight in Portsmouth* (Portsmouth, City of Portsmouth, 1983), p. 14; van Helmond, *Votes for women*, p. 37; Leech, 'The feminist movement in Manchester', p. 30; Leneman, *A guid cause*, p. 126; Eustance, 'Daring to be free', 102.

25   Leneman, *A guid cause*, p. 40; *Dundee Advertiser*, 11 December 1907.

26   Leneman, *A guid cause*, p. 79.

27   L. Leneman, 'Dundee and the women's suffrage movement: 1907–1914', in *The remaking of Juteopolis* (Dundee: Abertay Historical Society Publication, 32, 1992), p. 82.

28   The minutes are available in the Shetland archive. I am grateful to Brian Smith for providing me with a copy.

29   In 1910 and 1911 militancy was suspended while two private members' bills were debated in parliament. (They were known as 'conciliation' bills because they were so limited it was hoped they could attract enough cross-party support to be passed.) After the failure of the second Conciliation Bill in March 1912 militancy was resumed, and after the ruling by the Speaker of the House that adding a women's suffrage amendment to Asquith's Franchise Reform Bill would so change its character that it would have to be withdrawn, militancy exploded into arson and bomb attacks on property. Rosen, *Rise up women!*, pp. 162, and 187–9.

30 *Ibid.*, p. 208.
31 Van Helmond, *Votes for women*, pp. 52–66.
32 L. Leneman, *Martyrs in our midst: Dundee, Perth and the forcible feeding of suffragettes* (Dundee, Abertay Historical Society Publication 33, 1993), pp. 21–6 and 30–3.
33 Leneman, *A guid cause*, pp. 196–7; Holton, *Feminism and democracy*, pp. 108–9; Cook and Evans, '"The petty antics of the bell-ringing boisterous band"', p.181.
34 Peacock, *Votes for women*, p. 9; Liddington and Norris, *One hand tied behind us*; Leech, 'The feminist movement in Manchester', p. 36; T. J. Berry, 'The female suffrage movement in South Lancashire with particular reference to Oldham 1890–1914' (unpublished MA dissertation, Huddersfield Polytechnic, 1986), p. 28.
35 Leneman, 'Dundee and the women's suffrage movement', pp. 81 and 87.
36 Annie Kenney was a cotton operative who became one of the first members of the WSPU central committee and remained devoted to the Pankhursts until the end. Her autobiography, *Memories of a militant*, was published in 1924.
37 Hannah Mitchell's unpublished autobiography was edited by her grandson Geoffrey Mitchell, and published as *The hard way up* (London, Faber, 1968). She was also one of the first WSPU central committee members, but she subsequently moved to the NUWSS.
38 Leneman, *A guid cause*, p. 94.
39 Brian Harrison interview with Jessie Stephen 1 July 1977, Harrison tapes collection, Fawcett Library; interview with Jessie Stephen by Suzie Fleming and Golden Dallas, in *Spare Rib*, February 1975, reprinted in *Spare Rib reader* (London, Penguin, 1982).
40 Brian Harrison interview, quoted in Leneman, *A guid cause*, p. 133.
41 S. P. Walters, 'Emma Sproson – a Black Country suffragette' (unpublished MA dissertation, University of Leicester, 1993).
42 N. Bonney, 'Essex women and the campaign for female suffrage 1850–1914 (Unpublished dissertation, Brentwood College of Education, 1971).
43 Angela V. John, '"A draft of fresh air": women's suffrage, the Welsh and London', in *Proceedings of the honourable society of Cymmrodorion for 1994* (1995). The activities of Welsh suffragettes in London is an important part of the story of Welsh suffragism but is not discussed further in this chapter which is looking at the suffrage movement outside the capital.
44 The point about Lloyd George comes from Cook and Evans, '"The petty antics of the bell-ringing boisterous band"', p. 180.
45 Leneman, *A guid cause*, pp.103 and 67; Cook and Evans, '"The petty antics of the bell-ringing boisterous band"', p.181.

3

Meanings of militancy: the ideas and practice of political resistance in the Women's Freedom League, 1907–14

IN 1906 Teresa Billington-Greig, a member of the Women's Social and Political Union (WSPU), rationalised the militant protests carried out by suffrage activists. Writing from a cell in Holloway Prison, she argued;

> To so be shut out from the rights and privileges of law is to be an outlaw. An outlaw must be either a rebel or a willing serf. Anyone who believes in human liberty and self-government is forced to rebel. There is no other way. It is either servile submission to tyranny or rebellion against it.[1]

The 'rebellion' alluded to by Billington-Greig, and the subsequent arrest and imprisonment of suffrage activists, signalled a new urgency and conviction among supporters. These militant acts generated a widespread expansion in women's suffrage societies, and the subsequent developments in female political activities were to have an enormous impact on gender relations in British society.[2] And yet, the diverse and multiple interpretations of female suffrage militancy in this period have received little detailed attention. This chapter sets out to redress this oversight by considering the 'meaning of militancy' for members of the militant suffrage society, the Women's Freedom League (WFL).

The WFL came into existence in November 1907 following a disagreement among the leadership of the WSPU two months earlier. The issue at stake was whether the expanding numbers of militant suffrage supporters should operate under democratic principles, or be controlled by an non-elected leadership. Those in favour of a democratic constitution, led by Teresa Billington-Greig, Charlotte Despard and Edith How Martyn, were strongly opposed by Emmeline and Christabel Pankhurst and their supporters, and the outcome was the emergence of two opposing WSPU committees. The pro-democracy committee, which was backed by twelve branches, did not manage to secure either the WSPU's finances or offices, and soon recognised that it would have to relinquish its claim to be the 'original' WSPU. Consequently, in November 1907, members voted to accept the new title of the Women's Freedom League.[3]

The attempt by WFL members to develop women's suffrage militancy through democratic processes raises important questions about broader interpretations of female militancy in the years leading up to partial enfranchisement in 1918. The records of the actions of, and discussion between WFL members in meetings, national conferences and the branches provides insights into militancy that have not been considered in the extensive – and often conflicting – accounts of the WSPU. Depictions of militancy as a purely political weapon that degenerated into a form of millenarianism, or as an exclusive tactic available only to a few well-off women, do not apply in the case of the WFL.[4] While analyses of suffrage militancy in relation to friendship networks are useful, those accounts that describe only the negative implications of militancy after 1912 are incomplete, and fail to do justice to the diverse programme of political resistance developed by the WFL.[5] On the contrary, in considering the meanings of militancy in the WFL, it is possible to trace its emergence as a forward-thinking and nationwide feminist organisation.

In later years, Teresa Billington-Greig was to claim that over and above the issue of internal democracy, the source of her disagreement with the Pankhurst leadership in 1907 lay in differences of opinion over militant tactics. Billington-Greig contended that WSPU actions failed to be directed sufficiently towards the institutions and practices that reinforced women's lack of equality with men.[6] Although this received little attention at the time of the split, a number of differences in the styles of WSPU and WFL militancy did emerge. First, in the latter months of 1907 the decision was taken by the WFL committee to discontinue the practice of interrupting speeches made by politicians at public meetings. Instead, in early 1908, members began calling on Cabinet Ministers at their homes in order to ask for an opportunity to put their case in favour of suffrage reforms. Second, new militant protests devised by Teresa Billington-Greig were implemented, and League members staged protests in police courts in London and Glasgow about the lack of justice women received in these 'man-made' courts.[7] In addition, tax resistance was reclaimed as a legitimate form of protest by unenfranchised women, and members were initially advised to resist paying income tax, property tax and inhabited house duty. Shortly afterwards, in March 1908, WFL member Dr Octavia Lewin became the first suffrage passive resister to be taken to court.[8]

The ideas contained in Teresa Billington-Greig's writings in Holloway in 1906 were enshrined in the WFL's constitution: the purpose of members' actions was to demonstrate a widespread refusal to be governed by the instruments of male authority until women were granted equality. Until women were enfranchised they were 'outlaws' and therefore justified in breaking laws instigated by men. The first indication of how the wider League membership viewed Billington-Greig's interpretation of militancy came during the League's annual conference in early February 1908. In accordance with the WFL's democratic principles, this was the opportunity for delegates representing branches to decide policies relating to all aspects of the League's organisation and work, and to elect the national executive committee.[9]

Discussions at the conference indicated that a need for clarity on the meanings and implications of militancy was an important concern among some members. In response to a request for a definition of 'the word "militant"', Teresa Billington-Greig referred delegates to the relevant clauses of the League's constitution. She added that what was justified by outlawry was 'anything from Police Court protests to the blowing up of the Houses of Parliament'.[10]

Although there was vocal endorsement of Billington-Greig's comments, it was apparent from subsequent actions that many delegates had not rigorously considered the implications of militancy. At a basic level, they understood militant protests as an expression of anger because the parliamentary political parties and particularly the government – had failed to act on women's demands. Yet it was also clear that some members had found it difficult to reconcile calls for militancy by WFL leaders with their own circumstances. The Middlesbrough delegate pointed out that it was 'impossible for all members to indulge in militancy', not least because those who were employed in paid work would find it difficult to take part in certain actions.[11] This dichotomy between a public image of outlawry and revolt and the practical barriers faced by many women's suffrage activists was an important factor in the development of WFL militancy in subsequent years.

At this early stage in the campaign, while the justification for militancy was not seriously questioned by WFL conference delegates, problems were apparent when attempts were made to justify particular actions. The most serious difficulties occurred when one delegate at the WFL's 1908 annual conference questioned what constituted legitimate protests for 'outlaws'. The Clapham branch delegate, Miss Murby, voiced her opposition to the protests that had taken place outside Cabinet Ministers' homes, claiming that such actions were those of 'ordinary street disturbers'.[12] Murby's comments were drowned out by cries from other delegates, and speakers rose to defend their imprisoned colleagues. Edith How Martyn stated unequivocally that government Ministers were answerable wherever they were.[13]

The issue was nominally resolved by an overwhelming vote in support of the League's militant policy, yet the potential pitfalls that had opened up when the policy was examined in detail remained. In response to concerns raised about the ability to participate in militancy, the conference accepted the condition that all members had to support militant policy, even if they did not actively take part.[14] However, this compromise failed to acknowledge the need to maintain the enthusiasm and commitment of the dispersed membership, and this was confirmed during 1908 when some newly formed branches disbanded.

Nevertheless, militant actions in 1908 continued to be dominated by high-

profile protests and the losses of some branches were obscured by the momentum in the campaign that produced new branches in other areas. Protests in the
vicinity of parliament and outside the homes of Cabinet Ministers were inter-
spersed with actions that were guaranteed to attract press attention. In October
1908 the League captured the headlines in a number of national newspapers
after members embarked on a night-time bill-posting campaign when copies of
the League's 'Proclamation' were stuck on to 'hundreds of public buildings in
London, Scotland and the provinces', including on the wall outside New Scotland Yard.[15] As one newspaper report commented, 'Nothing could have exceeded
the adroitness.'[16]

Shortly afterwards, on 28 October, two League members, Muriel Matters
and Helen Fox, chained themselves to the grille that segregated the Ladies'
Gallery from the chamber of the House of Commons, and attempted to address
MPs.[17] Nearby, simultaneous protests in the vicinity of St Stephen's Hall led to
the arrests of fourteen other League members, among them Mary Manning, a
teacher from Sale, who had travelled down to London in order to take part in
militant protests.[18] Although many of the militant actions undertaken by the
League were in London, members in Scotland and other areas did leave their
mark, and, if anything, members protesting in their own communities took relatively greater risks, as they lacked the anonymity possible in London. Nevertheless, the numbers involved in these protests were relatively few – in 1908
twenty-nine WFL members were imprisoned – compared with a membership in
the thousands spread across over fifty WFL branches.[19]

When delegates from forty of these branches met in London for the 1909
annual conference, there were clear indications that secretly planned and sporadic
London-based actions alone did not meet the needs of a growing and diverse
membership. Delegates from provincial branches spoke of their difficulties in
maintaining a distinct WFL identity in their communities, and appealed to the
League's London headquarters for more support for their branch activities.[20] In
response, the national executive committee admitted by way of an explanation
'that the office is agitated by periodic earthquakes in the form of militant protests'.[21]

Added to these difficulties, a resolution put forward by Finchley branch
members, recommending a temporary modification of militant tactics because
they were damaging public opinion, indicated that some members believed that
militancy was becoming less effective.[22] Although this resolution found no sec-
onder, it did demonstrate the concerns of some members about hostile public
reactions to militancy. The concerns expressed at the conference about militancy
and communication with WFL branches highlighted the oversights by the
League's national committee in registering the diverse circumstances of members. Nevertheless, the continued concentration on activities in London in 1909
demonstrated the lack of practical initiatives to remedy the imbalance between
headquarters and branches.

In 1909, attention was paid by the WFL's leadership to the declining impact of its militant protest, and new actions were planned that were designed to emphasise the failure of the government to respect long-standing democratic traditions. One action involved an appeal to a long-standing constitutional right to petition the King through the Prime Minister. Asquith's refusal to respond to this request led to another WFL protest, where members picketed the House of Commons continually between 6 July and 28 October 1909, in the hope that their presence and the attending press interest would force Asquith to meet them.[23] Although the WFL's peaceful picket was admired in many quarters, it was unsuccessful, and members' impatience spilled over into disturbances and arrests in nearby Downing Street.[24]

The disappointments encountered by the WFL during the summer of 1909 culminated in the attempt by two members to destroy ballot papers at a by-election in Bermondsey in late October. The impact of this action was profound, and press reports were especially condemnatory and exaggerated; the *Pall Mall Gazette* described it as an 'outrage unparalleled in English history'.[25] Attention focused on the minor injury suffered by a returning officer during the protest, and the protesters, Alison Neilans and Alice Chapin, were tried, found guilty of interfering with a ballot box and common assault, and sentenced consecutively to three and four months imprisonment.[26]

Reactions to the Bermondsey protest demonstrated both the antagonisms of the press and public to militancy, and the final straining of co-operation between the constitutional and militant sections of the suffrage movement, but more significant still were the reactions within the WFL. *The Times* reported that the League's Burton branch had severed its connections and had decided to affiliate to the constitutional National Union of Women's Suffrage Societies (NUWSS), because of the Bermondsey protest.[27] Although delegates at the next annual conference supported in varying degrees the actions of Neilans and Chapin, a note of caution was registered in the decision that militant protests in the future should not involve the risk of personal injury to bystanders.[28]

The expressions of support for militancy among delegates attending the 1910 annual conference belied the organisational difficulties in some WFL branches. Concerns again surfaced that the League was losing out to both the WSPU and NUWSS, and this was partly confirmed by recurrent financial difficulties and the lukewarm reaction to the launch of the League's own newspaper, *The Vote*, in October 1909.[29] While reorganisations in departments at the League's London headquarters and new instructions concerning regional organisation had produced some positive effects,[30] it had become obvious that militancy undertaken in the name of the WFL had little currency in the branches. In the face of the difficulties within the WFL, the issue uppermost in branch and national officials' minds at last merged into considering how to translate the message of militant resistance to a government which excluded women, into practical activities in branches.

The decision by the WFL and the WSPU to suspend militant activities in 1910 in order to monitor the progress of the all-party conciliation bill through parliament was timely. However, even though hopes were high that some measure of women's suffrage would be passed, the League's national committee did not entirely abandon its policy of resistance, and members were encouraged not to pay their taxes. Their inspiration was the WFL president, Charlotte Despard, who was threatened with imprisonment in June 1910 in relation to her non-payment.[31] Although there was no official acknowledgement by the NEC, it was evident that militant protests along existing lines had reached the limits of their effectiveness.

Particularly significant during the 1910 truce was the lessening of the imbalance between attention given over to militant protests and arrests and the activities in the League's sixty-plus branches that were spread across the British Isles. This development was not purely coincidental, because although militancy had not been widespread in the League, without it members and officials had to work much harder to get publicity and donations for the campaign. Opportunities both to publicise suffrage demands, and to bring members of the League together in large numbers arose in the WSPU processions in the summer of 1910. In June League members in their hundreds travelled to London to march in the impressive 'From Prison to Citizenship Procession', and joined their designated sections, which ranged from Ju-Jitsu to East End Sweated Workers.[32] Most indicative of the change in emphasis during the militant truce was the opportunity for League members to display their demands publicly and collectively in direct contrast to the secrecy that had surrounded many militant protests in the past.

With relatively greater levels of support from headquarters, WFL branch activities diversified during 1910. The most successful branches acknowledged the varied circumstances, interests and skills of their members, and branch meetings increasingly reflected this. For example, in Edinburgh, the WFL branch organised meetings specifically for students and in other branches the 'Mother and Baby At Homes' encouraged women with young families to take an interest in the League's work.[33] During 1910, branch meetings were much more likely to address subjects considered by members to have relevance to the WFL's work, and these included discussions on the Poor Law, women's municipal work and food reform. This diversification beyond the direct aim of female enfranchisement also saw the development in the branches of a social network. What was to be later described by the Portsmouth branch as the mixing of 'propaganda with pleasure' was manifested in musical evenings, fund-raising dinners and socials.[34]

Some branches chose theatrical means to challenge inequalities between men and women, which involved the participation of large numbers. Particularly successful were the performances of Cicely Hamilton's *A Pageant of great women*, which had first been produced in London in November 1909.[35] After its success, League branches in Sheffield, Ipswich, Middlesbrough, Sunderland, Eastbourne and Swansea were lent costumes and props in order to perform the *Pageant* in their own towns.[36] Although these social activities and diverse discussion topics were not consciously acknowledged as political resistance, branches were creating environments where an interest in challenging the barriers to women's equality could be reinforced and refined.

While the development of a political culture in the branches would prove to be crucial in the long-term future of the WFL, in 1910 the most pressing consideration remained achieving votes for women. In the face of government intransigence, the continuing inconsistencies in the WFL's militant policy once again became apparent following a return to militant protests by the WSPU in November 1910, in which a small number of WFL members took part. The WFL was bound by a commitment not to criticise the actions of its 'sister society', and its official policy, agreed at a special conference, was to continue supporting the truce in militancy until the government's intentions were clarified.[37] Less reticent about criticising the WSPU were Teresa Billington-Greig and Conciliation Committee chairman, Lord Lytton, who, through articles in *The Vote*, expressed dismay at of the resurgence in WSPU militancy. Their comments provoked equally critical counter-attacks from a small number of WFL members who expressed support for the WSPU.[38] The war of words fought out in the columns of *The Vote* emphasised the lack of consensus in the WFL, and the bitter round of accusations and counter-accusations culminated in Billington-Greig's resignation from the League at the end of 1910. Her resignation was backed up with the publication of scathing criticisms of the entire militant movement shortly afterwards in 1911.[39]

In Billington-Greig's *The militant suffrage movement* Emmeline and Christabel Pankhurst and the WSPU were subjected to a fierce attack. Furthermore, given the crucial role Billington-Greig had occupied in the WFL, her assault on her former colleagues was particularly harsh. In the chapter entitled 'The Freedom League Failure' the WFL was condemned for failing to distinguish itself sufficiently from the WSPU. While supportive of the work of the Conciliation Committee, Billington-Greig also contended that crucial opportunities had been missed to adopt wider concepts of militant feminist revolt against inequality and male power, and that instead of allowing democracy to work for them, the League had suffered through the weakness of its leaders and had stagnated in red tape and bureaucracy.[40]

The impact of Billington-Greig's departure and criticisms was surprisingly limited, especially given her central role in the development of the WFL since 1907. Although the lack of clarity in purpose had infuriated Billington-Greig, many WFL members did not appear to share her radical ideas, and, equally, her visions of all-out rebellion were too idealistic to be a tangible option for the diverse membership. The differences of opinion apparent among members of the NEC and delegates at the 1911 annual conference were more a product of the tense political situation than with Billington-Greig's departure. Moreover, as in previous moments of potential crisis in the League, a majority of members managed to pull together in a display, albeit tenuous, of outward unity, and after a number of forthright discussions, conference delegates backed their national committee.[41] Nevertheless, Billington-Greig did leave an important legacy in her identification of a broad-based policy of political resistance that extended beyond confrontational militant protest undertaken exclusively towards achieving the vote. Although not as radical as Billington-Greig had envisaged, during 1911 aspects of her ideas began to come to fruition as greater numbers of WFL branches endorsed protests that involved larger numbers in resistance to government without consent.

With a militant truce once again in place, but with a greater awareness that the campaign might not be imminently successful, League members turned in greater numbers to passive resistance. Early in the year Laurence Housman, a member of the Men's League for Women's Suffrage, put forward proposals for a large-scale disruption of the 1911 census and this was immediately taken up by the WFL.[42] The numbers of women taking part increased considerably following the subsequent endorsement of the WSPU and support from some members of the constitutional societies. On census night branches all over the country took part, and in Manchester it was reported that sixteen houses had been placed at WFL members' disposal so that they could absent themselves from their homes to avoid taking part in the census. In Edinburgh it was reported by the secretary, Miss Sidley, that the numbers taking part in the protest had reached 'four figures'.[43] The publicity generated by the protests was widespread, and with justification Edith How Martyn writing in *The Vote* commented that it was 'the most effective protest yet made by women against government without consent'.[44]

Passive resistance by suffrage supporters extended the established tradition of civil disobedience, and, in particular, appealed to League members who could not or did not want to take part in active militancy. Due to the efforts of the Women's Tax Resistance League, which had been formed in 1909, and the continuing work of the WFL, tax resistance had become a feasible alternative to violent confrontation for greater numbers of women, particularly when dog licences and other minor taxes were included in the campaign. This inclusion made it possible for women with low incomes to take part, and working-class member, Emma Sproson, was one of a number of women who resisted paying her dog licence, along with wealthy WFL treasurer, Elizabeth Knight.[45] Entire branches took part in tax resistance: in Edinburgh members abstained from paying taxes on the branch's bank account, and at the other end of the country, the Brighton branch of the WFL rallied around their secretary and treasurer who had goods seized in lieu of non-payment of inhabited house duty.[46]

Women's Freedom League supporters boycott the census 1911

Branch members' support for passive resistance proved crucial for the WFL following the WSPU's resumption of militancy in 1912 and the subsequent arson and destruction that ensued. Appealing to those self-declared militants who did not endorse the new direction of WSPU members, Despard clarified the position of the League;

> We occupy a unique and peculiarly difficult position, but a useful one ... We are in the middle of two opposing principles ... Militancy to the WFL is an elastic weapon ... We can use it or we can refrain. When we use militancy we put forward the logic behind it.[47]

In spite of severe and damaging difficulties among national committee members which focused on unsuccessful attempts to challenge the growing influence of Charlotte Despard, the special conference of April 1912 did have a more positive outcome in terms of a clear definition of WFL militancy.[48] Distinctions between the WSPU and the WFL were formerly outlined when delegates endorsed a policy of militancy without violence. Furthermore, WFL militancy officially included passive resistance with the statement that militant actions involved 'any protest involving the risk of imprisonment'.[49] This inclusion of passive resistance in definitions of militancy marked an explicit acknowledgement by members of a wider spectrum of civil resistance, and plans were made to boycott goods produced and sold by opponents of women's suffrage.[50]

However, conference delegates continued to convey their belief that the need for women's suffrage was immediate and many did not want to relinquish a commitment to return to more directly confrontational, 'active' militancy. In response to Despard's plans to cripple the economic system through a 'Producers and Consumers League', the remark of one delegate emphasised the sense of urgency: 'we should be working for the vote for our great-great-grandchildren'.[51]

In the months that followed, the impetus towards active militancy, together with a desire for caution among members, was skilfully balanced by Charlotte Despard in the enticing rhetoric she used in articles in *The Vote*. She continually implied that a return to militancy was imminent by calling for members to volunteer for 'danger duty', but asserted that the League's actions would be logical and considered.[52] This policy served to maintain the active involvement of members who tended to support WSPU actions and vocally condemned the treatment of suffragette prisoners, yet it also reassured members who did not want the League to follow the path set by the WSPU.

Although there was a danger that the WFL's actions might be submerged beneath those undertaken by WSPU members, they nevertheless succeeded because many branches had by this time developed their own campaigns and critiques against the exploitation and disabilities suffered by women, and were therefore less dependent on instructions issued by their leadership in London. These ranged from the Swansea branch's campaign for women's lodging houses in their town, to the Portsmouth branch's decision to boycott Huntley and Palmer goods because of its discrimination against unionised workers.[53] Charlotte Despard's comment, 'We are "builders" as well as "fighters"', crucially reflected the development in the WFL's policy of resistance.[54] The leadership and members of the WFL had negotiated this dual emphasis on 'building' the militant campaign to attack a range of barriers to women's equality, and 'fighting' the government in their refusal to do justice to women and acknowledge them as citizens.

The WFL leadership marked their eventual loss of patience with the political manoeuvres of the government and parliament at the end of January 1913, when Charlotte Despard and Elizabeth Knight led a protest march to Westminster, and were subsequently arrested.[55] The impact of this protest was measured not by the degree of militancy, compared with the WSPU, but by the impact on WFL members across the country: the message was that the WFL was once again in active, militant conflict with the government. The developments that had taken place in the WFL between 1909 and 1913 were evident in the numbers taking part in subsequent militant actions and the lessening of the imbalance between actions in London and the rest of the country. Branches in Portsmouth, Middlesbrough, Manchester and Brighton organised secret billposting campaigns in their towns which were reminiscent of those carried out in London in 1908.[56] Members in all parts of the country conducted a 'war against law' and entered police courts to record proceedings related to women's lack of equal treatment before the law, and protested against the forced exclusion of women from courts when cases with explicit sexual references were discussed.[57] Tax resistance continued with well-attended public meetings organised at the sale of goods. The most publicised protest was undertaken by Kate Harvey, who in May 1913 barricaded herself into her home in Bromley.[58]

The militant policy pursued by the WFL was deemed disruptive enough by the authorities to warrant counter-measures to minimise the impact of members' protests. To their anger, tax resisters found their fines were anonymously paid. Further attempts to hinder the League's work were made when they were banned from holding meetings in Caxton Hall in London. However, in spite of these measures, which provided useful publicity for the League, the greater underlying significance of the WFL's resumption of active militancy in 1913 lay in the acknowledgement by members of the need to develop broader challenges to the social, economic, legal and political barriers to women's equality.

At what proved to be the final conference before the outbreak of the First World War, plans were discussed for a series of deputations to parliament to protest against women's lack of economic power in marriage, and the disabilities women faced in local government.[59] Another suggestion was proposed which entailed crippling the Bank of England by depleting its gold reserves. Although it never came to fruition, this plan, which clearly drew on older radical traditions of protest, was well received by conference delegates.[60] Much less popular was the suggestion to initiate a campaign to assist working women to limit the size of their families – until women were enfranchised. The reservations that it would lead to 'unlimited licence' reflected a more general ambivalence about birth control among members of the League.[61] In the event, the outbreak of war in August 1914 meant that members were never required to choose whether to support such radical plans.

After the declaration of hostilities the WFL leadership announced a suspension of active militancy, but there was no call to cease all actions, and some members continued their tax resistance.[62] The secretary of the WFL, Florence Underwood, was one of a number of members who continued to refuse to pay income tax during the war.[63] This pattern of individual action by members replaced the large-scale militant resistance at all levels of the WFL, and was compounded by the decline in confrontational references to militancy in The Vote and other suffrage publications. The last discussion on political resistance that included WFL branches took place in 1915, when a plan to resist compulsory registration was discussed, and it was eventually announced that while, individually, members could resist, no official, co-ordinated action would be organised.[64]

The remaining years of war confirmed the culmination of active militant protests and the use of a provocative rhetoric of militancy, yet, significantly, the

emphasis on resistance to the instruments of female oppression had been sufficiently ingrained in the identity of the WFL to ensure its continued influence in
the years after 1918. Through this process the WFL developed from a militant
suffrage society to a post-suffrage, feminist organisation.

This chapter has traced aspects of militancy that have largely been overlooked
by historians. The opportunity for the membership of the WFL to be democra-
tically represented in discussions on female militancy led to a diversification in
policies and actions. Although at times a difficult and divisive issue, militancy in
the WFL developed into a policy of non-violent resistance against women's
oppression. It also ensured, for those members who desired it, the maintenance
of a confrontational militant identity. Although after 1912 the WFL rarely dominated the headlines, and its members did not commit, and were not subjected
to the violence experienced by members of the WSPU, it played a crucial role in
the developing of a broader feminist agenda. The widespread endorsement of
this meaning of militancy by WFL members had a lasting legacy that deserves
its place in 'new' histories of the women's suffrage campaign in Britain.

NOTES

1 T. Billington-Greig, 'The militant policy of Women Suffragists', Manuscript, 12 November
   1906. Written in Holloway Prison and reprinted in C. McPhee and A. FitzGerald (eds), *The
   non-violent militant: selected writings of Teresa Billington-Greig* (London, Routledge and
   Kegan Paul, 1987), pp. 113–14.
2 For details of the suffrage societies in this period, see A. J. R. (ed.), *Suffrage annual and
   women's who's who* (London, Stanley Paul and Co., 1913).
3 *Women's Franchise*, 14 November 1907, p. 227.
4 A. Rosen, *Rise up women! The militant campaign of the Women's Social and Political
   Union 1903–1914* (London, Routledge and Kegan Paul, 1974), pp. 196, 245; and L. Garner, *Stepping stones to women's liberty: feminist ideas in the women's suffrage movement,
   1900–1918* (London, Hutchinson, 1984), pp. 44–9.
5 A. Morley with L. Stanley, *The life and death of Emily Wilding Davison* (London, Women's
   Press, 1988), p. xiii; S. S. Holton, *Feminism and democracy: women's suffrage and reform
   politics in Britain 1900–1918* (Cambridge, Cambridge University Press, 1986), pp. 34–5.
6 See T. Billington-Greig, 'The militant suffrage movement: emancipation in a hurry', (1911)
   reprinted in FitzGerald and McPhee, *The non-violent militant*, pp. 143–70.
7 *Women's Franchise*, 28 November 1907, p. 253, and S. Newsome, *A history of the Women's
   Freedom League 1907–1957* (London, WFL, 1958), p. 4.
8 *The Daily Chronicle*, 17 December 1907 and 28 March 1908, Maud Arncliffe Sennett Collection of Press Cuttings, Pamphlets, Leaflets and Letters on Women's Suffrage, British
   Library, London (hereafter referred to as MAS), vol. 2, p. 41 and vol. 3, p. 15. Holton had identified tax resistance actions by women suffrage campaigners that pre-dates this. See
   S. S. Holton, 'From anti-slavery to suffrage militancy: the Bright circle, Elizabeth Cady Stanton and the British women's movement', in C. Daley and M. Nolan (eds), *Suffrage and beyond:
   international feminist perspectives* (New York, New York University Press, 1994), p. 228.
9 WFL Constitution (1912).
10 Verbatim Minutes, 3rd annual conference of the WFL, 1 February 1908 (VM 1908), p. 12
   (Fawcett Library, London).

11 *Ibid.*, pp. 13–15.
12 *Ibid.*, pp. 45–6.
13 *Ibid.*, pp. 46–9.
14 *Ibid.*, pp. 13–15.
15 WFL, *Annual Report*, 1908 (*AR* 1908), p. 11; *Daily Graphic* 13 October 1908; MAS, vol. 5, p. 36.
16 Unknown press cutting, MAS, vol. 5, p. 31.
17 *Daily News*, 29 October 1908, p. 5.
18 *The Times*, 29 October 1908, p. 10, and 30 October 1908; MAS, vol. 5, p. 88.
19 *AR* 1908, p. 21.
20 Verbatim Minutes, 4th annual conference of the WFL, 9 January 1909 (VM 1909) pp. 7–9, 16–19, 21, 46–7.
21 *AR* 1908, p. 6.
22 VM 1909, p. 32.
23 Mrs Gerard, 'Hats off to the past, coats off to the future' (London, WFL [1932]), pp. 2–3.
24 *The Times*, 10 July 1909; MAS, vol. 7, p. 95.
25 *Pall Mall Gazette*, 28 October 1909; MAS, vol. 8, p. 82.
26 Alison Neilans, *Ballot box protest: defence at the Old Bailey*, (WFL, London, c. 1910).
27 *The Times*, 1 November 1909; MAS, vol. 8, p. 90.
28 Verbatim Minutes, 5th annual conference of the WFL, 29 January 1910, pp. 11–16.
29 *Ibid.*, pp. 9–17.
30 National Executive Committee Minutes, Fawcett Library, London (NEC), 20 November 1909, p. 112.
31 WFL, *Annual Report*, 1910 (*AR* 1910), pp. 10–11.
32 The Vote, 4 June 1910, p. 69, 18 June 1910, pp. 93–94, 25 June 1910, pp. 98–107.
33 *The Vote*, 26 November 1910, p. 56; WFL *Annual Report*, 1910, p. 25. See also C. Eustance, 'Daring to be free: the evolution of women's political identities in the Women's Freedom League, 1907–1930' (unpublished Ph.D. thesis, University of York, 1993), Ch. 2.
34 *Ibid.*,
35 See J. Holledge, *Innocent flowers: women in the Edwardian theatre*, (London, Virago, 1981), pp. 69–71.
36 *The Vote*, 30 April 1910, p. 11, 14 May 1910, p. 26, 15 October 1910, p. 294, 22 October 1910, p. 305, 29 October 1910, p. 3; *AR* 1910, p. 19.
37 *The Vote*, 5 November 1910, p. 21, and 26 November 1910, pp. 50, 51.
38 *Ibid.*, 26 November 1910, p. 54, 10 December 1910, p. 81, and 17 December 1910, p. 95.
39 NEC, 6–7 January 1911, p. 30; *The Vote*, 28 January 1911, p. 164, 4 February 1911, p. 183, 11 February 1911, p. 194.
40 Billington-Greig, *The militant suffrage movement*, pp. 171–8, 185–93.
41 Verbatim Minutes, 6th annual conference of the WFL, 28 January 1911, pp. 47–8; *AR* 1910, p. 8.
42 *The Vote*, 11 February 1911, pp. 187, 190.
43 *Ibid.*, 15 April 1911, pp. 299, 302.
44 *Ibid.*, 8 April 1911, p. 286.
45 Untypically, in Sproson's case this resulted in a harsh sentence: six weeks imprisonment in the Third Division. M. Wynne Nevinson, *Five years struggle for freedom: a history of the suffrage movement, 1908–1912* (London, WFL, 1912), p. 16. Other accounts of members tax resistance can be found in *The Vote*, 1911–15.
46 WFL, *Annual Report* 1911 (*AR* 1911), pp. 19–20, 22.
47 *The Vote*, 3 February 1912, p. 172.
48 Verbatim Minutes, special conference of the WFL, 27–8 April 1912 (VMSC 1912), pp. 2–76.
49 VMSC 1912 (Sunday), p. 27.
50 *Ibid.*, pp. 32, 34–5.
51 *Ibid.*, p. 36.
52 For example, *The Vote*, 14 August 1912, p. 292.

53 *Ibid.*, 24 February 1912, p. 214, and 23 March 1912, p. 267; *AR* 1911, p. 31.
54 *The Vote*, 7 December 1912, p. 98.
55 NEC, 8 February 1913, pp. 33–4.
56 *The Vote*, 14 February 1913, pp. 269, 270; WFL, *Annual Report*, 1914, pp. 24, 26.
57 *The Vote*, 23 May 1913, p. 55, 13 June 1913, p. 107, 27 June 1913, p. 137.
58 WFL, *Annual Report*, 1913, p. 16.
59 Verbatim Minutes, 9th annual conference of the WFL, 28 March 1914, pp. 15–31.
60 *Ibid.*, pp. 80–1.
61 *Ibid.*, pp. 61–71.
62 *The Vote*, 14 August 1914, p. 278.
63 WFL, *Annual Report* 1915–1919, p. 8; *The Vote*, 1 January 1915, p. 455.
64 *The Vote*, 26 November 1915, p. 829.

4

'Pay the piper, call the tune!': the Women's Tax Resistance League

> [A] law which compels persons debarred from Representation to pay taxes violates one of the fundamental principles of that Constitutional Spirit for which English-men have fought – that 'Taxation and Representation must go together'.[1]

TAX resistance as a form of protest had an illustrious history. John Hampden, the constitutional reformer, was the major inspiration of the Women's Tax Resistance League (WTRL). His refusal in 1635 to pay 'ship money', a tax imposed by Charles I, had helped precipitate the constitutional crisis which led to the English Civil War. Edwardian women tax resisters saw themselves continuing a proud tradition of dissent and opposition to unjust government. This chapter outlines the origins of the WTRL and examines its contribution to the suffrage campaign.

In its publicity material, the WTRL stressed the unconstitutional nature of a system which made disenfranchised women pay taxes to a government in which they could not participate. It combined an appeal to individual conscience with an acute awareness of the logic of its cause. The WTRL argued that it was not merely the right of women to resist taxation; it was also their duty. Women had to teach their irresponsible rulers that government without consent was not only tyrannous but impossible. To refuse to pay taxes was more in keeping with the constitution than to subscribe willingly to an unconstitutional tyranny.[2] Only fools would attempt the coercion of awakened and defiant womanhood.[3]

One of the WTRL's leaders, Mrs Darent Harrison, who later kept up a long-running refusal which included barricading her house against bailiffs, set out the case in a pamphlet, *The right to resist.* Men and women who felt injustice keenly were, she said:

> the makers of new standards, the natural guardians of the people's liberties and the nation's honour. Resistance to organised injustice is to them not a matter of choice but a spiritual necessity, a social obligation dictated by the voices which govern all wise and virtuous human action. What Reason urges, with due regard for consequences, as a right to be asserted, the 'still small voice' more insistently

commands as a duty to be fulfilled. Man is a spirit and can only be compelled by
superior spiritual force; only in so far as laws are recognised to be just laws can
they have any binding force in the court of conscience.[4]

Darent Harrison used metaphors such as 'the court of conscience' to claim rational and spiritual dimensions to tax refusal. People who saw every reformer as a
crank, every resister and anarchist as an enemy, provided easy prey for tyranni-
cal rulers. Rebellion and revolt had preceded all great advances in national freedom, she went on, citing the Magna Carta, the Reformation, and Dissenters and
Covenanters in England and Scotland. These, then, were the precedents recalled
to explain and justify tax refusal as a political action in the Edwardian suffrage
campaign.

Some attempts to resist taxation for the cause of women's suffrage had been
made before. In 1870 Anna Maria and Mary Priestman, members of the first
women's suffrage society in England, refused to pay their taxes, as a result of which
some of their goods (dining chairs) were distrained – that is, taken by bailiffs to be
auctioned to recoup the amount owed. The sisters' strategy was foiled when a misguided sympathiser paid the outstanding tax bill before the sale began. This happened again the following year, so the sisters abandoned that method of protest.[5]
In 1884 Henrietta Müller, the wealthy daughter of a German businessman, had
refused to pay taxes.[6] Some of her furniture was seized and auctioned, but was pur-
chased by friends who returned it. A more sustained action occurred in 1904,
when Dora Montefiore, a member of the Social Democratic Federation and the
Women's Social and Political Union (WSPU), resisted taxation for two years. She
intensified her protest in 1906, barricading her house and refusing entry to bailiffs
for six weeks, an act that was perceived by some in the suffrage campaign as the
first of constitutional militancy. 'Fort Montefiore' attracted a good deal of publicity,
with newspaper reporters and police camped outside the house and large crowds
coming to listen to speeches from leading members of the WSPU.[7]

The question of what should be classed as militancy, its advantages and
disadvantages, was frequently debated within the movement. Gradually, a number of positions evolved, and in 1909 the WTRL was founded. This was an off-
shoot of the Women's Freedom League (WFL), which was formed in 1907 when
several leading activists in the WSPU, alarmed by Emmeline Pankhurst's
increasing autocracy and the shift away from socialist ideals, formed a breakaway
group. The WFL combined a reformist constitutional approach with a flair for
imaginative publicity tactics, some of which overstepped social proprieties and
some of which were illegal. In the WFL it was generally accepted that militancy
would be non-violent; in 1908 the national executive committee unanimously
supported the resolution that 'we do not set out to damage persons or property'.[8]
Legitimation for militancy was claimed by the WFL's leader, Teresa Billington-
Greig, who cited as influences historical cases such as the Non-Conformist Tax

Resistance League, the Chartists and the Corn Law League.[9] Thus tax resistance offered another avenue for civil disobedience, less controversial or strident than some forms of militancy, and, moreover, legitimated by historical precedent.

The possibilities of tax refusal had been discussed fairly early in the suffrage campaign and by 1907 some WFL members had begun to refuse to pay taxes. An article in the *Women's Franchise* by Edith How Martyn, WFL secretary and a founder member, recorded Lady Steel's refusal to pay income tax and urged others to consider tax resistance.[10] By 1908 the WFL was working out policies and tactics to support tax refusers. Charlotte Despard, the charismatic WFL president, was a close friend of Dora Montefiore, and may have been influenced by her. During this period Despard was searching for a way to express her disapproval of government in accordance with her pacifist principles. Several times during 1909 she met Mahatma Gandhi, with whom she shared ideals. At that time he was developing his principle of *satyagraha*, the 'truth-force', a form of spiritual resistance which might involve civil disobedience. Gandhi recognised the high moral value of the suffragettes' sacrifices. Despard viewed her tax refusal as 'a form of passive resistance'.[11]

The formation of the WTRL provides further evidence to refute earlier historiographical accounts of Edwardian suffrage campaigners as being perpetually at loggerheads.[12] Members were drawn from a number of societies, including the National Union of Women's Suffrage Societies (NUWSS), the WSPU, the London Society for Women's Suffrage, the New Constitutional Society, the Conservative and Unionist Women's Franchise League, the Church League for Women's Suffrage, the Free Church League, the Catholic Women's Suffrage Society, the Actresses' Franchise League, the Artists' Franchise League and the Women Writers' Franchise League, as well as individuals who belonged to none.[13]

Having canvassed all existing suffrage societies, the WTRL began in October 1909 with a meeting at the home of Dr Louisa Garrett Anderson, daughter of the respected doctor, Elizabeth Garrett Anderson. There were strong feelings that it should be simply another branch of the WFL, but it was established as a separate body so that members of all suffrage organisations could join yet retain their existing allegiances to other societies. A committee was formed to work out aims and strategies. The WTRL's rationale was so apparent that it was thought to be unnecessary to encumber itself with a written constitution, although members were asked for an annual voluntary subscription. Its objectives were to enrol, advise and support women prepared to resist payment of taxes; to research and expose anomalies and irregularities in the tax system; to publicise the consequences of resistance, distraint and sales; and to lobby parliament on taxation issues. The slogan 'No Vote No Tax!' was adopted as the WTRL's motto, and brown and black were chosen for its colours. A committee member, the artist Mary Sargant Florence, designed its processional banner of white silk emblazoned with the legend 'Pay the Piper Call the Tune'.[14]

It was hoped that publicity would accrue once a tax resister's goods were seized by bailiffs. By manoeuvering the state into an invasion of the private sphere, the WTRL could draw attention to a brutal violation of the sanctity of the home. They envisaged a powerful psychological impact on a public conditioned to the belief that a woman's place was in the home. That site of popular sentiment, the domestic hearth, would be invaded – in the name of the King! Surely, the image of a woman's personal and household goods being seized by bailiffs would impress on the public mind the sacrifices made for the 'cause', and underline the logic of the WTRL's case.

Tax resisters used every opportunity to highlight the law's illogicality and injustice. As a Poor Law Guardian, Miss L. E. Turquand was a respectable citizen, yet was unable to participate fully in the parliamentary process.[15] She sent this letter to the Income tax officers:

> Sir, I enclose amount due from my landlord as property tax, and apologize for the delay. If I were only in the same position as my landlord, that is a recognized citizen of the State for which I have to pay the same rate, if like him I had a voice in the spending of the money which I am forced to contribute, then, indeed, I should be pleased also to send the amount claimed from myself as 'Inhabited House Duty'. But as it is I cannot do so. I belong to the Women's Tax Resistance League, and am pledged to refuse to pay Government Taxes, for we believe that 'Taxation without Representation is Tyranny,' and though we have to submit to the Tyranny, we are not prepared to subscribe to maintain it. To force women out of their earnings to pay salaries to Cabinet Ministers and M.P.'s to legislate for men, who, through the Ballot Box, command attention and consideration, is to me such a gross injustice that I offer no apology for my action. Faithfully yours, L. E. Turquand.'

The tax officers failed to persuade Miss Turquand to abandon her position; she was taken to court and fined.[16]

The WTRL could also find fault with legislation, pointing to many obvious disparities in bureaucratic regulations. Miss Janie Allan, a very wealthy woman, argued that since she was not deemed to be a person for the purposes of the Franchise Acts, she ought not to be considered a person within the meaning of the Finance Acts. Brought to court for non-payment of taxes, she stated: 'Until the law decrees that a woman is always and unchangingly a person, I consider it my duty to refuse to be subject to the penalties attached to being a person.'[17]

Participating regularly in suffrage demonstrations and processions, members of the WTRL made the most of their links with the historic struggles for liberty and democracy. They were present when a statue of Hampden, champion of the people's rights, was erected at Aylesbury in 1913. Members led a procession and laid a wreath – a circle of white flowers enclosing a ship made from brown beech leaves – with the words 'From women tax resisters'. They addressed the watching crowd, selling more than two hundred copies of a booklet outlining Hampden's objections to unjust taxation written specially for the occasion.[18]

During the five years of the WTRL's existence, more than two hundred and twenty women took part in tax refusal. Many more gave their support, joining in public demonstrations, making donations and assisting individual resisters through local branches of other suffrage societies. In addition to their feminist commitment, what features did the membership share? The available evidence suggests that the bulk of members were from the middle classes. In the main it was those women who were wealthy or independent enough to be liable for taxation who could participate. Resisters included the very rich, such as Charlotte Despard, the WFL treasurer and heiress to the Knight's Castile soap fortune Dr Elizabeth Knight, and Janie Allan of the Allan shipping line. Professionals and working women, many of whom had to rely on their own earnings, were also involved, as were some very poor women, such as Emma Sproson, a member of the WFL executive, who had started work as a part-time factory hand at the age of nine.

Of the total number of resisters, twenty-three were doctors, including Louisa Garrett Anderson,[19] the Malthusian birth control pioneer Alice Drysdale Vickery, and Ethel Bentham, who campaigned for better lodging houses for working women. There were a number of graduates, including one professor, Miss Edith Morley. The writer Cicely Hamilton, author of *Marriage as a trade*, and the journalist Evelyn Sharp, editor of *Votes for Women*, belonged. Neither was wealthy. The actress Lena Ashwell, one of the first women theatre managers, was a League member. Mabel Atkinson of the Fabian Women's Group resisted taxes, as did Edith How Martyn, later a birth control propagandist, and Anna Martin, a welfare centre organiser. Other refusers included Adela Pankhurst, the Duchess of Bedford, the Honourable Evalina Haverfield and Princess Sophia Duleep Singh, daughter of a maharaja.[20] Those taxes to which no resistance was offered included local taxes such as poor law or water rates, etc., which were not resented because propertied women had some control over the expenditure of local councils, as they had the municipal vote. It was the direct taxation involved in what the WTRL described as imperial taxes which were resisted.

These annual taxes fell into two categories: first, property tax, inhabited house duty and income tax; second, taxes and licences on dogs, carriages and motor cars, male servants, armorial bearings, guns and game. Resistance to the first category of taxes was complicated. For example, to refuse a property tax on the annual value of houses or land was practicable only when the resister was both owner and occupier. Nevertheless, the WTRL documented twenty-one cases of property tax refusal. Because unearned income was taxed through deduction at source it was difficult to withhold. It was easier to refuse income tax levied on earned income, and more than 80 members refused this tax. Inhabited house duty, a levy on the annual value of a house payable by the occupier only, was the most popular and readily resisted tax. About 140 members, over half the WTRL's activists, refused to pay it. Once the resister had ignored the various official forms and demand notices, a notice threatening distraint in ten days would be sent by the Inland Revenue, at which point the resister would make an official statement explaining her refusal to pay. After this, the tax collector could levy distraint. Bailiffs could enter the resister's home to take property of sufficient value to cover the amount owed plus costs. Typically, these might be a levy fee of about 3s 6d (17½p), a bailiff's fee of half-a-crown (12½p) and costs of transport and sale of the goods by public auction, including 7.5 per cent for the auctioneer. Furthermore, the tax could be collected through various forms of seizure: of money in a bank, of English stocks and shares, or of the resister's interest in a business, estate or property. If no goods or property of any kind were available for seizure the resister could be imprisoned for an indefinite period until the tax was paid.[21] In the second category, licences and taxes were due on the first day of the year; if payment was refused the resister could be summoned to appear before local magistrates who could impose a fine and make an order to pay the tax. If, after a statutory period, resistance continued, tax collectors were empowered to seize goods without further recourse to public or court proceedings.

As can be seen, the processes of law were complex. They took time to complete: often eighteen months would elapse between the initial refusal and distraint procedures. Such lengthy processes may have discouraged many suffrage campaigners from adopting tax resistance as a political strategy.

However, from 1909 the campaign snowballed, gradually culminating in a number of distraint procedures. Publicity could be maximised at sales of goods or when resisters barricaded their houses against the bailiffs. By 1912 this tactic was having some impact across the country. Moreover, the public sales of resisters' goods attracted people not normally interested in suffrage issues. The press might ridicule resisters, but ordinary people often sympathised with grievances about taxation. The WTRL was well aware of this. Sales took place in or near the homes of resisters, in public auction rooms, hotels and country inns, in public halls, on village greens, in market squares, at cattle shows and horse sales. Local shopkeepers and tradespeople, neighbours, family friends and acquaintances, including fellow members of local societies or church congregations, would recognise a familiar figure. Resisters were advised to advertise their distraint sales in local papers, arrange for the press to attend, distribute handbills in the locality and inform all local suffrage societies, so that processions, preferably headed by a brass band, could walk with them to the auction rooms. Thus 'men and women who would never trouble to attend a suffrage meeting' could be made aware of the principles for which women were sacrificing themselves.[22]

A list of typical goods seized 'under distress for rates and taxes' evokes an elegiac picture of the lifestyles of Edwardian middle-class households: six plated afternoon tea-knives in a case, fish carvers, a plated fruit knife and fork, a silver cake-basket, silver candlesticks, salvers and teapots. A painting by

Rembrandt was sold for £75 to satisfy the state's claims on Miss MacGregor in Arboath.[23] When roughly £80 worth of goods belonging to Mrs Tollemache, including 'much valuable old china, silver and furniture', were to be auctioned, antique dealers were seen 'buzzing like flies around the articles they greatly desired to possess'. It seems that the tax collector's agents had taken the opportunity to seize such rare pieces. To prevent their sale, while still meeting the tax demand, the first lots of ordinary furniture were bought at grossly inflated prices, thereby ensuring that Mrs Tollemache kept her valuable antiques.[24] Other suffragists or suffragettes would often purchase the goods to return to their owners. For instance, Miss Roll had her silver spoons bought in and handed back in a bag of red, green and white silk, the colours of the NUWSS. Charlotte Despard's piano, frequently distrained, was sold and bought in by friends, and became a standing joke in the columns of The Vote, the WFL journal, as did Elizabeth Knight's persistent dog licence evasion. Resisters were advised to surrender to bailiffs small items such as jewellery and silver plate rather than heavy furniture, since they would be charged with the cost of transporting distrained goods. Miss Lelacheur of Henley-on-Thames avoided her transport costs by surrendering a cow.[25]

Reports of sales in The Vote convey either sardonic humour or an impression of genteel behaviour. It was recorded that tax officials 'invariably acted with the greatest kindness and courtesy'.[26] Decorated with flags, bunting and quotations from John Hampden, Woldingham village hall in Surrey was packed out for the sale of Miss Anderson's goods. After speeches from WFL and WTRL officials, the 'kindness and forbearance' of the King's officers was acknowledged and Miss Anderson thanked them 'for carrying out the stern duties of their offices with so little unpleasantness'.[27]

Official policy towards tax resisters was not consistent. Some were pursued relentlessly, others left alone. At times, vindictive behaviour was demonstrated. Clemence Housman's case exemplifies the triviality of bureaucracy. Eventually, after months of resistance, she was imprisoned for refusing to pay inhabited house duty. The taxi that took her to Holloway cost the government 4s 2d (21p), which was, ironically, the amount of the original debt.[28] Many officials handling the cases could see the legitimacy of the resisters' position or were already in favour of women's suffrage. When Janet Legate Bunten, treasurer of Glasgow WFL, became the 'first Scotch Tax Resister' in February 1912, the presiding magistrate was pro-suffrage; he had recently chaired a campaign meeting. Nevertheless, for keeping a dog without a licence, she was first fined then sentenced to ten days' imprisonment.[29]

When similar cases are compared there is evidence of class discrimination in the judiciary's response. Little was done about Princess Duleep Singh's refusal to pay for licences for her eight dogs, whereas Miss Andrews of Ipswich was gaoled in the First Division for one week for non-payment of a dog licence.[30] For the same offence, Emma Sproson was twice imprisoned for a total of six weeks at Stafford in the Third Division, until, by hunger-striking, she was transferred to the First Division. Her dog was subsequently shot by the police.[31]

On occasion, WTRL members received unpleasant treatment from the general public. When the WTRL's accountant, Ethel Ayres Purdie, placed a sign reading 'Women's Tax Agency' in her office window, her landlord and fellow tenants (all men) demanded she delete the word 'women'. They considered it offensive and objectionable. Refusing to remove the sign, Mrs Purdie rented another office across the road, whereupon the landlord threatened to sue for breach of contract.[32]

Mrs Kate Harvey, Charlotte Despard's long-time companion, barricaded her home against bailiffs, withstanding an eight-month siege. She refused to contribute national insurance payments on behalf of her gardener, and was the first woman to be imprisoned for a case of this nature. She was sent to prison for two months and became a *cause célèbre*, with mass meetings in Trafalgar Square and at Caxton Hall on her behalf. When her goods were to be sold, the event was so chaotic and the crowd so hostile to the tax collector that he had to relinquish his task, losing £7 over the whole process.[33]

Many women resisting tax were single or widowed. The most striking anomalies and injustices in tax legislation concerned married women. It is ironic that those major successes of the nineteenth-century campaigns for women's emancipation, the Married Women's Property Acts of 1870, 1874 and 1882, should have had such little effect on that symbol of a woman's status – her independent earnings. Despite the Acts, a married woman was not legally liable for income tax. Under the 1848 Income Tax Acts the separate incomes of husband and wife were aggregated and treated as one. Regulations required a man to make an income tax return on both his own and his wife's income. The wife was neither legally bound to make a return nor to tell her husband what her income was. Through her husband a wife could claim an abatement on tax she had paid, but this would be returned to him; he could keep it and often did. The WTRL brought these kinds of issues to public notice.

Dr Elizabeth Wilks, a WTRL committee member, and her husband Mark fully exploited the anomalies in a two-year campaign. Initially, Dr Wilks had paid income tax, but found her abatement was given to her husband. Some property was distrained, but because it actually belonged to Dr Wilks it had to be returned, since she was not liable for tax. She then refused to disclose her income to her husband, and Mr Wilks informed the Inland Revenue that he could not make a full return as he did not know what his wife earned. An estimate was made of the tax due, but Mr Wilks refused to pay because he, a teacher with London County Council, could not afford the amount levied on his own and his wife's much larger income. The case continued until a writ was served, and Mr Wilks was incarcerated in Brixton gaol. Two weeks later he was released. The tax was never paid. This was a golden opportunity for the WTRL; there were appeals to the King. A series of protest meetings was held, and parliament was lobbied to bring about changes in the law. When questions were asked in the House of Lords, Earl Russell took the chance to point out the legislative inconsistencies. He argued for 'natural justice and common sense', proposing that a law: 'which renders a man liable to indefinite terms of imprisonment for matters over which he is by statute deprived of any control is undesirable and should be amended'.[34] For the government, Lord Ashby St Legers admitted the lack of logic in tax assessment. Mr Wilks's imprisonment had been intended as a deterrent, although other husbands were not likely to put themselves to this sort of inconvenience. He suspected 'there was something in the incident in the nature of a political demonstration'.[35] In the House of Commons, the Chancellor of the Exchequer, Lloyd George, admitted that the tax system as it stood brought in much needed revenue. Changes in the law could mean serious losses to the Treasury and he was not prepared to instruct the authorities to refrain from administering the law. He retreated on the subject of Mr Wilks, promising no further action against him.[36]

In a similar instance, Ethel Ayres Purdie conducted a successful appeal in a test case over tax refusal by Dr Alice Burns, the assistant medical inspector for Co. Durham, and a member of both the WTRL and the WSPU. Her appeal began in June 1911 and, after letters and threats of imprisonment, culminated in October 1912. Although Dr Burns's husband lived in New Zealand, she was, in the strictly legal sense, 'living with him', and he was liable for her income tax. Since he was outside British jurisdiction, the tax could not be claimed from him.[37] Ethel Ayres Purdie recounted with glee the more absurd aspects of the case in a three-part account, 'A red tape comedy', in The Vote. To prove the couple were still 'living together', the court checked the situation with Dr Burns's mother-in-law. A letter to Dr Burns from her husband was produced in court. Gentlemanly reticence prevented the Commissioner for Taxes from reading a letter from husband to wife, although he did ask how it began. It began 'Dear Alice', Ayres Purdie told him, adding 'Pray don't hesitate to read it ... it is quite a nice, conjugal sort of epistle just such as a man would write to his wife.'[38] By using Ayres Purdie's expertise in this and other cases, the WTRL was able to run rings round the law.

But Dr Burns's case was typical in that it took seventeen months to come to fruition. It was difficult to keep such cases in the public eye over long periods. This was the greatest problem in using tax resistance as a form of non-co-operation to highlight the injustice of denying women the vote: its impact was vitiated by lengthy legal procedures.

As a form of protest tax resistance was a method of civil disobedience or passive resistance available to those who were unwilling or unable to take part in the more contentious militant demonstrations. Those who resorted to tax refusal as a matter of principle could gain great moral satisfaction. Many participants were precisely those women who had inherited the privileges won from earlier campaigns for women's emancipation; they were educated, economically independent and had careers. Women from a number of suffrage societies adopted the tactic and suffered the penalties; their homes were invaded, personal possessions auctioned. They were fined and imprisoned; they endured financial anxiety and hardship, the prospect of losing their jobs or livelihoods, as well as the ignominy of having their finances discussed publicly. There was, however, no guarantee that the original refusal would be effective in terms of publicity. In many cases no action, distraint, fine or imprisonment occurred.

Tax refusal had a strong nuisance value and could be used as a goad with which to impale the government. But it may have arrived too late in the suffrage campaign for its potential as a form of propaganda to be developed to the full. On the day war broke out on 4 August 1914 a propaganda meeting was being held at Barnstaple and seven new members were enrolled in the WTRL. On 26 August 1914 an emergency meeting of the WTRL committee was called in London, and there was heated debate over whether to continue to withhold taxes. As Kineton Parkes recorded:

> There was naturally a great deal to be said on both sides, and it argued much for the strong individuality of the women tax resisters that those who had stood side by side in Suffrage work for years were now sharply divided upon the relative importance of principles and patriotism.[39]

Women, who as prisoners had occupied adjacent cells in Holloway, held conflicting opinions about whether to pay imperial taxes during the war. As in the NUWSS and other suffrage societies, there were sentiments of patriotism and qualms about open hostility to government in wartime which proved divisive. It was also recognised that if women were granted the vote, the WTRL's particular battle cry of 'No Vote No Tax!' would become redundant. By a small majority it was decided to suspend action. A small watch committee was appointed to keep an eye on events, but the WTRL ceased its activities. Many of its members joined forces with the WFL and the Actresses' Franchise League to form the Women's Emergency Corps, and offered help with the war effort.

Some individuals, however, continued their resistance right up until 1918. Evelyn Sharp was finally forced into bankruptcy by the accumulation of legal costs after failing to declare income tax and was: 'the last tax resister to suffer persecution at the hands of unrepresentative government in the women's long struggle for citizenship'.[40]

NOTES

1 M. K. Parkes, *Why we resist our taxes* (pamphlet, London, WTRL, n.d.), p. 7. Unless otherwise stated, WTRL pamphlets are in the Fawcett Library archives, London. Box WTRL 396.11:336.
2 *Ibid.*, p. 7.
3 E. I. Harrison, *The right to resist* (pamphlet, London, WTRL, 24 April 1913).
4 Harrison, *The right to resist.*
5 M. K. Parkes, *The tax resistance movement in Great Britain* (pamphlet, London, WTRL, n.d.), pp. 1–2. The Priestman sisters lived on until 1914, witnessing the formation of the WTRL.
6 Müller was one of the first women to attend Girton in 1873. The sister of Eva McLaren, wife of the M.P. Walter McLaren, Müller was a member of several suffrage organisations, the National Vigilance Association, the founder and editor of the *Woman's Penny Paper* and a representative on the London School Board. L. Bland, *Banishing the beast: English feminism and sexual morality 1885–1914* (London, Penguin, 1995), pp.12–13.
7 Parkes, *Tax resistance movement*, p. 2; D. Mitchell, *Women on the warpath* (London, Cape, 1966), p. 19. See also Montefiore's autobiography, *From a Victorian to a modern* (London, E. Archer, 1927).
.8 WFL National Executive Minutes, November 1908. Fawcett Library.
9 T. Billington-Greig, notes on women's suffrage, Teresa Billington-Greig papers, Box 399, Fawcett Library.
10 E. How Martyn, *Women's Franchise*, 2 January 1908. This was a paper produced for all suffrage societies by the Men's League for Women's Suffrage.
11 A. Linklater, *An unhusbanded life: Charlotte Despard, suffragette, socialist and Sinn Feiner* (London, Hutchinson, 1980), pp. 141–2.
12 For a discussion on feminist networking, see 'Feminist friendship and feminist organisation' in A. Morley with L. Stanley, *The life and death of Emily Wilding Davison* (London, Women's Press, 1988), pp. 172–85.
13 Some prominent suffrage campaigners did not actually join the WTRL but adopted their tactics.
14 Sargant Florence was a specialist in fresco painting.
15 Miss Turquand belonged to the Free Church League for Women's Suffrage.
16 *A.B.C. of tax resistance* (pamphlet, London, WTRL, n.d.), pp. 9–10.
17 Janie Allan, quoted by Harrison, *The right to resist.*
18 *The Vote*, 6, 141, 6 July 1913. E. I. Harrison, *John Hampden* (pamphlet, London, WTRL, 1913, 2nd edn).
19 Later she became chief surgeon of a military hospital in the First World War.
20 After 1918 the WTRL secretary, Margaret Kineton Parkes compiled a list of active resisters. Haverfield founded and administered women's hospital units in Serbia in the First World War.
21 M. K. Parkes, *No vote no tax!* (pamphlet, London, WTRL, n.d.).
22 *A.B.C. of tax resistance*, p. 6.
23 *The Vote*, 6, 133, 26 May 1912.
24 *Ibid.*
25 *Ibid.*, 6, 132, 11 May 1912.
26 *Ibid.*, 6, 130, 20 April 1912.
27 *Ibid.*, 6, 144, 31 August 1912.
28 L. Housman, *The unexpected years* (London, Jonathan Cape, 1937), p. 285.
29 *The Vote*, 5, 127, 30 March 1912. Her fine was paid without her knowledge or approval.
30 Activists who were imprisoned felt they should be kept in the First Division as political prisoners, rather than in lower categories of imprisonment.
31 Parkes, *Tax resistance movement*, p. 23. M. W. Nevinson, *Five years' struggle for freedom: a history of the suffrage movement from 1908–1912* (pamphlet, London, WFL, n.d.), p. 16.
32 *The Vote*, 5, 127, 30 March 1912.

33 *Ibid.,* 9, 215, 5 December 1913.
34 *The Times,* 14 October 1912.
35 *Ibid.*
36 *Hansard* Fifth series, vol. XLII, 1912, col. 340.
37 Dr Burns had come to England from New Zealand to complete her medical education and gain experience in English hospitals. The couple were on good terms.
38 *The Vote,* 7, 160–2, 16–30 November 1912.
39 Parkes, *Tax resistance movement,* pp. 37–9.
40 *Ibid.,* pp. 40-1.

5

'A party between revolution and peaceful persuasion':
a fresh look at the United Suffragists[1]

THE existence of the United Suffragists (US) has been glossed over until recently by historians who have presented Christabel and Emmeline Pankhurst's decision that their Women's Social and Political Union (WSPU) would wholeheartedly support the British government during the First World War as the 'end' of the women's suffrage campaigns.[2] Those who recognise the US emphasise its small size and low level of public activity, presenting it as a tiny group of dissidents seeking to create a less militant group in opposition to the WSPU.[3] The confusion surrounding its aims extends to its origins. Brian Harrison identifies it as a progression from the Votes for Women Fellowship, formed some time after 1912, Ann Morley and Liz Stanley locate its formation in June 1914, 'soon after ... Votes for Women became its official newspaper'.[4] The US, however, was formed in February 1914, six months before the outbreak of the First World War.[5] It has attracted the attention both of feminist historians who focus largely on women's anti-militarism and of non-feminist historians who find in women's war work further proof that suffrage campaigns never constituted a serious political strategy.[6] The US, which continued suffrage campaigning throughout the war, has become lost within these deliberations. Even those historians who are willing to recognise that it was 'more than a disgruntled group of former WSPU activists squeezed out of the inner circle' pass swiftly over the organisation to an analysis of the war years without pausing to consider exactly how much more the US actually represented.[7]

It can be argued that we find within the US a new direction in suffrage politics in that it formed an important part of what Sandra Stanley Holton describes as a 'realignment of militancy' within British suffrage.[8] Moreover, through its aim to be the only totally inclusive suffrage body, it became the sole organisation to call for a return to single-issue suffrage politics. This stance made it an obvious rallying ground for any dissenters from the wartime policy of other suffrage groups, and an important, almost unique site of suffrage activity during the First World War.

The US was founded in response to the plethora of views within the suffrage movement by 1914. By then a seemingly infinite variety of political identities was available to suffrage campaigners. Most obviously, the movement was divided into militant and constitutionalist wings. Christabel Pankhurst brought militancy into the suffrage campaign on 13 October 1905 when she spat at a policeman outside Manchester's Free Trade Hall following her ejection from a Liberal Party meeting for heckling. Although she later described her spit as a 'pout', she opted to go to prison rather than atone by paying a fine, in order to gain maximum publicity for this new direction in suffrage activity.[9] From that point on, various militant tactics were selected. Early varieties were often borrowed from the socialist movement, as Christabel acknowledged, and included heckling at public meetings, delivering impromptu suffrage addresses at street corners, attending mass demonstrations and (from 1907) selling *Votes for Women* in the street.[10] As the WSPU recruited women across many classes, much of the 'militancy' of these actions came from the attack they represented on the gender conventions of their time rather than the actual action itself.[11] Although this initial type of so-called 'passive' militancy was never totally eclipsed, the WSPU pursued more extreme forms over a period of time.[12] Mary Leigh and Edith New adopted window-smashing in June 1909 and were applauded by Emmeline Pankhurst for reclaiming 'a time-honoured method of showing displeasure in a political situation'.[13] More 'active' forms of militancy then joined the earlier 'passive' kinds: arson, damage to pillar-boxes, vandalism of major works of art and even bombing became legitimate WSPU tactics. This switch from 'passive' to 'active' militancy aroused outraged comment from the increasingly oppositional constitutionalist wing of the suffrage movement. At this stage, the two wings appeared irreconcilable.

As June Purvis and others have recently pointed out, the fact that divisions between the leadership of the militant and constitutional wings of the movement were so total has led to a rigid split within suffrage historiography, which has tended to be constructed from either a militant or a constitutional perspective.[14] Recent feminist research has attempted to overcome this problem in different ways. Morley and Stanley focus on the strength of friendship networks, presenting a web of suffrage workers whose activities transcended organisational barriers.[15] Holton, who succinctly questions the effectiveness of the terms 'militant' and 'constitutionalist', also devotes close attention to 'those currents within the suffrage movement which cut across' the alleged divide.[16] A plethora of local studies also exists which attempt to celebrate the diversity of suffrage rather than focus on its narrowness.[17] Welcome as these developments are, however, they can still be problematic. Attempts to reclaim the interorganisational links which undoubtedly existed at grass-roots level, and were facilitated by friendships between individual suffragists, can sometimes ignore the fact that there were very real differences in policy and tactics between the suffrage organisations of Edwardian Britain.

These divisions were so many that by January 1914 the 'Suffrage Directory' of *Votes for Women* listed fifty-three suffrage organisations.[18] Such diversity did not necessarily bring strength. Many leading suffrage workers were becoming convinced that the breadth of the movement was hampering the campaign, as resources were spread too thinly and work was frequently replicated. Also, the societies were often exclusive, catering for suffragists who felt that their primary public identity was defined through factors such as their political allegiance, ethnic origin, religion or metier.[19] Then there was the problem of militancy. By 1914 even its more passionate adherents recognised that the actions of the WSPU were driving the organisation further and further underground, as the state reacted with increasing stringency to its terrorist tactics.

Some supporters of militancy outside the WSPU could see that there was a real danger of its being cut adrift, especially if perpetrators of legal militancy were to be laid open to prosecution merely on the grounds of their association with the Union. Emmeline Pethick-Lawrence, now estranged from the WSPU, feared that 'the adoption of more drastic militant policy [would force] the WSPU into underground channels'.[20] This, combined with the problem of suffragists spreading themselves too thinly through too many groups, convinced certain activists that the time had come to found a new suffrage organisation. Hence, the US was intended to draw suffragists together, helping both increasingly isolated militants and also constitutionalists. Pethick-Lawrence explained:

> Now it is absolutely essential to the welfare of the whole movement that as the militant section is driven underground there should arise a strong intermediate party, occupying a position between the revolutionary section and the party of peaceful persuasion – an intermediate party determined of front, strong of action, politically militant and ready if need be to challenge oppression – yet with a stable organisation that remains above ground and intact for constitutional agitation.[21]

The US declared itself as the 'one kind of suffrage society that did not exist ... one that *any* suffragist could join'.[22] It was open to men and women 'irrespective of membership of any other society, militant or non-militant'. It also sought to recruit 'those suffragists ... who have not hitherto joined any suffrage society', believing that there remained many whose isolation made their suffrage work 'ineffective'.[23] The first list of US vice-presidents published in *Votes for Women* supports this. As well as such well-known WSPU 'exiles' as Evelyn Sharp and the Pethick-Lawrences, it also boasted 'among the personnel some ... well-known men and women who have not hitherto been identified with suffrage societies'.[24] Mrs Pethick-Lawrence was 'most interested to see the Hon. Phyllis and the Hon. Audrey Coleridge, daughters of the judge who had sentenced my husband, Mrs Pankhurst and myself in the conspiracy trial'.[25]

After its launch, the US flung itself enthusiastically into the type of high-profile suffrage work initiated by the early WSPU. Its first official work was in two

London by-elections at Poplar and Bethnal Green. In both constituencies it engaged in the 'canvassing, open-air meetings and paper-selling' which had become integral to any suffrage election campaign.[26] Yet significant differences are apparent which indicate that the US was achieving its aim of working with rather than against existing suffrage societies. Although Sylvia Pankhurst was not overly warm towards the new organisation (she later claimed that Mrs Ayrton Gould, US honorary secretary, had flirted with her East London Federation (ELF) before helping to form a new organisation), the US still managed to arrange a joint demonstration with the ELF during the Poplar campaign.[27]

It is partly this association with the ELF coupled with the presence of men like John Scurr and George Lansbury within its ranks that has led to the US being classified as a 'further attempt to link the suffrage movement with the "rebel" socialist politics' connected with the *Daily Herald* and its supporters.[28] Yet although some socialists were amongst the earliest recruits to the ranks of the new society, it must be remembered that the US was explicitly 'non-party', its party politics restricted to the opposition of 'any government which refuses to introduce a suffrage measure' or party supporting such a government.[29] Its main concern was to unite as diverse a body as possible. John Scurr himself called for the need to subjugate all political and organisational differences to the single issue of the vote, believing that it would only be achieved if campaigners would 'permit discussion on no other matter'.[30] Further to this he was involved (with other US supporters) in the Suffrage First Committee, which eschewed party politics to demand 'a body of electors in every constituency who are prepared to put suffrage first and to vote exclusively on this issue at the next election'.[31] Therefore, the use of a socialist model of militant campaigning practised by the US did not signify a wholesale political shift, but, rather, a return to suffrage militancy's earlier passive forms. It was this ability successfully to separate passive militancy from the active form which freed US members to continue militant work without the threat of guilt by association, and represented a realignment of militancy within the organisation.

Early US work concentrated on the Greater London area, reflecting its initial base. Members' meetings were held regularly in the New Constitutional Society's Hall in Knightsbridge. They were not simply intended to replicate larger public meetings, but to promote 'the exchange of ideas and enrolment of new members, both men and women'.[32] Within three weeks they were popular enough to necessitate moving to a larger hall. Vigorous work amongst the London electorate followed. Here, the US again returned to the tactics of early, passive militancy. In March 1914 it announced the commencement of a vigorous campaign of heckling, and appealed for 'anyone prepared to put suffrage questions at public meetings either with a view to silencing the speaker or to eliciting an answer ... to apply at once'.[33]

Another important part of US campaigning which again had formed a cornerstone of earlier suffrage work was its emphasis on education. This was a multi-faceted affair. Part of it involved regular contact with the public through meetings, paper sales and poster-parades. Another strand was concerned with effectively convincing other organisations of the need for suffrage. In this, the US was most successful in reaching groups on the left, although speakers were offered to any organisation. The New Barnet branch of the National Union of Railwayservants was the first to apply for a US speaker in April 1914. They were soon followed by other trade-union branches, and London branches of the British Socialist Party. Simultaneously, the US also stressed the importance of self-education amongst its supporters, turning them from raw recruits into active workers. Here, it followed a policy common amongst other political organisations, encouraging 'speaking debutantes [to] begin by taking the chair for [experienced] speakers', before launching out on their own.[34] This again shows the US achieving its aim to recruit from those who were new to public political life, with no previous experience in a suffrage organisation, as well as from the membership of other suffrage bodies.

Whilst London remained its power base, the US was intended as an organisation, not a small regional group. One month after its launch it began provincial work, first in Stroud, Saffron Waldon and Leeds, then in Scotland.[35] By June, branches had formed in Amersham, Stroud and Edinburgh. Every attempt was made to recruit from as broad a base as possible. No potential support was to be excluded on grounds of sex or class. To emphasise this, the opening of a US shop and offices in Edinburgh was accompanied by the further announcement that it was to sell brooches in the organisation's colours of purple, white and orange to suit all pockets, at twopence, sixpence or, for the more affluent members, a shilling.[36] The US was quick to publicise occasions when it felt that the aim of broad-based support had truly been achieved. A typical report of a meeting in Votes for Women goes as far as mentioning with pride the audience at an early Amersham open-air meeting which consisted of 'whole families including old age pensioners and babies in perambulators'.[37]

Yet despite such optimistic accounts, there are some indications that the US was having problems in putting what modern commentators might describe as clear blue water between themselves and the many other suffrage groups. These were greatest when provincial work was undertaken by US organisers suddenly exposed to unfamiliar environments and networks of strangers. In April 1914 the leaders had to place an official plea that any supporter planning a US canvassing centre 'in any constituency ... should communicate with us first to avoid overlapping ... and to ensure organisation and support'.[38] There appears to have been a very real possibility at this stage of the US being eclipsed in the provinces altogether, had it not been for the decision of Emmeline and Fred Pethick-Lawrence to hand Votes for Women over to the new group. In this action, the Pethick-Lawrences were not simply playing the role of generous benefactors, despite their undoubted support for US policy. The merger, Emmeline explained, was intended to be mutually beneficial. *Votes for Women* was in dire financial straits. Since losing its position as the official organ of the WSPU, it had not attracted sufficient readership in its new role as an independent publication. Now:

> The paper will have once more the backing and support of a powerful and rapidly growing society; and the United Suffragists will have an official medium by means of which they will be able to keep their own members and the outside public in constant and regular touch with the whole of their activities.[39]

The date chosen for the final handover of the paper, was 21 August 1914. Unfortunately, unbeknown to the US leadership in June, that forthcoming August was to be remembered by historians for an event far larger than the return of *Votes for Women* to the status of an organisational paper, namely the outbreak of the First World War.

War had a tremendously dislocating effect, especially on the militant wing of the suffrage movement. The unilateral decision of Christabel and Emmeline Pankhurst immediately to suspend militancy and offer support to the government removed the WSPU's organisational network from many activists at a time when wartime restrictions made any form of communication more difficult. Eunice Murray, a Women's Freedom League (WFL) organiser in Scotland, recalled that the ensuing confusion was so great that many WSPU organisers were stranded without wages and forced to turn to sympathetic suffragists in the League to borrow their fares to get home.[40] Several of the other suffrage organisations, whilst not following wholeheartedly along the Pankhursts' jingoistic path, also suspended their suffrage agitation, although others, including the Church League for Women's Suffrage, encouraged members to 'wear their badges when doing any public work'.[41] Only the WFL continued a national political campaign in districts where they were strong.[42] WSPU members wishing to continue suffrage campaigning faced a more difficult task. The efforts of groups such as the Suffragettes of the WSPU and the Independent WSPU were hampered through the loss of the original WSPU central records, lost during successive police raids on the Union's headquarters.[43] Personal networks were the only way these groups could attempt to contact the old WSPU membership, but they were aware that these only covered a proportion of potential support. In an early *News Sheet*, the Suffragettes of the WSPU claimed: 'By untiring efforts as many women as could be reached were approached personally or by letter. Those who received no communication may take it that their postal addresses could not be obtained.'[44]

Such basic problems made it very difficult to get any fresh campaigns based on an existing disaffected membership off the ground. However, unlike larger and longer-established suffrage organisations, which had developed a much broader women-centred political agenda by 1914, the single-issue focus of the US gave it a clear mandate to 'keep the suffrage flag flying'.[45] Its main founding principle had been to unite members of the many smaller suffrage societies for common work. This made its existing framework ideal to facilitate the efforts of individual members of societies suspending suffrage work who wished to continue. The US committee decided to undertake no relief work. It stated:

> [The Committee are not] going to put the purple white and orange into cold storage for the period of the war ... they intend to do their best to keep together as an organisation for the propaganda of Women's Suffrage, and they believe that the war makes it even more necessary than usual that the woman's point of view should be emphasised.[46]

Certain areas lost no time in commencing suffrage work under a new organisational banner. In Bolton it was reported that: 'Two or three suffragists dismayed at the prospect of other suffrage societies laying down their arms in the "Greater War" at once decided to form a branch of the US. Others quickly rallied round, and the work was carried on without any break.'[47] In other districts, US branches were slower to form, as suffragists found new directions for their public activities. However, as the initial excitement and upheaval of the outbreak of war settled down and it became apparent that no immediate end was in sight for hostilities, some turned back to campaigning for the franchise. At the beginning of 1915, *Votes for Women* proudly announced:

> We may claim that our efforts to keep the suffrage flag flying in spite of the war have met with a gratifying and stimulating measure of success. In several instances we have through the columns of the paper and by means of meetings, deputations & etc been able to draw public attention to serious abuses which have made the lot of women in wartime harder even than in peace; but never for a moment have we lost sight of our single goal; the enfranchisement of women.[48]

Four regional branches, in Stroud, Amersham, Bolton and Edinburgh, were mentioned in support of the US claim that there was still interest in campaigning for the franchise alone outside of its London power base. These were joined during the year by a further fourteen branches.[49] Although this figure approaches the regional structures of neither the National Union of Women's Suffrage Societies (NUWSS) nor the WSPU, the gentle increase it represents refutes further the view that the war brought an end to all suffrage work.[50] Within the branches themselves, work appears to have become easier over a period of time. The Glasgow US, which formed with fifteen members in March 1915, had increased its ranks to forty by November.[51] A similar situation occurred in Birmingham. There, the branch only managed an average total sale of twenty-five copies of *Votes for Women* at first, and found it necessary to issue public words of comfort: 'Members who were in doubt as to whether or no it would be wiser to drop suffrage now will be reassured by the sympathy with which the work of the branch has met during its first week.'[52] Extra workers responded to this, and within five months one person alone reported selling five and a half dozen papers.[53]

In many districts, the US managed to sustain a higher level of activity through the war than suffrage organisations that attempted to retain their formal structure whilst prioritising other issues such as relief work. The Birmingham US held two meetings a month, one technically for members which was also open to supporters, and one public meeting, whilst Manchester managed to match the London branches with a weekly meeting programme. Weekly paper sales, poster displays, public meetings and open-air campaigns in the summer were undertaken throughout Britain in the name of the US by women and men who felt it essential that the suffrage flag be kept flying at this time. Many of those involved has already seen active service with the WSPU, including Mary Richardson who joined the US in March 1915. Her recruitment was obviously seen as a great coup by the US, as she had previously been counted as an extremely loyal Pankhurst militant. *Votes for Women* gave several column inches to her appointment as organiser in Kensington, culminating in a description of her triumphant first meeting there where she 'had a great reception, the audience remaining on their feet for several minutes'.[54] Other well-known WSPU figures who migrated into the US during the war included ex-organisers Ada Flatman and Mary Phillips, Mary Neal of the first London WSPU committee and ex-prisoners Bertha Brewster and Dr Alice Ker.[55] The US also attracted some non-militant suffragists to its ranks, notably in January 1915 when the entire Chorley Wood and District Women's Suffrage Society became the Chorley Wood and District United Suffragists.

As well as providing a natural focus for those who were disillusioned with the turn that their own organisations had taken at the outbreak of war, there is evidence that the US managed to fulfil some of its potential in recruiting those who had previously not been associated with any other suffrage society. The Liverpool branch was able to recruit Mrs M. Edwards, a well-known local socialist. Although associated with many progressive causes in the city and a staunch suffrage supporter, this was the first time that she felt able to commit herself to a suffrage organisation. In other areas, too, the US recruited fresh faces into the suffrage campaign. Such individuals do not appear to have comprised anything more than a small proportion of the overall US membership, but that they were recruited at all in wartime indicates that the organisation was having a degree of success in this direction.

Despite these optimistic factors, it is also true that the US, as a newer organisation with a less well-established structure, suffered during the war. *Votes for Women* always put up a brave front and increased its funds steadily from £469 7s 1d in January 1915 to £1,968 15s 11d the following year.[56] However, it was by no means untouched by the general malaise that appeared to infect all areas of British political life at this time, slowing down levels of activity and hindering recruitment. The change was most apparent to those who recalled the high points of WSPU activity. US committee member Evelyn Sharp wrote to her ex-WSPU comrade Ada Flatman in 1916: 'You must sigh over our depleted advertising columns! Our only consolation is that I do think we get more than most people, but our finance is not our strong point at the present moment. The war gets more frightful every day. Prices go up, up, up: and incomes go down.'[57] It was finally decided that the paper should change from a weekly to a monthly publication in 1916. This appears to have kept it buoyant. It also lightened the load of regular sellers, as it was only necessary to organise one big sale each month, although notices within the paper encouraged them to regard an issue as current for at least the week following its publication. The organisation continued to expand gradually and form new branches, with Henley, Ashford, Portsmouth and Corsham joining in 1916. It is tempting to read such expansion as insignificant when compared with that achieved by other societies prior to 1914. Only when set against the upheavals of the war do the achievements of the US as a suffrage society become apparent, as Evelyn Sharp explained:

> We are doing what we can to keep the suffrage flag flying during this terrible war, though it is very difficult with the mass of suffragists doing other things. But they do say the United Suffragists have kept the thing from being overwhelmed altogether and I know we have made some societies come back into the right path and that is perhaps worthwhile.[58]

It was the determination of the US to keep the suffrage flag flying and to prioritise suffrage work above any other concern which led to its demise before the end of the war. It kept up a rigorous propaganda campaign around the agonisingly slow progress of the Representation of the People Bill from its initial stages in the guise of the Conference of Electoral Reform in January 1917. However, the passage of the Bill into law in 1918 removed the US's *raison d'être*. Once the franchise was won, there was no further requirement for a single-issue suffrage campaign. *Votes for Women* announced the Bill triumphantly in its edition for February 1918, at the same time informing its readership that this was to be its final issue. 'There could be', it declared, 'no better end for any paper that stands for a great cause' than to see its cause achieved, thereby obviating any need for itself. Furthermore, it was decided that 'the United Suffragists ... will close down at the end of March in order to set free its men and women for public work of a wider and more varied order'.[59] Whilst there were many possible directions that this work could take, clearly there remained no need for a body dedicated to achieving the franchise alone. Hampstead US poignantly discussed 'What equality means' at its final meeting. This topic, so typical of many at US branches since their inauguration, was suddenly tempered with a harder edge of reality. Elsewhere in London, members met for a large celebration on 16 March before stopping all US work. And in Bolton, members discussed future work and recorded: 'Whilst nothing definite can be settled the general desire seemed to incline to the Women's International League as the policy of that League includes adult suffrage and also offers a wide field of service not only in the interests of women but of humanity generally.'[60] This was not the end of the road for individual activists, but it did draw a line under their collective activity as United Suffragists.

Looking afresh at the US it is clear that it represented much more than a loose oppositional coalition of disgruntled WSPU activists. It offered an alternative form of suffrage campaigning in 1914; a realignment of militancy involving a return to early militant tactics. Although many of these were lifted from the socialist movement, the US also offered a genuine bridging organisation between suffragists of different political viewpoints, despite the presence of well-known socialists in its ranks. Its potential was certainly recognised by the government of 1914, which took it seriously enough to include it with the ELF in franchise negotiations in that year.[61] It has been suggested that the government only did this to undermine the WSPU. However, the US, as has been seen, not only engaged in some militancy itself but also never condemned the most violent action nor excluded its perpetrators from its ranks. Both the US's attempts to unite public suffrage campaigning and underground militant work and its stated aim to be inclusive and open to all suffragists emphasise that it was in no way a safer option for politicians to court. Rather, it represented the one thing lacking in Edwardian suffrage politics: an organisation that could unite disparate activists together in a concentrated campaign for the franchise alone. It was its potential in this respect that led the government to negotiate with the US immediately after its formation.

The US was eventually hampered by the outbreak of the First World War more than by deficiencies in its own policy. Yet even operating within wartime stringencies it achieved more suffrage work than groups such as the Independent WSPU or the Suffragettes of the WSPU, which both attempted to reactivate from within existing organisations. This was due to its success as a bridging group. The US was uniquely placed to keep the suffrage flag flying, as it was an organisation dedicated to the promotion and prioritisation of suffrage above all else.

Finally, the US also serves as a reminder of how diverse suffrage politics had become by 1914. So various were the issues concerning franchise campaigners that it was now necessary to have an organisation which campaigned for the vote alone, believing that 'with the process of sectionalisation should also go one of coordination'.[62] The US therefore merits serious study not simply in its own right, but also by those who believe that suffrage politics represented far more than just the campaign for the vote.

NOTES

1 *Votes for Women*, 10 July 1914. I am indebted to Jim Sharpe and Jane Rendall for their comments on this essay, and to Kerrie Donohoe for her practical help during its completion.

2 For instance David Mitchell, *Women on the warpath: the story of the women of the First World War* (London, Jonathan Cape, 1966), mentions only the Independent WSPU.

3 See for example Brian Harrison, *Prudent revolutionaries: portraits of British feminists between the wars* (Oxford, Oxford University Press, 1987), p. 228; Andrew Rosen, *Rise up*

women! The militant campaign of the Women's Social and Political Union 1903–1914 (London, Routledge and Kegan Paul, 1974), p. 224.

4 Harrison, *Prudent revolutionaries*, p. 251; Ann Morley with Liz Stanley, *The life and death of Emily Wilding Davison* (London, Women's Press, 1988), p. 83.

5 *Votes for Women*, 6 February 1914.

6 For feminist histories which examine women's anti-militarism, see Ann Wiltsher, *Most dangerous women: feminist peace campaigners of the great war* (London, Pandora, 1985); Jo Vellacott, *From Liberal to Labour with women's suffrage: the story of Catherine Marshall* (Montreal, McGill-Queens University Press, 1993). Suffrage histories which examine anti-militarism include Jill Liddington and Jill Norris, *One hand tied behind us: the rise of the women's suffrage movement* (London, Virago, 1978); Sandra Stanley Holton, *Feminism and democracy: women's suffrage and reform politics in Britain 1900–1918* (Cambridge, Cambridge University Press, 1986). Non-feminist interpretations of women and the First World War include Mitchell, *Women on the warpath*.

7 Holton, *Feminism and democracy*, p. 128.

8 *Ibid.*

9 Christabel Pankhurst, *Unshackled: the story of how we won the vote* (London, Hutchinson, 1959), p. 52.

10 Interview with Christabel Pankhurst, *Sunday Times*, 6 April 1906.

11 See Rosen, *Rise up women!*, p. xvii, which describes militancy as the use of 'tactics sufficiently combative as to be widely regarded as shocking'.

12 For distinctions between 'passive' and 'active' militancy, see Ray Strachey, *The cause: a short history of the women's movement in Great Britain* (London, Virago repr. 1978), p. 313.

13 Antonia Raeburn, *The militant suffragettes* (London, Michael Joseph, 1973), p. 61.

14 June Purvis, 'Researching the lives of women in the suffragette movement' in Mary Maynard and June Purvis (eds), *Researching women's lives from a feminist perspective* (London, Taylor and Francis, 1994), p. 169.

15 Morley with Stanley, *The life and death of Emily Wilding Davison*.

16 Holton, *Feminism and democracy*. p. 4.

17 See Leah Leneman, *A guid cause: the women's suffrage movement in Scotland* (Aberdeen, Aberdeen University Press, 1984), Angela John, *Our mother's land: essays in Welsh women's history* (Cardiff, University of Wales Press, 1991), Krista Cowman, 'Engendering citizenship: the political involvement of women on Merseyside 1890–1920' (DPhil thesis, University of York Centre for Women's Studies, 1994).

18 *Votes for Women*, 6 February 1914. The figure included the United Suffragists.

19 More exclusive groups included the Women Sanitary Inspectors' Suffrage Association, the Conservative and Unionist Women's Franchise Association; the Irishwomen's Franchise League.

20 *Votes for Women*, 10 July 1914.

21 *Ibid.*

22 *Ibid*, 21 August 1914.

23 *Ibid*, 6 February 1914.

24 *Ibid.*

25 Emmeline Pethick-Lawrence, *My part in a changing world* (London, Victor Gollancz, 1938), p. 303.

26 *Votes for Women*, 20 February 1914.

27 E. Sylvia Pankhurst, *The suffragette movement* (London, Virago, repr. 1977), p. 520. Further evidence of Sylvia's dismissal of the US in favour of her own group can be found in Patricia Romero, *E. Sylvia Pankhurst: portrait of a radical* (London, Yale University Press, 1987), p. 103.

28 For more detail on this line of argument, see Holton, *Feminism and democracy*, p. 128; Rosen, *Rise up women!*, p. 224.

29 *Votes for Women*, 6 February 1914.

30 John Scurr, letter in *ibid.*, 24 July 1914.

31 Suffrage First Committee policy statement, *ibid.*, 13 March 1914.
32 *Ibid*, 3 April 1914.
33 *Ibid.*, 6 March 1914.
34 *Ibid.*
35 *Ibid.*, 20 March 1914. See also Holton, *Feminism and democracy* p. 181 note 52.
36 *Votes for Women*, 10 July 1914.
37 *Ibid.*, 22 May 1914.
38 *Ibid.*, 3 April 1914.
39 Emmeline Pethick-Lawrence, editorial statement, *ibid.*, 10 July 1914.
40 Eunice Murray, private diary quoted in Leneman, *A guid cause*, p. 209.
41 *Church League for Women's Suffrage monthly pamphlet*, September 1914.
42 *Votes for Women*, 1 January 1915.
43 The Suffragettes of the WSPU and the Independent WSPU were two separate breakaway groups of former WSPU members who opposed the Pankhursts' support for the war and attempted to continue suffrage campaigning during this time. Two separate publications chronicle their activities: *The Suffragette News Sheet* and *The Independent Suffragette*. No history exists as yet of either organisation. Brief details are in Leneman, *A guid cause*, pp. 209, 262; D. Mitchell, *Queen Christabel* (London, Macdonald and Janes, 1977) p. 251; Morley with Stanley, *The life and death of Emily Wilding Davison*, pp. 181–2, Rosen, *Rise up women!*, p. 254.
44 *The Suffragette News Sheet*, December 1915.
45 This phrase which became common shorthand for any political suffrage work which continued during the war was also the title of a long article explaining the United Suffragists' war policy, *Votes for Women*, 21 August 1914.
46 *Ibid.*
47 *Ibid.*, 20 August 1915.
48 *Ibid.*, 1 January 1915.
49 According to the local branch reports in *Votes for Women* US branches formed in 1915 at Chorley Wood, Birmingham, Manchester, Glasgow, Southport, Liverpool, Reading, Hampstead, Kensington, Streatham, Wendover, North West London, Hull and Letchworth. Organised activities were also reported at Cardiff and Bristol.
50 The NUWSS was the large constitutional women's suffrage society which kept its organisational structure in place during World War One.
51 *Votes for Women*, 19 November 1915.
52 *Ibid.*, 19 February, 1915.
53 *Ibid.*, 2 July 1915.
54 *Ibid.*, 21 May 1915. Mary Richardson herself later omitted any mention of her US experience in her autobiography *Laugh a defiance* (London, Wiedenfeld and Nicholson, 1953).
55 Bertha Brewster was imprisoned at Walton Goal in August 1909 and was force fed. She broke cell windows as a protest against this, was rearrested and served a further six weeks' hard labour in Walton in January 1910. Dr Ker was an ex-NUWSS member who joined the WSPU in Birkenhead and spent time in Holloway for her part in the window-smashing in London in March 1912.
56 *Votes for Women*, 15 January 1915; 14 January 1916.
57 Evelyn Sharp to S. Ada Flatman, 3 March 1915. Suffragette Fellowship Collection, Museum of London. MOL 50.83/1134.53.
58 *Ibid.*, 13 May 1916. MOL 50.82/1134.56
59 *Votes for Women*, February 1918.
60 *Ibid.*
61 Holton, *Feminism and democracy*, p. 126.
62 *Votes for Women*, 21 August 1914.

DIANE ATKINSON

6

<hr>

Six suffragette photographs

THE photographs featured in this chapter are from the Museum of London's Suffragette Fellowship Collection. It is a unique and important archive of the Women's Social and Political Union's (WSPU) campaign for the vote. The aims of the Fellowship governed its collecting policy: 'to perpetuate the memory of the pioneers and outstanding events connected with ... women's emancipation and especially the militant movement'.[1] These six images are a very small part of the several thousand items which include banners, newspaper cuttings, jewellery, badges and brooches, Holloway Prison mementoes, typescripts, correspondence, handbills, 'relics' of Emmeline and Christabel Pankhurst, and photographic and printed images.

First, Annie Kenney in her mill clothes, a working woman and the only woman of her class to join the senior hierarchy of this largely middle-class organisation. Second, three women about to take direct action in Whitehall, tying their bulky propaganda posters to the railings – the edge where the establishment physically began – which could lead to arrest and imprisonment. Third, the delirious joy of suffragettes being released from Holloway. If you look carefully you can hear their cheers and share their emotions. Fourth, publicity stunts were a trademark of the suffragette campaign, and this photograph of ex-prisoners in replica prison clothing gives an idea of the impact they must have had on Edwardian passers-by. Fifth, a photograph that conveys the curiosity of the many men present about the woman making a speech on the cart; we can infer the remarks which would have been made about her politics, her looks and her dress, her place and her temerity in taking up such a visible position in the public domain. It is a man's world that is depicted – the suffragettes are the only women in this scene of men and boys. For women, being an active suffragette was a 'coming out'. It could mean social and financial hardship and isolation, and this is suggested by the isolated figure. While there are a few other suffragettes present, she is exposed to a potentially hostile crowd on her own. It took bravery to 'come out' of the private domain and claim one's space in an alien world: the public domain of men, boys, sexual innuendo and politics. The sixth photograph is evidence of the scope of the WSPU's marketing activities. It is a tender, informal scene; a snapshot of mother and child, possibly daughter, proud to be identified with a militant political movement that was already unpopular with most members of the public. By 1910 suffragettes had already smashed windows, been involved in running battles with the police, chained themselves to railings, gone on hunger strike and been force-fed, and had taken part in rooftop protests all over the country. The gentleness of this image belies the real dangers suffragettes were exposed to on many occasions.

Figure 1   Annie Kenney is wearing iron-tipped, wooden clogs, a long skirt, smocked blouse and woollen shawl. Her hair is parted in the middle and covered. The photograph is signed near the bottom, but her marital status, Miss or Mrs, is not given. This is a studio portrait by 'Schmidt', of 26 Victoria Street, Manchester. It is a photograph of a working-class heroine with a half-smile, bright eyes and a faraway look. She does not look at the photographer but beyond him to a different and distant place. An ungloved hand, that of a working woman, emerges from a smocked blouse to clutch her shawl: this is the uniform of a mill 'lass' in the North of England. The hand and the shawl denote the coldness of her working life, though she is photographed not at work, but in a photographer's studio.

Schmidt's studio is basic, even shabby, in its appearance and equipment. The lack of a painted background or props, and a ragged mat on the floor, reinforce the poverty of this woman. Her expression reminds us of the representations of Dickens and others, of warm sentiment about poverty and labour.

This, an early photograph of Annie Kenney, was taken in late 1907. Manchester's trade directories tell us that Frederick W. Schmidt took the premises in 1907 and remained there until 1917; his business probably suffered from anti-German feelings during the First World War. Such sentiments were sometimes expressed in attacks on businesses with German or German-sounding names. Maybe he inherited some goodwill when he took on these premises – it had been a photographic studio for four of the six years preceding his time there. He may even have inherited the torn rug.

Annie Kenney's autobiography, *Memories of a militant,* bound in purple, white and green, was published in 1924. It is a stirring story of her early life as a mill-girl and her recruitment and career as a suffragette. Her descriptions of the day-to-day, behind-the-scenes activities illuminate her life and that of the thousands of women who joined the WSPU, this most daring of women's suffrage organisations:

> Nuns in a convent were not watched over and supervised more strictly than were the organisers and members of the Militant Movement during the first few years. It was an unwritten rule that there must be no concerts, no theatres, no smoking; work, and sleep to prepare us for more work, was the unwritten order of the day. These rules were good, and the more I look back on those early days the more clearly I see the necessity for such discipline. The changed life into which most of us entered was a revolution in itself. No home-life, no one to say what we should or should not do, no family ties, we were free and alone in a great brilliant city, scores of young women scarcely out of their teens met together in a revolutionary movement, outlaws or breakers of laws, independent of everything and everybody, fearless and self-confident.'[2]

Kenney's working-class family background and working life were highly prized by the Pankhurst family. She was deeply loyal to them, especially to Emmeline Pankhurst and her daughter, Christabel. Their close relationship is not surprising: Annie's own mother had died in early 1905, and that was the year she met the Pankhursts. The instructions that she was given to wear her mill clothes for this photograph (Figure 1) sent out a message: working women should adopt Annie as a role model and join their movement. The public was thereby reminded of the potential numerical strength of this determinedly modern campaign if its membership derived from women like Annie and her working 'sisters'.

Annie Kenney was 'extremely popular wherever she speaks and draws enormous crowds'.[3] Her life, as far as we can tell, was atypical, which is the one reason why her place in suffragette history is assured. Her bustling entry in the *Suffrage annual and women's who's who,* published jointly by Stanley Paul and Selfridge's department store in 1913, puts flesh on the bones of this photograph (the entries were supplied by the women themselves). Her biography, a very brief sketch of her life and career up to that date, tells us that she was born at Springhead, near Oldham, Lancashire in 1879. She was the fifth of twelve children and began to work part-time in a cotton mill at the age of eight and full-time by the age of thirteen. An active trade-unionist, she sat on the district committee of her cotton workers' trade union. On 13 October 1905 she and Christabel Pankhurst became the first two militants when they interrupted Sir Edward Grey's electioneering meeting at the Free Trade Hall in Manchester, asking when the Liberal Party would give women the vote. They were thrown out of the meeting, arrested, and sent to Strangeways Prison, Kenney for three days and Pankhurst for seven. On her release, Kenney moved to London and became the first paid

WSPU organiser. In 1906 she was arrested for trying to interview Asquith, the Chancellor of the Exchequer, and was sentenced to six weeks in Holloway Prison. Later that year she was arrested (with nine other suffragettes) and served another term there for protesting outside the House of Commons. In 1908 she went to prison again for a month, arrested while accompanying Emmeline Pankhurst to parliament.

In 1912 she took charge of the WSPU after the Pethick-Lawrences and Emmeline Pankhurst were arrested for conspiracy to incite violence. Christabel, acting on a warning, fled the country and lived in Paris, directing WSPU operations there for the last two hectic years of the campaign. Kenney 'still continues to superintend the organisation of the Union' at the time of the publication of the *Suffrage annual*.[4] Later in 1913 she was arrested and sentenced to eighteen months in prison for conspiracy to incite violence following a police raid on WSPU headquarters. She went on hunger and thirst strikes and was released several times under the Prisoners' Temporary Discharge for Ill-Health Act, known as the 'Cat and Mouse Act'. Her health suffered as a result of her actions and treatment in prison. During the First World War she allied herself with Emmeline and Christabel Pankhurst's jingoistic activities in encouraging men to join up, and helping the government's drive to recruit women into war work, especially into munitions factories.[5]

Figure 2　Three well-dressed, middle-class women wearing hats: one with a bird in it, another with feathers, and warm winter clothing of overcoats and leather boots, gloves, a muff and double fox-fur and fur stole. They have arrived at their destination carrying posters. They have a purposeful look. The year is given as 1909. Two men are present: one looks straight at the photographer, another, carrying a package, stands behind. Partly obscured by two of the women is probably a tradesman's cart. The man looking at the camera may be the tradesman. The little bit of architecture visible suggests that the buildings are government offices in Whitehall.

The image shown in Figure 2 has for many years been described as 'Railings Chainers'. It comes from Nurse Pine's collection of six photograph albums in the Suffragette Fellowship archive. Pine was one of two nurses who ran a suffragette nursing home in Campden Hill Square in West London. Most of her photographs are captioned and dated, sometimes at the time, others after the events depicted. Research has shown that most, but not all of her annotations are correct. It is difficult to see why she called this photograph 'Railings Chainers'. We cannot see any padlocks and chains. It is likely that she is describing what she knew retrospectively about this event, rather than what is visible. What seems most likely is that the suffragettes first tied the posters and then chained themselves to the railings. The 'chauffeuse' of the WSPU's purple, white and green car, Vera 'Jack' Holme, is the woman on the right. The suffragettes deliberately cultivated a feminine and fashion-conscious appearance to counter the public's perception of their campaign as 'unwomanly' and 'unsexing'. From the earliest days Mrs Pankhurst instructed WSPU members how to dress: she and her daughter Christabel were shining role models in this strategy. Even when engaged in 'guerrilla warfare' against the government, suffragette window-smashers and vandals and arsonists were well-dressed and wearing a hat.

Chaining themselves to the railings of government buildings in Whitehall was a favourite tactic in the early years of the WSPU's campaign. This direct action enabled women to make a visible and noisy protest at key locations. Their ability to make speeches lasted as long as it took policemen to cut them out of their chains. An early issue of *Votes for Women* explained the thinking behind this form of protest: 'Railing chainers ... tells the world that women are not prepared to submit tamely and without protest to political tyranny ... It arrests attention and arouses thoughts and quickens perception of a wrong hitherto ignored and slothfully accepted.'[6]

Figure 3 records the release of suffragettes from prison on the morning of 31 July 1908, having served a month for obstruction while on a deputation to the House of Commons on 30 June. All wear the WSPU's colour scheme of purple, white and green: purple for dignity; white for purity; green for fertility and hope for the future. The initials 'WD' belong to Marion Wallace Dunlop, who we see overjoyed at being free after her first prison sentence. She was a Scottish artist and member of the Fabian Women's Group, as well as of the WSPU, who was imprisoned for stencilling the words of the Bill of Rights on the wall of St Stephen's Hall at Westminster. Her entry in the *Suffrage annual and women's who's who* says for 'recreations': 'no time for them – till the vote is won'.[7] A year after this triumphant photograph was taken she would be back in Holloway, becoming the first hunger striker to protest at the government's refusal to grant suffragette prisoners political status. Instead of being given privileges as political prisoners, won during the nineteenth century, suffragettes were treated as 'common criminals'. Between

Figure 3 Fifteen women leave Holloway Prison early one summer's day. A number of
them have broken into a run, three fling their arms in the air, one of whom is waving a
handkerchief. It is a joyous occasion. Two wear sashes saying 'Votes for Women'. All are
wearing hats. This is a snapshot probably taken by a fellow suffragette or family
member or friend of one of the released women. They are walking and running towards
freedom and may be about to be met by a large crowd. An arrow points up at a woman,
ninth from the left of the group. The initials 'WD' have been added suggesting her
identity. Two of the women carry printed matter of some kind, books or pamphlets, or
perhaps their own writing.

The women are between 20 and 40 years old. They are fashionably dressed,
joyous, and optimistic. In contrast to this twentieth-century image of women running in
the streets, the crenellated fortification of Holloway Prison behind them presents a
medieval picture.

1906 and 1914 over a thousand suffragettes served their sentences in Holloway, which had been built in 1852 as the City House of Correction for men and women serving short terms in prison. From 1902 it was used exclusively for women prisoners: in 1970 it was demolished and a new women's jail was built on the site.

Votes for Women described what happened to these women following the moment captured in the photograph:

> On Friday morning the first batch of prisoners to be released from Holloway were met at the prison gates, and escorted in triumph, banners flying, and bands playing, to Queen's Hall, where some 250 friends and supporters were waiting to give them a warm welcome ... A bouquet of purple and white sweetpeas and purple heather was presented to each of the prisoners.[8]

At the breakfast reception at the Queen's Hall, Langham Place, the leaders of the WSPU paid tribute to the women, each of whom made a speech describing their time in Holloway. These were rousing and guaranteed to bond those present closer together for the struggle ahead. At eleven o'clock the prisoners were taken by Emmeline Pankhurst and the Pethick-Lawrences to Shoreditch in East London where the WSPU was campaigning at a by-election against the Liberal candidate. They were given 'an enthusiastic welcome from the women [suffragettes and local supporters] of the constituency'.[9] Wherever possible, the leadership always exploited the propaganda potential of the testimony of released prisoners. It was good for morale and recruitment.

Figure 4 captures an image of the WSPU's Chelmsford by-election campaign in action in December 1908. Mrs Drummond was known as 'The General' because of the uniform and regalia presented to her by the London medal and regalia-makers Toye, Kenning and Co. in recognition of her military manner. She is not wearing her uniform because it did not fit her: she was pregnant with her first child, a son she named after Keir Hardie, the leader of the Independent Labour Party in parliament, and a loyal supporter of the suffragettes. Flora Drummond had trained as a postmistress, joining the WSPU after being disqualified for being too short when the General Post Office changed the minimum height regulations.

Even though some Liberal Members of Parliament were active supporters of women's suffrage, in 1906 Christabel Pankhurst announced that the WSPU would henceforth campaign against Liberal candidates at by-elections and general elections until women got the vote. It was hoped that this strategy would cause Liberal politicians to exert pressure on their party colleagues who were hostile or ambivalent to the idea of votes for women. The suffragettes were impressive political campaigners: they hired the best halls, wrote compelling propaganda and arranged publicity stunts to convert public opinion.

The results at Chelmsford pleased the WSPU leadership. The Liberal MP

Figure 4 The scene is outside an inn in Chelmsford, Essex, where a political meeting and demonstration is about to take place. Three flags, and four 'Votes for Women' and WSPU banners flutter in the breeze. A poster urges voters to 'Keep the Liberal out'. There are two other larger posters on the right which may well be connected to this group of women. They are propped against the wall of the building next door to the inn, possibly a meeting hall for which this event is being organised.

Eleven of the demonstrators wear replica prison uniforms to show that they are ex-prisoners. Mrs Drummond, a senior WSPU organiser, known as 'The General', stands on the right-hand end of the line. Everyone is warmly dressed, suggesting it is a cold day. There are a couple of women sympathiser standing next to the ex-prisoners.

A brass band with a dozen musicians has been hired to accompany the procession through Chelmsford. A single policeman is there to keep order. The driver of the omnibus is very proud of his motor which is of 'British Design and Manufacture'. A number of curious male onlookers watch the photograph being taken by the local photographer Fred Spalding. A large space has been cleared to record this political moment. Out of the window of the inn look two women who are probably speakers at the meeting. There is a strong sense that everyone wants to be in this photograph, to be captured at this historic event.

polled 2,565 fewer votes than the Conservative who took the seat.[10] Although it was impossible to prove, the suffragettes always claimed their campaign was the cause of lost Liberal votes, sometimes leading to the defeat of a sitting MP. *Votes for Women* describes the WSPU's work in the constituency:

> The special feature of the week was the demonstration which was held on Satur-
> day last, when the local party, under Mrs Drummond, joined forces with four
> motor-bus loads of suffragettes coming down especially into the constituency from
> London. Mrs Drummond has had charge of the ... arrangements, and divided the

constituency in to two halves ... Each centre was supplied with a motor-car ... Everywhere the women have been received with the utmost consideration and kindness, and the most hearty support has been given by the local people, who have come to their assistance in all kinds of ways. The shops have displayed the Union colours, and have exhibited for sale many articles in the familiar colours of purple, white and green.[11]

Figure 5   A lone woman is making a speech on a cart belonging to the White Lion Hotel. The vehicle, without its horse, has stopped in front of the premises of the printers Hill and Dolling, and the auctioneers and valuers Elworthy and Son. The man with his back to the camera leaning on the cart, between the shafts, is there to help the women on and off their impromptu platform. Another woman stands behind holding handbills or newspapers. There are only three other women in the photograph – the rest are men (four of them pipe-smokers) and boys, all wearing flat caps or bowler hats, which indicate their social class. It is probably winter – everyone is warmly dressed and buttoned-up. All the women wear hats; the most splendid one is worn by the woman whose face we see in profile standing near to Hill and Dolling's window.

About ten members of the audience take an interest in the person who is taking the photograph. They sense it is an important moment. The photographer is probably positioned in an upper room across the street, possibly in a room in the White Lion Hotel itself.

No information accompanies Figure 5. It is possible to identify the speaker on the cart as the suffragette Isabel Seymour, who was a close friend of Emmeline and Frederick Pethick-Lawrence, who probably recruited her into the WSPU in 1906. Soon after she went to work at the London headquarters at 4 Clement's Inn, the Strand. Her entry in the *Suffrage annual and women's who's who* is very brief. We learn that her full name is Isabel Marion Seymour, that she was born in 1882, making her about twenty-six years old when this photograph was taken in about 1908. Her talents were public speaking as the *Who's who* declared that 'she has taken a prominent part as a speaker for the WSPU in England, Austria, Germany, Belgium and Canada'.[12]

Personal courage was required of the suffragette speaker. Unused to the open and frank stares of men and boys in such numbers, and in public, suffragettes had to quickly master a range of skills to overcome the prejudice against women daring to speak on politics. Frequently, they were accused of being prostitutes; they had to contend with ridicule, threats of violence, and being pelted with rotting fruit and vegetables and clods of earth. Sylvia Pankhurst had dead cats and dogs thrown at her when she campaigned in the East End of London.

Annie Kenney's *Memories of a Militant* conveys an idea of the work required of an organiser: 'In the early days I thought nothing of having a hard morning's work sending out handbills and chalking pavements, of speaking at a factory gate at 12 o'clock, of speaking at the docks at 1.30, of holding a women's meeting at 3 and a large open-air one at 7, and when it was over I would address envelopes for letters which I sent out to the sympathisers in the district.'[13]

In February 1910 the Putney and Fulham branch of the WSPU opened at 905 Fulham Road. Their campaign during the general election, a month earlier in January 1910, was so successful that their move to 'these new and commodious premises has been rendered absolutely necessary'.[14] The shop and office were run by the two honorary secretaries, Miss Cutten and Mrs H. Roberts (the latter is possibly the subject of the photograph shown in Figure 6.6). The 'Shop Warming' took place on 12 February when the Mission to Women, a series of afternoon and evening meetings in the shop, was launched. Outdoor meetings were also held in the district. *Votes for Women* reported: 'The local interest was very great, and a policeman was on duty all day, keeping watch on the very friendly crowd which gathered round the window.[15] The banner 'Taxation Without Representation Is Tyranny', in startling black letters on a white ground, across the shop was a centre of great interest.'[16] A month later the honorary secretaries asked local suffragettes: 'will any friend kindly lend some palms to improve the appearance of the shop?'[17]

By the time this photograph was taken, probably in the summer of 1910, the shop was well stocked. Cutten and Roberts understood the importance of their windows to the ambivalent, curious and uninterested shopper who might call at their premises: 'A hint to other shopkeepers who wish to attract customers, comes from this local Union, the frequent window dressing has a miraculous effect.'[18] The WSPU had shops like this all over the country. They were nerve-centres of local activity; sometimes co-ordinated from the headquarters,

Figure 6 A young mother stands with her baby outside a shop, which the caption tells us is run by the Putney and Fulham branch of the WSPU. She may be the manager showing off her bonny new baby. She has popped out of the shop without her hat, the door is still open. The shop is festooned with purple, white and green flags, and much tricolour merchandising. Photographic portraits and propaganda postcards hang from 'washing-lines' strung across the two bay windows of the shop. Postcards of the 'stars' of the movement are strung from vertical strings. Several posters attached to a table in the middle of the shop advertise the fact that *Votes for Women* is sold there. The sheet music for the song 'Purple, White and Green', is visible. There is a silk scarf, a muff, stationery edged in the colours, a postcard album, a basket of farm eggs, pots of jam and marmalade, pamphlets and books. A banner hangs on the back wall bearing a slogan which includes the words 'Representation ... is Tyranny'. There may be people at work in the basement of the shop, which is lit partly by the 'pavement lights' which give additional light from the street, At least three of its windows are open.

they often operated autonomously, devising activities tailor-made to a particular local community. All the shops and offices recruited new members and raised funds for the WSPU's 'War Chest'. They also did propaganda work, including 'chalking parades' which sent suffragettes out to chalk notices of meetings on pavements, in purple, white and green chalk. 'Bicycle scouts' would join a 'bicycle corps' and ride out to outlying districts to 'rouse' women's interest in the struggle for the vote. 'Umbrella parades' took place in winter, and 'parasol parades' in summer, to increase sales of *Votes for Women*. As well as the banner that we can see in the photograph, this shop would have had its own banner, which members would have embroidered and appliquéd with imagery and mottoes of particular relevance to their own branch.

In each photograph shown in this chapter there is someone missing: the photographer. At the time of these photographs the photographer was a relatively new and important person who could stop time and keep it in his or her box. The photograph could be used to show many other people who were not there what it was like to have been in a particular place. John Tagg emphasises the power of the press when it reproduced photographs.[19] The photographs themselves are compelling mementoes of the people depicted in their shadows.

NOTES

1 *Calling all Women* (London, The Suffragette Fellowship, 1930), p. 1.
2 Annie Kenney, *Memories of a militant,* (London, Edward Arnold, 1924), p. 110.
3 *The Suffrage annual and women's who's who* (London, Stanley Paul, 1913), pp. 282–3.
4 *Ibid.,* pp. 282–3.
5 Olive Banks, *The biographical dictionary of British feminists, vol. 1, 1800–1930* (Brighton, Harvester/Wheatsheaf, 1985), pp. 107–8.
6 *Votes for Women,* March 1908, p. 81.
7 *The suffrage annual and women's who's who,* p. 386.
8 Votes for Women, 6 August 1908, pp. 358–9.
9 *Ibid.,* p. 259.
10 *Ibid.,* p. 363.
11 *Ibid.,* 3 December 1908, pp. 164–5.
12 *The suffrage annual and women's who's who,* p. 354.
13 Kenney, *Memories of a militant,* p. 156.
14 *Votes for Women,* 28 January 1910, p. 284.
15 *Ibid.,* 18 February 1910, pp. 311–12.
16 *Ibid.,* pp. 311–12.
17 *Ibid.,* 4 March 1910, p. 360.
18 *Ibid.,* 25 February 1910, p. 344.
19 John Tagg, *The burden of representation: essays on photographies and histories* (London, Macmillan, 1988), pp. 233–4.

7

Suffragette fiction and the fictions of suffrage

THE figure of the suffragette is ubiquitous in the mainstream culture of twentieth-century Britain. From *Fame is the spur* to *Kind hearts and coronets* and *Mary Poppins* the suffragette has served as an immediately recognisable icon of strong-minded English womanhood or audacious female eccentricity. This essay is predominantly but not exclusively concerned with suffragette fiction – that is, fiction written by the suffragettes and their supporters in the period between the onset of Women's Social and Political Union (WSPU) militancy in 1903 and 1928, when all women received the vote. By 1908 the public impact of suffragette militancy had already become such that *all* forms of rebelliousness exposed women to the possibility of being associated with the suffragettes. At the end of E. M. Forster's *A room with a view* the heroine Lucy Honeychurch breaks her engagement and resolves to become more independent – 'one of the women whom she had praised so eloquently who care for liberty and not for men'.[1] Although the expression of Lucy's desire for more personal freedom is quite unconnected with the question of votes for women it nevertheless elicits this response: '"And mess with type-writers and latch-keys," exploded Mrs Honeychurch. "And agitate and scream, and be carried off kicking by the police. And call it a Mission ... when no one wants you! And call it Duty ... when it means that you can't stand your own home!"'[2]

The years between 1903 and 1928 were a time of impassioned public contestation over the meanings of the women's suffrage movement and the representations of the suffragette which are reflected and mediated in the writing of the time. But the relationship between any work of fiction and the historical situation to which it may refer is complex and contradictory. Not all writing by suffragettes and their supporters will afford a complimentary view of the suffrage movement, and as the ideological project of an author is not necessarily that of her text, writers with no investment in that movement will sometimes offer positive representations of the suffragettes and their struggles, and vice versa. The novels of two disillusioned suffragettes, May Sinclair's *The tree of heaven* and Cicely Hamilton's *William – an Englishman*, for example, while exhibiting many of the familiar characteristics of suffragette fiction, appear so hostile to the movement that they might well be taken as the work of anti-suffragists.[3] In contrast, a work of fiction by an anti-suffragist, Mary Augusta Ward, president of the Anti-Suffrage League, provides one of the most attractive depictions of a young, idealistic suffragette in the character of Delia Blanchflower in the eponymous novel.[4]

However, the tendency of much mainstream fiction written at the time of suffragette militancy was to discredit the movement by exposing the personal defects of its supporters or exploiting the entertainment value of militancy to the full. The various guises in which the suffragette appears are often those which are reliant on the notion of fixity in the construction of otherness. Nettie Miniver in *Ann Veronica*, Gertrude Marvell in *Delia Blanchflower* and Olive Chancellor in *The Bostonians* are all representations of the suffragette/ist as a manipulative, frustrated spinster who exercises an unhealthy hold over the young whom she influences.[5] Susan Higgins has discussed the differences between the strident Clara Dawes in *Sons and lovers* (1911) and the respected suffragist Alice Dax on whom she is modelled.[6] The actress Isabel Joy, who accepts a wager to sail around the world and get herself arrested three times in order to win money for the 'cause' in *The Regent*, embodies the stereotype of the suffragette as a publicity-seeking exhibitionist and the potential of militancy as an amusing spectator sport.[7]

Whereas the authors of mainstream fiction frequently construct the subjectivities of the subordinated to serve their own interests, suffragette fictions are written by the disempowered out of their own experience. It is, therefore, useful to maintain a working distinction between the fictions of suffrage – that is, works like *A room with a view* and *The Regent* – which provide examples of the suffragette as a sign from which a variety of socially and culturally determined meanings can be read, and suffragette fiction – that is, work written by suffragettes and their supporters which furthers our understanding of the 'cause' and provides a view of the women's suffrage movement from within. At their best, suffragette writings are fictions of cultural resistance and social transformation which can be seen to offer a challenge to two crucial areas of patriarchal power – its control of language and representation, and its control of gender meaning and gender difference.

In one of the early discussions of suffragette writing Elaine Showalter contends that on balance the 'women's suffrage movement was not a happy stimulus to the woman writer'.[8] She is right to assert that much of the writing produced under the influence of the women's suffrage movement was simply propagandist and of strictly limited aesthetic or literary interest. However, as Lisa Tickner has pointed out, the art/propaganda divide is of questionable value within the context of the cultural production of the women's suffrage movement because this demarcation is in itself a kind of propaganda for art which 'secures the category of art as something complex, humane and ideologically pure through the operation of an alternative category of propaganda as that which is crude, institutional, partisan'.[9] What is needed is a carefully differentiated analysis of suffragette fiction which assesses its relationship to existing power structures and the wider social, historical and political relationships of which it forms a part, and not in relation to preconceived ideas about 'propaganda' and 'art' or the inherent value of particular modes of writing.

Some distinctive qualities of suffragette fiction may be pinpointed in relation to its moment of production. The fact that suffragette fiction was written at a time when votes for women appeared finely in the balance, usually in the hope of influencing a heated public debate, makes it significantly different from earlier representations of suffrage. As Martha Vicinus has pointed out, most chartist fiction written by working men was produced after the great chartist demonstrations of 1848.[10] The industrial novels of the 1850s and 1860s, of which George Eliot's *Felix Holt: the radical* (1866) is probably the most obviously connected to the suffrage agitation of the 1840s, also followed, rather than anticipated, the social and political disturbances upon which they can be seen to depend.

For much of the nineteenth century women's enfranchisement had been considered a subject of ridicule. When Mrs Jellyby in *Bleak House* (1853) abandons her utopian schemes for the welfare of the natives of Borrioboola-Gha on the left bank of the Niger to pursue the right of women to sit in parliament, Dickens leaves the reader in no doubt that her second project is as foolish and ill-starred as the one which it supersedes. Indeed, Mrs Jellyby is the prototype of the suffragist as an irresponsible wife and mother, an image that was to become increasingly familiar in nineteenth- and twentieth-century culture. "'But you never have large families now: I suppose you are too busy with your suffragetting'", is one of the platitudes about the English recited by a German widow in Katherine Mansfield's short story, 'Germans at meat'.[11]

The suffragette fiction produced during the period of militant agitation served the 'cause' by contesting the popular image of the suffragette as a deluded harridan or street-brawler. It often pleaded, albeit melodramatically, for the rights and wrongs of women to be recognised. It sometimes posited the question of commitment unambiguously as a leitmotif. And it sometimes chose to deal explicitly and self-consciously with the formation of the suffragette's identity. Within the women's suffrage movement authors with national reputations, such as Elizabeth Robins, who was a prestigious recruit to the WSPU national committee in 1909, were highly respected and often enjoyed a special relationship with the leadership. Moreover, creative writing was highly valued as an expression and extension of political identity and commitment, and played a key

role in affirming and reiterating the feminist communal ideals to which the suffragettes and their supporters subscribed.

In the preface to *A pageant of great women* Cicely Hamilton contends that
the women's suffrage movement 'was the first political agitation to organise the
arts in its aid'.[12] Proselytising for the vote by 'the means proper to writers the use
of the pen'[13] was one of the declared objectives of Women Writers Suffrage
League (WWSL), founded in 1908 by Cicely Hamilton and Bessie Hatton, the
membership of which included many well-known authors such as Olive
Schreiner and Sarah Grand. The very act of subscribing to the WWSL constituted not only a public challenge to the hallowed autonomy of the creative artist,
but also a public declaration to the effect that the woman author did not view
art as a special activity divorced from the political. As membership of the WWSL
was restricted to the professional or semi-professional writer who had received
payment for her work, the acquisition by women of the status of professional
writer and of economic independence came to be seen as interrelated issues in
ways which bring to mind the connections made in Virginia Woolf's much later
essay, 'Professions for women'.[14]

Suffragette authors, amateur and professional, saw it as their particular responsibility to challenge the popular prejudices against the suffragettes through
the production and dissemination of booklets, leaflets and tracts, etc. May Sinclair's pamphlet, *Feminism*, for example, was commissioned and published by
the WWSL as a riposte to Sir Almroth Wright's virulent diatribe against suffragette 'hysteria' in *The Times*.[15] One common misconception was that militant
activity constituted an affront to womanliness. In *Pages from the diary of a militant suffragette* Katherine Roberts pointed out that the stage was the only place
where women had equal rights with men in their professions and asked if there
were any place 'where women retain their womanliness more than on the
stage?'[16]

The importance of ideological contestation over representations was never
underestimated by the women's leadership. The various suffrage newspapers –
Votes for Women (the WSPU), *The Vote* (the Women's Freedom League (WFL))
and *The Common Cause* (the National Union of Women's Suffrage Societies
(NUWSS)) – regularly carried reviews of new plays and books. Influential suffragettes and suffragists, including Emmeline Pethick-Lawrence, Emmeline
Pankhurst and Millicent Fawcett, attached sufficient importance to imaginative
writing to review new fiction themselves.

The better-known titles of suffragette fictions, some written by prominent
activists – Constance Maud, *No surrender*, Charlotte Despard, *Outlawed*,
Gertrude Colmore, *Suffragette Sally*, Elizabeth Robins, *The convert* and Evelyn
Sharp, *Rebel women*[17] – were welcomed and read avidly by women who had
become habituated to seeing the behaviour and motives of the suffragette
maligned in public elsewhere. In *Prisons and prisoners* Lady Constance Lytton

complains that 'our movement has had to combat all the conditions of an era of darkness, ignorance, and barbaric oppression ... newspapers will not accept, publishers will not print, and booksellers will not sell the true facts concerning us'.[18]

But not all the press was hostile to the suffragettes: the *Manchester Guardian* and the *Daily Chronicle* both published Evelyn Sharp's short stories before they appeared in a single volume, *Rebel women*, in 1910. The popularity of Sharp's good-humoured accounts of suffragette activity did much to dispel the popular misconception of the suffragettes as ladies of leisure, cranks, or humourless feminists, as well as boosting the morale and self-esteem of the suffragettes. 'The crank of all the ages' ends with the observation that 'it is sometimes helpful to remind yourself, if you are the crank who stands at a street corner selling papers for a cause, that cranks are the salt of the earth'.[19]

I have argued elsewhere that the women's suffrage movement is an example of what Rita Felski has termed a public feminist sphere, a discursive space in which the shared experience of gender-based oppression provides the impetus for the development of a self-consciously oppositional identity among its members.[20] Like the wearing of the suffrage colours, a woman's choice of reading matter became a symbolic marker of her oppositional identity. In *The wife of Sir Isaac Harman* (1914), for example, Ellen Harman's possession of a novel by Elizabeth Robins is an outward signifier of inner dissidence. Books that were perceived to oppose the double standard, to offer a critique of patriarchal values, or to contain a feminist vision of the future – including Olive Schreiner's 'Three dreams in a desert', George Meredith's *Esther Waters*, Charlotte Perkins Gilman's *The man-made world*, and George Eliot's *The mill on the Floss* – were taken into the women's prisons and read there by suffragettes.[21] While the numbers of women prepared to break the law to effect changes in the social order were always limited, they were augmented by many others prepared to help the 'cause' in whatever lawful ways they could: by subscribing to the funds of the various suffrage organisations; by lobbying and 'letter-writing; and by using their power as consumers to purchase suffragette publications, including fiction.

Although suffragette fictions are formally and ideologically diverse, they share an explicit rhetorical foregrounding of the relationship between the woman writer and her reader. The attempts of writers of fiction to reproduce the items of the suffragette calendar – street-meetings, paper-selling, demonstrations, arrests, etc. – in 'authentic' semi-documentary detail were popular in suffragette/ist circles because they provided their audience with the pleasures of recognition: the wry sense of humour displayed by the first-person narrator of Evelyn Sharp's suffrage tales added much to the readers' enjoyment of her carefully observed descriptions of the velleities of a suffragette's life. In 'Patrolling the gutter' the suffragettes return from a day's work with their hair damp and skirts and boots caked in mud, to be greeted by the postman's cry: "'votes for a few rich

women that's all you're after'".[22] In 'Votes for women – forward!' the suffragettes
have to contend with the street humorist who assumes that 'the name of every
woman in the shop, not excluding the charwoman was Pankhurst'.[23] Moreover,
the distinction between fact and fiction was sometimes deliberately blurred or
abandoned in the author's quest for topical subject-matter and verisimilitude. In
Gertrude Atherton's popular *Julia France and her times*, for example, the fictional heroine ('picturesque without being sensational, a brilliant powerful per-
suasive speaker'[24]) is made to speak in the Albert Hall alongside the WSPU
leaders, including Emmeline Pethick-Lawrence.

The frequent references to persons and events outside the literary text
which characterise suffragette fiction resist the readers' efforts to extricate the literary text from history, and therefore from politics. Thinly veiled portraits of public figures, which would have been immediately recognised by readers of the
time, are a recurring feature of many works. The model on which Ernestine
Blunt is based in Robins' *The convert* is the schoolteacher Mary Gawthorpe, and
the labour leader Lothian Scott is a fictional version of Keir Hardie. But, as one
might expect, the most common representations are of the Pankhursts. Ellen
Melville in *The judge* attends a meeting in Edinburgh addressed in a 'hoarse,
sweet North-country voice' by Mrs Ormiston, 'the mother of the famous rebels
Brynhild, Melissa and Guendolen'.[25] Christabel Pankhurst is transposed into the
charismatic Christina Amhurst in Colemore's *Suffragette Sally* and into the
fanatical Maud Blackadder in Sinclair's *The tree of heaven*. Annie Kenney, the
Lancashire mill-girl, becomes Annie Carnie in *Suffragette Sally* and Fanny Kelly
in Maud's *No surrender*.

The novels written by the suffragettes and their sympathisers were topical,
impassioned, polemical and easily accessible. They were not usually experimental or self-consciously literary, and their authors, unlike the women modernists of the time, did not usually question the traditional ideas about the
mimetic and representational functions of art. This is not, of course, to assume
the leading women modernists were unsympathetic to the women's suffrage
cause. On the contrary, May Sinclair, Dorothy Richardson, Virginia Woolf and
others all made practical contributions to the struggle at various times: Woolf by
addressing envelopes, Sinclair by taking part in a 'self-denial appeal' and
Richardson by visiting the suffragettes in Holloway prison. But the women modernists were dedicated primarily to literary and artistic innovation and, as Gillian
Hanscombe and Virginia Smyers have observed, 'to activists, artistic radicalism
seems all too often traditionalist in its assumption of the primacy of art over the
other workings of the world'.[26]

Suffragette novelists, therefore, usually eschewed irony, parody, any
extended use of symbolic language and elaborate narrative structures. Instead,
they used vivid dialogue and/or interior monologue to formulate their arguments and to reach a wide readership. This was sufficiently large to sustain the

Women's Press, a feminist publishing house which published or distributed the work of Cicely Hamilton, Elizabeth Robins, Beatrice Harraden, Charlotte Perkins Gilman, Helen Blackburn, Constance Lytton and others, and occupied the same building in London as the WSPU after 1912. The readership of suffragette fiction included many unsophisticated factory girls to whom suffragette authors wished to offer the pleasures of a good story and not to discourage from reading books by the use of inaccessible or unfamiliar forms of writing. This is the preferred audience to which the *Votes for Women* series of novels advertised by the publishers Stanley Paul in 1913 was directed.

Although questions of literary form are not usually raised explicitly in the fictions of suffrage, an interesting exception is *Intellectual Mansions SW1*, a satire on an avant-garde writer whose progressive ideas about art are contrasted to his proprietorial attitudes to his wife and his hostility to the suffragettes. *Intellectual Mansions, SW1* warns of the dangers of the 'philosophical, non-committal attitude of mind which characterises literary and artistic people in relation to contemporary facts'.[27] But another novel by the same author, *In the eighth year*, appears much more critical of activism and attributes the support of married women for the suffragettes to marital boredom in the eighth year of marriage.[28]

The plots of suffragette fiction articulate a kind of counter-discourse which has the capacity to situate and question the authority of the dominant value system. This is particularly marked in relation to the double standard which, as Susan Kingsley Kent has argued, was the single greatest issue in the suffrage campaign, serving as a symbol that best exemplified women's subject status and the dangers consequent to it.[29] In her autobiography *The flurried years* Violet Hunt complains about the 'anomalies of our so constipated divorce law' and the injustices in relation to the custody of children which the suffragettes would alter when they got the vote.[30]

The iniquity of the double standard is the issue that resonates through virtually all the suffragette fictions: in *The cost of a promise* Germaine Damien is required to appear in public in support of her husband who is standing for parliament, but is forbidden to speak on suffragette platforms in her own right;[31] in *Outlawed* Beryl Marchmont is one of many women in prison 'sent there by men – judged, condemned, by men – whom no woman would have condemned';[32] in *The call* male chemists display an undercurrent of hostility to Ursula Wingfield's scientific work because they 'may have unconsciously resented a woman's claim to discovery'.[33] Like Vida Levering in *The convert*, Mrs Hetherington in Annie Tibbits's *At what sacrifice?* is revealed to be a victim of double standards – a woman with a past. Her personal experience of marriage to an abusive husband, and subsequently of sweated labour, poverty and near starvation as a single breadwinner, account for her impassioned advocacy of the militant cause.[34]

Suffragette fiction differs from earlier suffragist fiction in many important respects. Much nineteen-century suffragist fiction had attempted to show how the acquisition of votes by women would secure a 'millennium of public righteousness and the end of private vice'. As A. V. Dicey put it: 'There are virtues, such as modesty, ready sympathy with, and compassion for poverty and suffering, which, though possessed in some degree by most human beings are deemed, whether rightly or not, to be specifically feminine.'[35] The tone of high Victorian moral rectitude is exemplified in a series of eight updated short stories published by the National Society for Women's Suffrage which equate women with thrift, industry, good housekeeping and sobriety, and men with intemperance, idleness, profligacy and corruption. In A woman's duty, for example, the six hundred woman householders in the ward of St Mary's oust the appropriately named Mr Boosey and return a candidate who supports the temperance movement in the local government elections.[36]

But by the turn of the century the Victorian obsession with respectability had come to seem increasingly outmoded to many observers. A criticism frequently levied against the leaders of Victorian and Edwardian suffragettes/ists by sexual radicals was that they supported the repressive codes of Victorian morality rather than demanding full sexual and emotional freedom for women. The dual obsession with sexual purity and social propriety is satirised in The wife of Sir Isaac Harman. When Ellen Harman leaves her husband and seeks support from the suffragette Miss Alimony she is advised to return home to avoid a scandal: '"It will be a Matrimonial Case. How can I be associated with that? We mustn't mix up Women's Freedom with Matrimonial cases. Impossible! ... Think of the weapon it gives our enemies. If once other things complicate the Vote, – the Vote is lost".'[37]

As Lesley Hall argues in chapter 13 of this book, 'recent historiography on the late nineteenth- and earlier twentieth-century women's movement has tended to assume a dichotomy between "social purity" and "sexual reform". In practice this was less than absolute.'[38] Rather than thinking of them as two irreconcilable opposing factions, she suggests that it is more helpful to approach 'social purity' and 'sex reform' as 'elements within a spectrum of opposition to conventional assumptions of the day about sexual relations and the role of women' which different women chose to occupy and articulate at different times.[39] In 1913 Wilma Meikle drew attention to the rift which had developed between some younger suffragettes, of whom the young Rebecca West is one example, and their older counterparts who 'ignored with a brazen decorum the revolutionary claims that feminism involved'.[40]

Such differences had become apparent much earlier in women's responses to Grant Allen's controversial novel The woman who did (1896) which Millicent Fawcett had reviewed unfavourably in the Contemporary Review. Fawcett claimed that Allen had never 'given any legal help by tongue or pen to any practical effort to improve the legal or social status of women', and that it was 'as an enemy that he claims to link together the claim of women to citizenship and social and industrial independence, with attacks upon marriage and the family'.[41]

Suffragette fictions testify to the complexity of the debates about sexual morality within the suffragette/ist ranks and to the passions which they engendered. Although Cicely Hamilton cautioned her readers against the 'confusion of one virtue with virtue in general', arguing that 'no natural ethical code emanating from within could have summed up woman's virtue in a virtue – physical purity',[42] virginity was a source of pride for many suffragettes. Valentine Wannup in Ford Madox Ford's *Some do not* boasts that "'I was a slavey and am a suffragette ... I'd like you to understand that in spite of it all I'm pure! Chaste, you know ... Perfectly virtuous".'[43]

While H. G. Wells chose to ridicule the suffragette Nettie Miniver for her strong aversion to the physical in *Ann Veronica* ("'Bodies! Bodies! Horrible Things! We are souls. Love lies on a higher plain. We are not animals. If ever I did meet a man I could love I should love him" – her voice dropped again – "platonically"'[44]), writers like Rebecca West, who were associated with the journal *The Freewoman* (1911–13), were challenging conventional sexual attitudes and demanding the right of women to express their sexuality outside the context of marriage.

Ellen Melville, the young suffragette heroine of West's *The judge*, is an unmarried mother. For Dulcie Ellice, who chooses to enter into a legal pact instead of a conventional marriage in Percy White's *To-day*, the causes of national divorce and women's suffrage are inextricably linked: "'I'm a woman defying opinions that the next generation will scrap-heap ... Do you expect me to cringe to or to hide from palsied moralists, out of whose hands the power to ban is rapidly slipping?'".[45]

Suffragette fiction was instrumental in forging sisterhood across the lines of class, and several novels strenuously attempted to establish working women as the cause and support of the women's suffrage movement. The best known of these, Elizabeth Robins's *The convert*, attempts to establish that it was in the interests of working women to support the suffragette by presenting the vote as something which would solve a wide range of social problems and by connecting its acquisition to a wide range of social reforms which would benefit the working class. Both *The convert* and two other novels, *Suffragette Sally* and *No surrender*, address the criticism directed at the suffragette leadership from within the labour movement to the effect that working women stood to gain little from supporting the militants and that working people as a whole would benefit more by demanding full adult suffrage rather than the limited franchise sought by supporters of the WSPU and the WFL.

The convert appeals to the conscience of those raised above the need for economic struggle by emphasising the desperate plight of working-class women. A series of speakers cite topical examples of women's exploitation in a number of notorious sweated industries and condemn the government's failure to enforce minimum working hours. In the semi-documentary Trafalgar Square scenes, which were based on Elizabeth Robins's transcriptions of speeches she had heard at the suffragettes' open-air meetings, the socialist/suffragist position is eloquently put by Ernestine Blunt: "'All women suffer – but it's the woman of your class who suffer most. Isn't it? Don't you men know – why, it's notorious! – that the women of the working class are worse sweated even than the men?'"[46]Wendy Mulford has observed that 'the worlds of *The convert* are inter-linked, economically, sexually and politically. The same set of power relations encircle the middle-class women as exploit the labour, the reject the basic human needs, of the working-class women.'[47]

The convert grapples with another difficult problem that the suffragettes faced: the privileged woman who was conscious of the influence she exerted and anxious to avoid its dilution by the extension of power to others of her sex. The romantic novelist Marie Corelli claimed that 'as matters stand at present, I can win for any candidate in whom I may happen to be interested, at least forty or fifty votes – perhaps more'. Corelli added: 'If I did secure my own one vote, should I be better off than I am now, with the certainty of forty or fifty male voters at my beck and call, ready to do precisely as I bid them?'[48] But many anti-suffragist women were nothing like as confident or competent as Marie Corelli. As Janet Courtney later noted in *The women of my time*, it was 'our fate, as antis, to attract all the ultra-feminine and the ladylike incompetents'.[49]

The aristocratic house parties in *The convert* dramatise the means whereby privileged women were able to exercise power in two roles, which Brian Harrison has pointed out were much favoured by anti-suffragists: the female philanthropist and the political hostess;[50] and they dramatise the problems that conservative women of this type presented to the suffragettes: "'Now, if we got our maids to do those women's hair for them – if we lent them our French hats – ah, then ... they'd convert you creatures fast enough'", says Lady Whyteleaf. While Vida Levering declaims that 'the aim of the movement is to get away from the need of just these little dodges',[51] the aristocratic matrons take pride in their abilities to exercise their wiles on men. Not the least of the *The convert*'s many ironies is the fact that Vida's success in converting her rich and powerful lover to the women's cause demonstrates the effectiveness of the very manipulative techniques that feminists decried.

Constance Maud's *No surrender*, which takes its title from the words made famous by the militant suffragette Mary Leigh, and Gertrude Colmore's *Suffragette Sally* are concerned with dispelling the myth that the suffrage movement was only of interest to middle-class women. Each dramatises the story of Lady Constance Lytton (Lady Geraldine Hill in *Suffragette Sally* and Mary O'Neil in *No surrender*) who had disguised herself as a seamstress and subjected herself to the ordeal of forcible feeding to prove the suffragettes' claim that middle-class women were receiving more lenient treatment in prison than their working-class sisters. Both novels avoid an exclusive focus on one central protagonist, but are concerned with suffragettes from a cross-section of social backgrounds in order to show how friendships between women can be formed, and sisterhood sustained, across class divisions.

Sally Simmonds in *Suffragette Sally* is a domestic servant who responds fervently to Lady Geraldine Hill's 'call to all women; to stand together; to be full of courage; to fight for themselves and for each other; most ardently for the poorest, the most oppressed of all'.[52] *No surrender*, which is dedicated to Charlotte Despard, focuses on the strong support for women's suffrage among the poor women factory workers in the textile mills of Lancashire, and on the prejudice against votes for women on the part of many men in the labour movement, exemplified by the trade-unionist and Labour MP, Joe Hopton.

Rather than laying any claims to originality, suffragette fiction is frequently formulaic. As John Cawelti has suggested, the concept of a formula is useful as a means of making historical and cultural inferences about the collective fantasies shared by specific groups of people.[53] The fact that the fictions of suffrage often conform to a limited number of narrative patterns not only illuminates the 'collective fantasies' to which suffragette authors and their first readers subscribed, it also tells the reader much about the determinations imposed upon the texts by their historical moment of production. In *The morphology of the folk tale* Vladimir Propp has referred to a reiterant plot function as 'an act of character, defined from the point of view of the significance for the course of action'.[54] A common reiterant plot function in the texts which I have discussed is the experience of prison as the pivotal event which accounts for a suffragette's withdrawal from active politics. This happens in a number of texts, including *Ann Veronica, From Hampstead to Holloway, The tree of heaven* and *To-day*. A second reiterant plot function is the rescuing of the damsel in distress; here, chivalry prompts a man to rescue a suffragette who is threatened by ruffians or has fallen among women. This is the case in *The declension of Henry D'Albiac, Intellectual Mansions, SW1, A fair suffragette, The cost of a promise,* 'The soul of a suffragette' and *Delia Blanchflower* – Blancheflor is the name of the damsel rescued by Sir Percival in Arthurian legend.

There is a third reiterant plot function. Delia Blanchflower in *Delia Blanchflower*, Ann Veronica in *Ann Veronica*, Dorothea Harrison in *The tree of heaven*, Kate Denver in *From Hampstead to Holloway*, Una Blockley in 'The soul of a suffragette', Julia France in *Julia France and her times*, Katharine Hilbury in *Night and day*, Germaine Damien in *The cost of a promise*, Ursula Wingfield in *The call* and Gipsie Grey in *A fair suffragette* are all caught between conflicting desires: the desire to be loved and the desire to be active and independent.[57]

In some novels the suffragette appears unable to find a femininity in which she can co-exist with the patriarchal order. When presented with a choice between the claims of her male admirer and the claims of political commitment, the suffragette usually opts for love. This is the case in *A fair suffragette*, in which the cost of Gipsie Grey's marriage to Vernon Mowbray is a promise that her suffragette activities will end, and also in 'The clear call', in which Sara Cummings stops her suffrage work to avoid giving offence to her husband's supporters in his parliamentary constituency.[58] But sometimes she is able to dispense with an unsympathetic man's services, as Sally Simmonds does in *Suffragette Sally* and Anne Sherard does in 'The choice',[59] or else to convert a seemingly intractable opponent of women's suffrage to the suffragette cause, as Jenny Clegg converts Joe Hopton in *No surrender*, and Flora Evans does Henry D'Albiac in *The declension of Henry D'Albiac*. In Constance Smedley's *The daughter* the wealthy suffragette Delia Willett contracts a marriage to a penniless young artisan to prove that she is capable of living on a pittance and experiencing the lot of a woman of the people.[60]

Suffragette fiction is also richly illuminating on the divisions within the ranks, particularly in relation to the later stages of militancy and the WSPU arson campaign. The latter was peculiarly fraught with tensions and contradictions that found their way into fiction. As Ray Strachey put it in *The cause*, 'on the one hand the suffragettes challenged physical violence, as if they were real fighters, and yet they refused any real contest because they were women'.[61] The rhetoric of the WSPU leadership often relied heavily on military metaphors: 'fighting orders', 'guerrilla warfare', the 'women's army', 'military discipline', etc. But if suffragette rhetoric made liberal use of military metaphors it also made much of the deep respect with which women held human life, 'for we know what life costs'.[62] Una Bateson in W. L. Courteney's short story 'The soul of a suffragette' describes herself as a soldier in an army who must carry out her orders: '"What would happen if private soldiers began to question and discuss the commands given them by their leaders? It is not my business to argue. I have been enrolled in a militant force, and I should be a deserter if I refuse to obey."'[63]

But for other women such analogies were unacceptable. Cicely Hamilton found herself listening to their speeches and wondering 'what the "warriors" would feel if they were pitchforked into the real thing'.[64] *William – an Englishman* is about an idealistic young socialist (William) and a naive young suffragette (Griselda), who think of their 'little political scuffles as war'. William and Griselda stumble accidentally on 'the other kind of war – of bullets and blood, and high explosives'[65] on their honeymoon in the Ardennes. Here they are made to face the realities of war – the rape of Griselda, which brings about William's disillusionment, and the enemy bombardment which results in his death.

The emphasis in both *William – an Englishman* and May Sinclair's *The tree of heaven* is on the folly of abdicating individual responsibility to the collective whole as dedication to the 'cause' sometimes seemed to require of its devotees. As Christabel Pankhurst once exclaimed, 'to lose the personal in a great impersonal is to live!'.[66] In *The tree of heaven* Dorothea Harrison observes as 'the little vortex of the Woman's Movement is swept without a sound into the immense vortex of the War'.[67] It is the First World War which prompts Dorothea, whose fiancé is killed in action, to think of her time in the campaign for women's suffrage retrospectively as time foolishly wasted: '"All the years – like a fool – over that silly suffrage ... I told him he didn't care for freedom. And he's died for it".'[68]

Both Sinclair and Hamilton are able to draw upon inside knowledge of the women's suffrage movement to achieve strikingly naturalistic detail. May Sinclair is particularly skilled in evoking an orgy of wanton destructiveness, as hysterical women are seen to run amok under the auspices of the Women's Franchise Union: 'Now and then, just to show what violence it could accomplish if it liked, it burned down a house or two in a pure and consecrated ecstasy of Feminism.'[69] It is the 'terror of the collective soul' and the threat of 'massed emotion' which are made to account for Dorothea's antipathy to communal modes of organisation.[70]

May Sinclair and Cicely Hamilton are sensitive, scrupulously so, to the slightest failing on the part of the political radicals – 'cocksure, contemptuous, intolerant, self-sacrificing after the manner of their kind'. But neither *The tree of heaven* nor *William – an Englishman* is equally attentive to the unacceptable face of patriarchal society that consigned women dying of cancer to prison for symbolic acts of defiance or to the unacceptable face of patriotism that consigned men to slaughter in their millions in the First World War. So strong was the identification of Hamilton and Sinclair with Britain's war effort that they were no longer able to recognise principled dissidence but only unbridled fanaticism in the movement that both had once enthusiastically supported.

Not all suffragette writers regarded the demands of the nation and women's suffrage as antithetical. Quite the opposite – many saw the claims of women's freedom and of the nation as complementary. In *The call*, for example, Ursula Wingfield explains to her fiancé that '"I had to fight in the woman's Cause. It seemed a sort of – call, and I nearly died for it. And you had to fight in the war, that was a call, too, and you nearly died for it".'[72] While the extreme militant tactics in use after 1910, and the autocratic conduct of Christabel and Emmeline Pankhurst, may help to account for the disenchantment that we find in Hamilton and Sinclair, their fiction, as Jane Marcus has observed, is 'the field on which we may see a great ideological battle fought, where the struggle for sexual freedom becomes "silly" and the leaders, like the Pankhursts, are called protofascists, as the war mentality condones militarism, nationalism and patriotism'.[73]

There is a marked contrast between *The tree of heaven* and *William – an Englishman* and the pacifist Evelyn Sharp's pre-war short story, 'The women at the gate'. This extended meditation on the complex nature of warfare begins with a woman bystander in a crowd, who observes as, one by one, twelve suffragettes attempt to gain entry into the House of Commons and each is turned back and arrested. The woman converses with a sympathetic artisan about the properties of Greek tragedy and 'real wars'. Real wars, it is agreed, are generally inconclusive. There is never any glory in war – "'at least, not where the war is'".[74] She then reveals herself to be the thirteenth suffragette who has come to offer herself up for arrest. And the question – how does anybody know which side has won? – is answered by the man who has fought in 'real wars': "By looking to see which side pays the price of victory".[75]

NOTES

1 E. M. Forster, A room with a view (London, Edward Arnold, 1908), p. 28.
2 Ibid ., p. 298.
3 May Sinclair, The tree of heaven (London, Cassell, 1917); Cicely Hamilton, William – an Englishman (London, Skeffington, 1919).
4 Mary Augusta Ward, Delia Blanchflower (London, Ward Lock, 1915).
5 H. G. Wells, Ann Veronica (London, T. Fisher Unwin, 1909); Ward, Delia Blanchflower, Henry James, The Bostonians (London, Macmillan, 1886).
6 Susan Higgins, 'The suffragette in fiction', Hecate, 2, 1976, pp. 31–46: 35–6.
7 Arnold Bennett, The Regent: a five towns story of adventure in London (London, Methuen, 1913).
8 Elaine Showalter, A literature of their own: British women novelists from Brontë to Lessing (London, Virago, 1978), p. 236.
9 Lisa Tickner, The spectacle of women: imagery of the suffrage campaign 1907–14 (London, Chatto and Windus, 1987), p. xi.
10 Martha Vicinus, 'Chartist fiction and the development of a class-based literature', in H. Gustav Klaus (ed.), The socialist novel in Britain towards the recovery of a tradition (Brighton, Harvester Press, 1982), pp. 7–25:7.
11 Katherine Mansfield, 'Germans at meat', In a German pension (New York, Alfred Knopf, 1926), pp. 13–21: 16.
12 Cecily Hamilton, foreword, A pageant of great women (London, Marian Lewis, 1948), p. 7.
13 Elizabeth Robins, Way stations (London, Hodder and Stoughton, 1913), p. 225.
14 Virginia Woolf, 'Professions for women', in Leonard Woolf (ed.), The collected essays of Virginia Woolf (London, Hogarth Press, 1966–7), vol. 2, 1966, pp. 284–9.
15 May Sinclair, Feminism (London, The Women Writers' Suffrage League, 1912); Sir Almroth Wright, The Times, 28 March 1912, pp. 7–8.
16 Katherine Roberts, Pages from the diary of a militant suffragette (Letchworth and London, Garden City Press, 1911), p. 143.
17 Constance Elizabeth Maud, No surrender (London, Duckworth, 1911), Charlotte Despard and Mabel Collins, Outlawed: a novel on the woman suffrage question (London, Henry J. Drane, 1908); Gertrude Colmore, Suffragette Sally (London: Stanley Paul, 1911), Elizabeth Robins, The convert (London, Methuen, 1907); Evelyn Sharp, Rebel women (London, A. C. Fifield, 1910). Gertrude Colmore appears to have belonged to both the WSPU and the WFL.
18 Lady Constance Lytton, Prisons and prisoners: some personal experiences by Constance Lytton and Jane Warton, spinster (London, William Heinemann, 1914), p. 66.
19 Evelyn Sharp, 'The crank of all the ages', in Sharp, Rebel women, pp. 68–74: 74.
20 See Rita Felski, Beyond feminist aesthetics: feminist literature and social change (London, Hutchinson Radius), pp. 166–7 and Maroula Joannou, "'She who would be politically free herself must strike the blow": suffragette autobiography and suffragette militancy', in Julia Swindells (ed.), The uses of autobiography (London, Taylor and Francis, 1995), pp. 31–45: 38.

21 Lytton, *Prisons and prisoners*, pp. 121, 156, 187, 333.

22 Evelyn Sharp, 'Patrolling the gutter', in *Rebel women*, pp. 75–82: 82.

23 Evelyn Sharp, '"Votes for women – forward!"', *ibid.*, pp. 92–100: 96–7.

24 Gertrude Atherton, *Julia France and her times* (London, John Murray, 1912), p. 289.

25 Rebecca West, *The judge* (London, Hutchinson, 1922), pp. 50, 52.

26 Gillian Hanscombe and Virginia L. Smyers, *Writing for their lives: the modernist women 1910–1940* (London, Women's Press, 1987), p. 12.

27 Philip Gibbs, *Intellectual Mansions, SW1* (London, Chapman and Hall, 1910), p. 236.

28 Philip Gibbs, *In the eighth year: a vital problem of married life* (London, Williams and Norgate, 1913).

29 Susan Kingsley Kent, *Sex and suffrage in Britain 1860–1914* (London, Routledge, 1987), p. 209.

30 Violet Hunt, *The flurried years* (London, Hurst and Blackett, 1926), p. 129.

31 Gertrude Reynolds, *The cost of a promise* (London, Hodder and Stoughton, 1914).

32 Despard and Collins, *Outlawed*, foreword, p. ix.

33 Edith Ayrton Zangwill, *The call* (London, George Allen and Unwin, 1924), p. 155.

34 Annie O. Tibbits, *At what sacrifice?* (London, Digby, Long and Co., 1912).

35 A. V. Dicey, *Letter to a friend on votes for women* (London, John Murray, 1909), pp. 41, 42.

36 Carey Search, *A woman's duty* (London, National Society for Women's Suffrage, n.d.), Suffrage Stories, no. 3, held in Girton College Library, Cambridge at p. 396.3.36.

37 H. G. Wells, *The wife of Sir Isaac Harman* (London, Macmillan, 1914), p. 7.

38 See p. 190.

39 See p. 198.

40 Wilma Meikle, *Towards a sane feminism* (London, Grant Richards, 1917), p. 83.

41 Millicent Garrett Fawcett, 'The woman who did', *Contemporary Review*, 23, 1896, p. 630.

42 Cicely Hamilton, *Marriage as a trade* (London, Chapman and Hall, 1909), p. 86.

43 Ford Madox Ford. *Some do not: a novel* (London, Duckworth, 1924), p. 105.

44 Wells, *Ann Veronica*, p. 176.

45 Percy White, *To-day* (London, Constable, 1912), p. 238.

46 Robins, *The convert*, pp. 161–2: 162.

47 Wendy Mulford, 'Socialist-feminist criticism: a case study, women's suffrage and literature, 1906–1914', in Peter Widdowson (ed.), *Re-reading English* (London, Methuen, 1982), pp. 179–93: 185.

48 Marie Corelli, *Woman, or – suffragette? A question of rational choice* (London, C. A. Pearson, 1907), p. 13.

49 Janet Courtney, *The women of my time* (London, Lovat Dickson, 1934).

50 Brian Harrison, *Separate spheres: the opposition to women's suffrage in Britain* (London, Croom Helm, 1978), p. 83.

51 Robins, *The convert*, p. 223.

52 Colmore, *Suffragette Sally*, p. 16.

53 John Cawelti, *Adventure, mystery and romance: formula stories as art and popular culture* (Chicago and London, University of Chicago Press, 1976), p. 7.

54 Vladimir Propp, *The morphology of the folk tale*, trans. Lawrence Scott (Austin, University of Texas Press, 1968), p. 21.

55 Wells, *Ann Veronica*; W. Barton Baldry, *From Hampstead to Holloway: depicting the suffragette in her happiest moods* (London, John Ousley, 1909); Sinclair, *The tree of heaven*; White, *To-day*.

56 V. Goldie, *The declension of Henry D'Albiac* (London, Heinemann, 1912); Gibbs, *Intellectual Mansions, SW1*; Adrienne Mollwo, *A fair suffragette* (London, Henry J. Drane, 1909); Reynolds, *The cost of a promise*; W. L. Courtney, 'The soul of a suffragette', in *The soul of a suffragette and other stories* (London, Chapman and Hall, 1913), pp. 3–44, Ward, *Delia Blanchflower*.

57 Ward, *Delia Blanchflower*; Wells, *Ann Veronica*; Sinclair, *The tree of heaven*; Barton Baldry, *From Hampstead to Holloway*; Courtney, 'The soul of a suffragette'; Atherton, *Julia France*

and her times; Virginia Woolf, *Night and day* (London, Duckworth, 1919); Reynolds, *The cost of a promise*; Zangwill, *The call*; Mollwo, *A fair suffragette*.

58 Annie S. Swan, 'The clear call', in *Margaret Holroyd or the pioneers* (London, Hodder and Stoughton, 1910), pp. 139–63.

59 Annie S. Swan. 'The choice', *ibid.*, pp. 45-67.

60 Constance Smedley, *The daughter* (London, Constable, 1908).

61 Rachel Strachley, *The cause: a short history of the women's movement in Great Britain* (London, R. K. Bell and Sons, 1928), p. 313.

62 Emmeline Pankhurst, *My own story* (London, Eveleigh Nash, 1914), p. 241.

63 Courtney, 'The soul of a suffragette', p. 31.

64 Cicely Hamilton, *Life errant* (London, Dent, 1935), p. 84.

65 *Ibid.*, p. 85.

66 Christabel Pankhurst, *Unshackled: the story of how we won the vote* (London, Hutchinson, 1959), p. 78.

67 Sinclair, *The tree of heaven*, p. 261.

68 *Ibid.*, p. 276.

69 *Ibid.*, pp. 203–4.

70 *Ibid.*, p. 197.

71 Hamilton, *William – an Englishman*, p. 25.

72 Zangwill, *The call*, p. 378.

73 Jane Marcus, 'Corpus/corps/corpse: writing the body in/at war', in Helen M. Cooper, Adrienne Auslander Munich and Susan Merrill Squier (eds), *Arms and the woman: war, gender and literary representation* (Chapel Hill and London, University of North Carolina Press), pp. 124–68: 134.

74 Evelyn Sharp, 'The women at the gate', in *Rebel women*, pp. 7–19: 12.

75 *Ibid.*, p. 19.

DEBORAH TYLER-BENNETT

8

Suffrage and poetry: radical women's voices

Beyond the bars I see her move,
A mystery in blue and green,
As though across the prison yard
The spirit of the spring had been.

Laura Grey, 'To D.R. in Holloway', *Holloway jingles* (1912)[1]

THE above poem by Laura Grey was first fully reprinted in Louise Berkinow's 1974 anthology of women's poetic writing.[2] Despite the inclusion of Grey's work in this ground-breaking study (which also reprinted poems by her fellow hunger strikers and Sylvia Pankhurst), and despite works by 'suffrage' poets being included in recent anthologies by Angela Leighton, Margaret Reynolds and Glenda Norquay, links between the fight for enfranchisement and women's poetry concentrating on themes of disenfranchisement are still overlooked by many current anthologists and critics.[3] Studies of the cultural iconography of suffrage, such as those compiled by Lisa Tickner and Midge Mackenzie, consider visual artefacts (such as those produced by the Suffrage Atelier) but do not address the impact of the struggle for the vote on women poets who were both pro- and anti-suffrage.[4] It is interesting to note how Tickner begins her study by listing where women artists involved in suffrage work developed their talents (e.g., commercial art, the arts and crafts movement), as one could suggest that a similar technique could be used to outline the careers of poets such as Grey, Emily Wilding Davidson, Sylvia Pankhurst, Eva Gore-Booth, Augusta Webster and Alice Meynell.[5] It is impossible, in one short chapter, to provide a full overview of poetry produced by women involved in suffrage campaigns between 1906 and 1914. Thus, I intend to divide this chapter into three sections, locating dominant themes, images and sources for poems under discussion.

It is unsurprising that poets such as Pankhurst and Gore-Booth capitalised on themes developed by earlier radical poets such as Isa Craig (Knox), Bessie Rayner Parkes, Adelaide Anne Procter and the anarchist Louisa Bevington. The first section of this chapter studies how much of what can be termed 'suffrage poetry' extended the existing debate as opposed to creating a new one. Second, I intend to challenge the notion that prose was the most subversive literary form available to women writers involved in suffrage movements for, as is noted by Kate Flint, poetry was read avidly by women for its 'subversive', challenging qualities.[6] Third, I shall consider themes, images and poetic form as employed by two of the best-known 'suffrage poets', Eva Gore-Booth and Sylvia Pankhurst, comparing works by these to anonymous or 'obscure' suffrage 'jingles' and verses. By so doing, I hope to indicate how themes use by Victorian women poets came to be developed in aid of suffrage, and also to consider methods by which posterity has dealt with connections between suffrage and women's poetic voices.

In the outwardly conventional narrative verse 'A woman's answer', Adelaide Anne Procter creates a female voice forced to respond to her male lover's complaint that her love for him is not exclusive.[7] Like Shakespeare's Cordelia, the woman uses her reply to 'prove' her love, whilst at the same time exposing the frailty of basing one's life on the construct of romantic affection. As with much poetry by women written during the nineteenth century, an outwardly conventional plot reveals thinly disguised subversion. By using narrative form, Procter (an associate of many women of the Langham Place group) manages to tell a love story, whilst questioning the very ground upon which romanticism is based, and making reference to Elizabeth Barrett Browning's epic concerning women, poetry and work, *Aurora Leigh* (1857).[8] The poem's narrator loves *Aurora Leigh* both because her lover gave her the volume, and also because Aurora insists on the importance of autonomy and work for women. Just as Browning's Aurora avers her vocation in economic terms as 'work to do', so Procter's speaker asserts that her heart, love aside, answers 'a thousand claims beside your own'.[9] Verses such as this can be used to indicate aesthetic shifts in poetry by nineteenth-century women. Indeed, aesthetic shifts as demonstrated in women's poetry between 1858 and 1928 would intimate that questions of identity, enfranchisement and economics are not solely related to women working within suffrage movements (such as Pankhurst and Gore-Booth), but are also emphasised by earlier women poets such as Procter, and by later poets who were not necessarily active in the struggle for the vote.

In a recent article on the anthologist Mrs William (Elizabeth) Sharp, I indicate that the above questions are continuously foregrounded by a diverse array of women poets from the 1850s onwards.[10] When considering key themes explored by women writers prior to the rise of suffrage movements by women such as Dinah Mullock Craik, better known as the author of popular novels such as *John Halifax, gentleman* (1858), and Bessie Rayner Parkes, Isa Craig and Adelaide Anne Procter, ideas concerning women, social mobility and economics are continuously foregrounded. Obviously, treatment of these themes is often determined by the poet's age, class, race or geographical location; nevertheless the 'thousand claims' which press upon Procter's speaker prevail. In many cases, patriarchal literary theorists have buried a continuous tradition of women's poetic social commentary. For example, Dinah Mullock Craik is remembered as a sentimental novelist, not as a poet who tackled subjects such as infant mortality, female vagrancy and women's mental illness.[11] Adelaide Anne Procter's fate appears to have been likewise sealed by sentimentalised, posthumous memoirs of her by Charles Dickens, which prefaced reprintings of her verses from 1859 until 1914.[12] Here, Dickens employs the familiar figure of woman poet as Christian martyr, neglecting to mention Procter's political links with Barbara Bodichon, Bessie Rayner Parkes and Langham Place.[13] Despite Candida Anne Lacey's reprinting of Procter's 'Now', which highlights the poet's belief in women's rights, employment and the need for the vote, and the placing of this as her obituary in *The English Woman's Journal* (1864), Dickens's picture of the ailing, sentimental 'poetess' still conditions her literary reputation today.[14] Procter's call to arms in 'Now' pre-dates the familiar image of Joan of Arc, so popular with later suffrage movements, and the poem's words and stirring rhythm perhaps indicate that it influenced poems such as Cicily Hamilton's lyrics for Ethel Smyth's 'March of the women' (1911), Emily Wilding Davidson's 'L'Envoi' (1912) and W. A. N.'s 'The vote'.[15]

In much the same way, production of both poetry and illustration by predominantly female collectives, which was to become such a feature of suffrage movements, can be traced back to another Langham Place worker, the printer Emily Faithfull. Her Victoria Press (run by her between 1860 and 1867) predates both the arts and crafts presses (such as the Irish Dun Emer Press, run by women's rights advocate Evelyn Gleeson, and the Cuala Press, developed by the Yeats sisters between 1908 and 1946) and print shops such as those run by the Suffrage Atelier, which were also pre-dated by the rise of the woman printer in cities such as Edinburgh.[16] This not only mirrors the political concerns of workers for women's rights, such as Isa Craig's work for the Lancashire cotton hands, for whom she published an anthology in 1863, but also the activity of pro-suffrage writers in other political struggles, such as Eva Gore-Booth's involvement with Irish independence movements.[17] What I have hoped to draw attention to here are aesthetic strategies and traditions of production which suffrage poets were able to draw upon for both practical ideas and poetic substance. Next, I shall briefly indicate the subversive power of poetic forms for women readers, demonstrating links between the woman poet and her perceived female audience.

As Kate Flint indicates, from the 1830s onwards, traditional educationalists often regarded poetry as a dangerous form.[18] She cites a novel of 1847 (Grace Aguilar's *Home influence: a tale for mothers and daughters*) as highlighting this, by having a mother warn her daughter against poetic achievement which will jeopardise her domestic duties.[19] Likewise, in Mary E. Braddon's immensely popular novel, *Vixen*, Lady Mabel Ashbourne silences her own poetic voice after the critical failure of one volume.[20] Hostile literary critics are held partly responsible, but Lady Mabel's parents and her fiancé exhibit similar prejudices, as they advise her to aim for simplicity, not the long intellectual narrative structure which she has produced (in fact, for many years the sonnet was regarded as the most suitable form for women). Lord Mallow, her final choice of husband, advises 'a volume of ballads and idylls' as opposed to an epic, and it is significant that, upon marriage to him, Mabel abandons poetry for the image of the perfect wife, becoming 'altogether his second self'.[21] Whilst the Victorian poet A. Mary F. Robinson condemns the narrow range of poetic forms open to women (in her poem 'Cruel fate', she says 'my sweets and sonnets cloy / I'm tired of being coy'), twentieth-century critics such as Flint indicate that poetry often represented romantic alternatives to parental values, hence the inclusion of Shelley among lists of favourite poetic works compiled by young female readers.[22] For middle-class readers the pleasures of poetry dealing with violent emotion (when conduct-books and parental authority advocated a repression of 'self') is obvious. One can assume that, for many women, the subversive appeal of poetry continued into adulthood. Yet for a late twentieth-century reader, even the most outwardly conventional volume of nineteenth-century women's poetry can challenge dominant social perceptions of women. For example, 'Moonlight sonata', by Christian poet Frances Ridley Havergal, tells the story of Alice, a female musician who is reluctant to take up her gift.[23] Despite an outward simplicity, Havergal's poem is double-edged: on the one hand, the Christian message of not neglecting God's gifts is clear; on the other, the poem appears to be a plea for careers on behalf of artistically inclined young women like Alice. It is, perhaps, unsurprising that Braddon, a writer of sensation fiction, found use for Havergal's poems as codas to novel chapters.

When one considers the radical history of suffrage texts, plays and novels most readily spring to mind: Gertrude Colmore's *Suffragette Sally* (1911), Elizabeth Robins's *The convert* (1907) or Cicely Hamilton/Edith Craig's *A pageant of great women* (1909).[24] Poetry is seldom mentioned in critical works on suffrage, and plays a secondary role to prose in Glenda Norquay's recent anthology, yet it was the locus of radical aesthetic strategies used by both Sylvia Pankhurst and Gore-Booth. As Flint indicates, both poetry and prose could convey messages which were avidly sought out by women readers. To illustrate this, she uses the words of suffrage reviewer S. Bullen, who recalled reading Charlotte Perkins Stetson's (Gilman's) poems with 'pleasurable wickedness'.[25] Communication, connection and networking are, as most commentators on suffrage acknowledge, cornerstones of campaigns for the vote. Poems published in single volume by established poets such as Gore-Booth are only one part of communication networks linking suffrage writers and readers. As verses from Holloway prison – *Holloway jingles* (1912) reprinted by both Berkinow and Norquay, indicate, poems provided a means of demonstrating solidarity, and also of communicating and responding to emotions created by incarceration. Indeed, one could suggest that, by depicting imprisonment as a collective experience, the Holloway hunger strikers of 1912 transform the intentions of the law, by making a solitary punishment a collective bonding process. In the final section of this essay, I shall outline themes and concepts shared both by well-known poets and by anonymous poets, and consider the differing forms and techniques by which these are expressed.

I wish to begin by returning to those anonymous, or obscure, hunger strikers, the 'jingle' writers of 1912. What interests me about them is the use which they make of lyric genres. For example, an anonymous poem on a woman who has smashed windows and has subsequently been sent to Holloway takes as its influence both the limerick and refrains from the Savoy Operas of Gilbert and Sullivan, using the latter's 'jolly' tone to make prison life appear bearable.[26] Another poem, by Edith Aubrey Wingrove, uses the motif of a college song, transforming the prison into a women's college, thus once more subverting the notion of imprisonment as a solitary punishment.[27] When one considers songbooks from what were then recently established women's colleges, such as Girton College, Cambridge, one realises how closely Wingrove adapted their rhythms, tone and the imagery of 'goals' and 'prizes' for her poem concerning Holloway.[28] Just as college prizes are regarded as 'goals' in Girton songs, the prizes cited by Wingrove are those of friendship and connection. Likewise, a poem by M. C. R. (possibly Madelaine Caron Rock) speaks of how silence (feared by the speaker when free) is revealed to be a myth concerning (actually noisy) prison life.[29] It is worth noting that all the poems mentioned above negate both popular images of Holloway as a location where one is made to feel solitary, and the idea that women (particularly of the middle classes) are destroyed by prison life. These poems often communicate at the level of simple emotion, giving cheer and solace to other women.

In poetry intended for both a pro-suffrage audience and a wider poetic readership, themes of connection are also present, but these are often contained within a more recognisably 'poetic' genre. Many images and ideas are repeated (such as those of women trapped, either in prison or within the confines imposed upon their gender by society), and these can be traced back to poetic 'foremothers' such as Procter. During a period when most magazines (from *The Girl's Own Paper* to *The Englishwoman's Journal*) published poetry, it is not surprising to discover that suffrage journals, such as that of the Women's Freedom League, *The Vote*, edited by Charlotte Despard, also carried verses. Again, magazines edited by women and aimed at both a specialist audience and a, hoped for, wider public arena were nothing new, as *Eliza Cook's Journal* (1849–54) indicates.[30] In this context, it is worth asking at what audience suffrage poets

Now in a cell
She sits and pines
And off thin skilly
Daily dines;
But still repeats,
As if by rote
"I want—I want—
I want a vote."

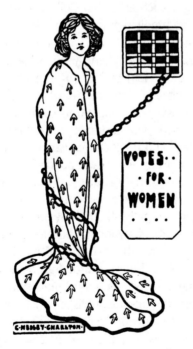

MORAL.

Take warning by
Her awful end.
And don't to poli-
Tics attend.
Don't earn your living—
If you can,
Have it earned for you
By a man.
Then sit at home
From morn till night,
And cook and cook
With all your might.

It may be slow—
But you can say,
"It's just as slow
In Holloway."

such as Sylvia Pankhurst, Gore-Booth and Adela Pankhurst were aiming. Unlike the small audience anticipated by the slight volume of 'jingles' produced by the Glasgow Branch of the Women's Social and Political Union (WSPU) in 1912, Sylvia Pankhurst's volume, *Writ on cold slate* (1922), was obviously aimed at both those who had lived through suffrage campaigns of 1907–14 and at a new readership attracted by the Pankhurst name.[31] Gore-Booth's poetry, it could be argued, is possessed by several known audiences, drawn from both suffrage connections and those interested in Irish literary and political concerns. Her *Poems* (1929) have been placed within the 'Celtic twilight' genre by critics, despite the poet having lived most of her adult life in Manchester.[32]

Sylvia Pankhurst's poems, although published in one collection after the major thrust of the suffrage movements, are inspired by her various experiences of prison and activism, including her 1906 incarceration in Holloway, the East End campaign of October 1912 and her arrest and removal to Holloway on 10 June 1914.[33] As Berkinow notes, *Writ on cold slate* (a reformation of Keats's epitaph, perhaps) can be interpreted as a revision of prison experiences.[34] What she fails to recognise is how the best-known poems of the collection, 'The mothers', can be directly related to the East End campaign of 1912 and its continuation. The chief theme of the poem is pregnancy whilst in prison. The dual meaning of 'pregnancy' is crucial, as the women in the poem are both literally pregnant, and pregnant with thought and ideas. The exhausted mothers' only hope is connection with each other, and the track of the pregnancy cycle is matched by the circle of the prison yard: 'O pregnant womanhood that scarce can drag / thy weary ripeness round the altered track.'[35] This is similar to Pankhurst's descriptions of East End mothers from 'sweated and unknown trades' in 1912, and echoes her concerns for the civil rights of pregnant women, as well as her prison experiences.[36] The poem, not included by Norquay, records the suffering of the many, as opposed to those of exclusively middle-class prisoners, and this also mirrors the poet's desire to organise and make militant working-class men and women in the East End of London. Links between the 'mothers' of the title exist in contrast to a solitary female figure in 'In lofty scorn', a poem in which Pankhurst illuminates an isolated woman, drawing upon classical allusions of female deities, which she then undercuts.[37]

Keats was a poet read by Sylvia Pankhurst to Annie Kenney, and it is therefore interesting that the woman in the poem resembles Keats's description of Thea in 'Hyperion' (1820).[38] The usage of a male poet as a key point of reference could be regarded as doubly subversive, as Keats's poem (literally idolising women) is used as the basis for a work in which one woman responds to the physical suffering of another. Pankhurst uses a section of 'Hyperion' (itself an epic fragment) to create a vignette of prison life, transforming the epic grandeur of Thea, Keat's imprisoned goddess, to an ordinary woman in Holloway. At times, the epic metre chosen by Pankhurst, replete with linguistic archaisms such as 'thy', stilts the flow of line, yet her deliberate use of heroic genres is calculated to undermine salacious reports in the popular English press on prison life, and to question the concept that epic images can only be attached to narratives of past masculine adventure.

Undoubtedly, the most recognised poet involved with suffrage movements is Eva Gore-Booth, whose poetry is versatile both in form and content.[39] As with Pankhurst, Gore-Booth combines both experience of the suffrage campaigns with personal pacifism (she was a member of the Women's Peace Crusade) and a commitment to working women (one of her lasting achievements being the foundation of Manchester's Women Textile Workers' Union).[40] However, throughout her poems runs a mythological thread, influenced by Celtic myths revived by (amongst others) Susan and Elizabeth Yeats, and Lady Augusta Gregory. Her works are also influenced by her non-militant attitudes and her lesbian relationship with Esther Roper, for many poems chart woman-to-woman relationships.[41] During her poetic career, Gore-Booth wrote verses denouncing landlords, outlining the results of child labour, celebrating the Irish landscape and highlighting her perceptions concerning the creative process.

The poem, 'Women's Trades on the Embankment' (written in response to Prime Minister Henry Campbell-Bannerman's appeal to the Women's Franchise Deputation on 19 May 1906, to 'have patience') likens disenfranchised workers to slaves who built the pyramids.[42] One work of Gore-Booth's which reveals the influence of another woman poet is 'The anti-suffragist', which bears clear overtones of Christina Rossetti's 'A royal princess'. It is worth recalling that Rossetti's work influenced many 'suffrage' poets, both in form and content; for example, A. A. Wilson's 'An end' (1912), appears to be a revision of Rossetti's 'A birthday'.[43]

Rossetti's 'A royal princess' is extremely interesting with regard to the work of Gore-Booth. First, it tells the story of a princess who leaves her royal home in order to stand at one with disenfranchised workers: 'I will go down to the people, I will stand face to face, I will stand / Where they curse king, queen and princess of this / cursed land'.[44] Second, the poem was published in Isa Craig's aforementioned anthology of 1863, in aid of the Lancashire cotton workers.[45] Gore-Booth's poem, like Rossetti's, deploys the Pre-Raphaelite device of a princess in a tower to convey a political message. Likewise, just as Rossetti's princess pines whilst surrounded by costly objects, so Gore-Booth's princess is here 'brazen caged' within an opulent castle.[46] Unlike Rossetti's princess, who takes action in order both to support the workers and gain her own autonomy in the face of death, Gore-Booth's princess resembles another Rossetti woman, the princess who dies waiting for her prince in 'The prince's progress' (1866).[47] Gore-Booth's princess is thus removed from her bower too late, and is revealed as an old woman with silver hair. Links between Gore-Booth's aesthetic and Rossetti are vital, as they reveal both the former's knowledge of a woman's literary tradition, and also demonstrate a poetic radicalism seldom associated with the latter.

In this chapter I have charted some aesthetic strategies used by women poets in their fight for the vote and, by so doing, have endeavoured to suggest some connections between women's poetry from the early part of this century and nineteenth-century women's writing. Some of the poetry quoted here has been reprinted, most recently in *Voices and Votes*, and is easily available to students, but other volumes of poetry are, unfortunately, more difficult to obtain, being located in the British Library, The National Library of Scotland, the Irish National Library, the Edinburgh Poetry Library and elsewhere. Consulting the Irish National Archives recent suffrage collection of prison lists and English news-cuttings, I was unable to locate the names of any woman poets involved in militant action (1912–14) in Ireland, although this does not mean that some unknown Irish poet does not occur in prison and court lists.[48] However, the study of links between female suffrage and women's poetry in Britain, and particularly in Ireland, is in its infancy. It may be hoped that, in the future, more works by suffrage poets will be discovered and reprinted, revealing, to use a phrase of Gore-Booth's, the variety of women's experiences during the years of struggle: 'All these I was; which one of these was I?'[49]

NOTES

Acknowledgements: Dr Martyn Bennett, for listening to drafts of the chapter, staff at the National Archive, Dublin, the Edinburgh poetry library, the National library of Scotland and the Irish National library.

1 E. Berkinow, *The world split open: women poets 1552–1950* (London, Women's Press, 1974), p. 149; G. Norquay, *Voices and votes: a literary anthology of the women's suffrage campaign* (Manchester, Manchester University Press, 1995).
2 Berkinow, *The world split open*, p. 149.
3 M. Reynolds and A. Leighton, *Victorian women's poetry: an anthology* (Oxford: Blackwell, 1995); Norquay, *Voices and votes*.
4 L. Tickner, *The spectacle of women: imagery of the suffrage campaign 1907–1914* (London: Chatto and Windus, 1987); M. Mackenzie, *Shoulder to shoulder* (New York, Vintage, 1975).
5 Tickner, *The spectacle of women*, p. 23.
6 K. Flint, *The woman reader: 1837–1914* (Oxford, Clarendon Press, 1993), p. 241.
7 A. A. Procter, *Legends and lyrics: second volume* (London, George Bell and Sons, 1985), pp. 187–9.
8 E. Barrett Browning, *Aurora Leigh* (London, Women's Press, 1978).
9 Procter, *Legends and lyrics*, p. 187.
10 D. Tyler-Bennett, 'Women's voices speak for themselves; gender, subversion and the *Women's Voices* anthology of 1887', *Women's History Review*, 4, 2, 1995, pp. 165–75.
11 D. M. Craik, *Thirty years: being poems old and new* (London, Macmillan and Co., 1880).
12 A. A. Procter, *Legends and lyrics: together with a chaplet of verses* (Oxford, Oxford University Press, 1914), pp. 1–10.
13 Procter, *Legends and lyrics*, pp. 1–10.
14 A. A. Procter, 'Now', in C. A. Lacey (ed.), *Barbara Leigh Smith Bodichon and the Langham Place Group* (London, Routledge, 1987), p. 19.
15 L. Whitelaw, *The life and rebellious times of Cicely Hamilton* (London, The Women's Press,

1990), p. 122; Norquay, *Voice and votes*, pp. 93, 94.

16 Lacey, *Barbara Leigh Smith Bodichon*, pp. 279–87; G. Lewis, *The Yeats sisters and the Cuala* (Dublin, Irish Academic Press, 1994); Tickner, *The spectacle of women*. pp, 24–5; S. Reynolds, *Britannica's typesetters: women compositors in Edinburgh* (Edinburgh, Edinburgh University Press, 1989).

17 I. Craig (Knox), *Poems: an offering to Lancashire* (London, Victoria Press, 1863).

18 Flint, *The woman reader*, p. 260.

19 *Ibid.*

20 M. E. Braddon, *Vixen* (Gloucestershire, Allen Sutton, 1993).

21 *Ibid*, pp. 474, 495.

22 A. M. F. Robinson, 'Cruel Fate', *Belgravia*, 38, March 1879, p. 43; Flint, *The woman reader*, p. 245.

23 F. R. Havergal, *Under the surface* (London, James Nisbet and Co., c. 1880s), pp. 24–48.

24 G. Colmore, *Suffragettes: a story of three women* (London, Pandora repr., 1984); E. Robins, *The convert* (London, Women's Press repr., 1990); Whitelaw, *The life and rebellious times of Cicely Hamilton*, pp. 84–7.

25 Flint, *The woman reader*, p. 242.

26 Berkinow, *The world split open*, pp. 146–7.

27 *Ibid.*, pp. 147–8.

28 E. Sargent *et al.*, *Girton College songs: a selections revised with additions* (Cambridge, R. Severs, 1980).

29 Berkinow, *The world split open*, pp. 148–9.

30 E. Cook, *Eliza Cook's poems* (London, Frederick Warne and Co., 1869).

31 Berkinow, *The world split open*, p. 151.

32 E. Ni Dhuibhne, *Voices on the wind: women poets of the Celtic twilight* (Dublin, New Island Books, 1995), pp. 106–28.

33 Mackenzie, *Shoulder to shoulder*, pp. 52–3, 206–8, 274–5.

34 Berkinow, *The world split open*, p. 151.

35 Quoted in *ibid.*

36 Mackenzie, *Shoulder to shoulder*, p. 207.

37 Berkinow, *The world split open*, pp. 151–2.

38 Mackenzie, *Shoulder to shoulder*, p. 33; J. Keats, *Poetical works* (Oxford, Oxford University Press, 1928), pp. 235–55.

39 A. A. Kelly, *Pillars of the house: an anthology of verse by Irish women from 1690 to the present* (Dublin, Wolfhound, 1988), p. 84; K. Donovan *et al.*, *Ireland's women: writings past and present* (London, Kyle Cathie, 1994), pp. 343–4; Catherine Reilly, *Winged words: Victorian women's poetry and verse* (London, Enitharmon, 1994), pp. 63–5; Ni Dhuibhne, *Voices on the wind*, pp. 106–28.

40 V. Blain *et al.*, *The feminist companion to literature in English* (London, B. T. Batsford, 1990), p. 444.

41 *Ibid.*

42 Ni Dhuibne, *Voices on the wind*, p. 113.

43 *Ibid.*, p. 115; C. Rossetti, *Goblin Market, the prince's progress and other poems* (London, Macmillan and Co., 1884), pp. 101, 168–75; Norquay, *Voices and votes*, p. 305.

44 Rossetti, *Goblin Market*, p. 174.

45 Craig, *Poems*, pp. 2–5.

46 Ni Dhuibhne, *Voices on the wind*, p. 115.

47 Rossetti, *Goblin Market*, pp. 21–41.

48 National archive, Dublin, *GPB suffrage files 1912–1914*, files A–P.

49 Ni Dhuibhne, *Voices on the wind*, p. 122.

Women's suffrage drama

The rediscovery of the drama of the British women's suffrage movement by feminists in recent years has led to the publication of eighteen short plays or mono-
logues which may be said to constitute a provisional canon of 'women's suffrage
drama'.[1] Plays such as Elizabeth Robins's *Votes for women* and *How the vote
was won* by Cicely Hamilton and Christopher St John were written and performed to raise awareness and money for the women's suffrage movement; most
were written by women and include characters who are invariably middle class
and involved in the women's suffrage agitation, either for or against it. If working-class characters are presented, they tend to be servants who do not develop
in their own right but merely function as the agent of a middle-class character's
conversion to the campaign. The number and type of roles in these plays
favoured the female performer, while male (and anti-suffrage) characters often
provide the dull background against which some crackling comedy or incisive
argument is staged.

This reappraisal of women's suffrage drama will look beyond the canon to
which I have referred to the diversity of plays performed in support of women's
suffrage, and will proceed from a perspective which is feminist and cultural-mate-
rialist. It will, therefore, suggest that women's suffrage drama was in many
respects subversive and that it served a variety of purposes. These included lending support to the suffrage movement by its treatment of the issue of votes for
women directly and indirectly; the use of drama to discuss wider issues which
affected women socially; and dramatising how women worked in the context of
political campaigning. Moreover, these plays questioned the view that aesthetic
considerations were more important than other concerns in the theatre.

The end of the nineteenth century and the beginning of the twentieth century, like the Renaissance, has been read as a period of transition and instability
in which drama, in particular, sees the emergence of new cultural forms.[2] Women
are both taken to represent this perceived social instability and are actually

involved in causing it. This reappraisal is founded on several propositions: that theatre is a social practice as well as an institution determined by economic relationships with its audience, its writers, its performers and its critics; that the causes of women's oppression both materially and psychologically are not reducible, but related to, the workings of the capitalist system; that women working in the theatre – in the past as in the present – enter into a complex and uneven set of (economic/class/racial/familial/emotional/sexual) relationships with each other and with others which have variously empowered and limited their work as individuals; and that the women working collectively in producing drama for the women's suffrage movement challenged dominant beliefs about the possible roles for women in society by acting out those roles on and off stage.

That major social changes ensued from the struggles represented by the drama of the women's suffrage movement should be a source of optimism for feminists today. Suffragists had good reason to believe that plays were effective in changing attitudes: a change in legislation was attributed to the production of one play.[3] However, the difficulties encountered by women in staging plays which dramatised unconventional ideas should not be under-estimated. Some compromises were involved.

Many women, including actresses active in the women's suffrage movement in Britain, wrote plays and sketches as an integral part of their political campaigns, especially between 1908 and 1914. They did not necessarily regard themselves as writers, but were moved to write for the first time because the vote promised to change women's lives in ways that went far beyond their participation in party politics. Enfranchisement, they believed, would represent a fundamental transformation of women's lives. It is this conviction which inspired specifically feminist interventions in the arts and the theatre, as distinct from the more generalised lobbying for democratic change. The need for women to organise themselves collectively in order to bring about change, rather than attempt to work as individuals, was identified. Consequently, numerous women's suffrage political organisations were established to represent the diverse interests of women (religious, party-political and professional) and to ensure their participation.[4] A number of cultural organisations specialised in different fields or aspects of agitation. Although the performance of Elizabeth Robins's play *Votes for women*[5] in 1907 could be said to mark the beginnings of women's suffrage drama, it was not until December 1908, when the Actresses' Franchise League (AFL) was formed, that the necessary infrastructure was available to promote women's endeavours on a large scale.[6]

Cicely Hamilton, actress and writer, claimed that women's suffrage 'was the first political agitation to organize the arts in its aid'.[7] For theatre practitioners such as Hamilton, writing and political activity were symbiotic; the transition from street processions and the visual arts to drama was straightforward. The move from one to the other constituted a statement about the diversity of

women's talents, and claimed for women the role of polymath. It signalled a
desire to remove the inequalities women endured in the workplace (notably the
theatre). The actresses who were accustomed to performing the role of the Womanly Woman in many plays authored by men felt compelled to counter this
restrictive image. Involvement in a diverse range of cultural activities in the
women's suffrage movement seemed inevitable and lent itself to developing a
feminist praxis which promised to challenge the competitive and individualist
ideologies of capitalism and the aesthetic.

As Lisa Tickner's study of the visual art of the women's suffrage movement
has shown, the movement was 'a sisterhood based on diversity'.[8] Women became
aware of the ideological battles being fought in the cultural arena and subsequently became adept at manipulating the press which had only recently constructed them as constituting a new market.[9] The use of press releases and
publicity stunts was commonplace. The suffragists' attempt to control their own
means of publication and performance was a strategy which marked the emergence of new relationships between producer and consumer in the women's suffrage movement. Some characteristic working practices were shared by many
who were producing drama and visual art for the movement: collaboration
rather than competition; removing the barriers between professional and amateur; and interrogating, if not rejecting, the aesthetic distinction between art and
propaganda which privileged 'genius' as the preserve of the individual middle-
class male.[10]

The cultural organisations of the movement worked independently of the
political organisations; artists and writers often collaborated and refused to take
credit for their work in order not to detract from the aims of the movement.
Edith Craig,[11] producer of many plays and pageants, worked for both the Suffrage Atelier and for the AFL,[12] before founding the Pioneer Players, a theatre
society which promoted women's suffrage together with other radical political
causes and experimental drama.[13] Craig directed on a freelance basis *A pageant
of great women*, the play which she co-wrote with Cicely Hamilton, at events
organised by both the Women's Freedom League (WFL) and the Women's
Social and Political Union (WSPU).[14] Craig resisted the partisan, believing that
'one cannot belong to too many suffrage societies'.[15] The priority for most suffragists was the success of the movement as a whole. Subsuming one's own identity in the movement, or the 'cause' as it was frequently named, was commended.
A suffrage newspaper noted that Craig's work 'has not always received its due
notice, owing to her habit of laughing self-effacement'.[16] The encouragement of
such generosity and collaboration was double-edged. It sponsored some radical
challenges to individualism, but it also encouraged the self-abnegation more
appropriate to Victorian ideas of femininity. Hamilton is careful to acknowledge
Craig's role in devising *A pageant of great women*, but her contribution has
often been overlooked, perhaps through Craig's 'self-effacement,' or through the

tendency to attribute authorship to one individual.[17]

The collaborative work made possible by the women's suffrage movement gave rise to several jointly written plays. Cicely Hamilton and Christopher St John co-wrote *The pot and the kettle* and one of the most successful of the movement's plays, *How the vote was won*.[18] In other fields, working together was a new priority for women, endorsed by the political movement. There were many instances of women-only cultural organisations, such as Lena Connell's photographic studio,[19] and the Aeolian Ladies' Orchestra led by Rosabel Watson.[20] Collaboration was also common between the various organisations: the Pioneer Players advertised the Woman's Theatre.[21] Lena Connell's photographs of participants in *A pageant of great women* were sold at the nationwide productions of the play to raise additional funds and promote awareness of the great women of the past which the play celebrated. These examples of co-operation and collaboration challenge the popular image of women involved in the sundry embittered factions of suffrage politics driven by personal ambition as well as corporate competition.

The idea of the artist as a uniquely gifted person was widely questioned by the women's suffrage movement through the endorsement of collaborative work and the encouragement of amateurs to participate. On other occasions, however, a claim was made by women for professional status in order to define their rights as workers. The demand to be included in the elite domain of the artist brought with it the burden of supplying proof that the quality of women's work equalled that of men. The rising status of acting as a profession led many women working in the theatre to question the role of the actress, to compare her status and her pay with that of the actor.[22] The critique (or temporary suspension) of conventional practices in the theatre and publishing, and the climate of cultural openness in the women's suffrage movement led to some extraordinary innovations. Actresses, such as Jess Dorynne, were freed from the constraints of convention and tradition which burdened professional writers. They used their experience of stagecraft and oppression to represent women in unconventional ways in drama. Dorynne's play *The surprise of his life* stages several outrageously broken taboos.[23] A pregnant, unmarried woman, Emily Jenkins, refuses to marry Alfred Williams, the father of her child, in order to protect her father's business reputation as well as her own. Emily not only finds voice assertive enough to say no, but also sufficient strength to use self-defence to resist an unwanted embrace from Alfred: 'she frees herself by a scientific jerk'.[24] Furthermore, she learns that her aunt Eliza regrets her own decision in marrying the father of her child. The sharing of experience between older and younger generations of women is shown to be transformative; Emily, having been influenced by the local suffragists, leaves her father's house to set up home with her aunt: 'I don't care nothin' about no votes, nor yet about no polerticks ... goin' to 'er an' the meetin's 'as taught me sure wot I felt before - ter respect meself as a woman, an' ter insist that I shall be so respected.'[25] This remarkable play does more than adapt an argument for women's suffrage for the stage. The 'woman-with-a-past' relished by the male-authored drama of the period is replaced by a woman who reclaims and narrates her own history, determining her future publicly in co-operation with other women. An autobiographical reading of this play[26] limits its critique to an isolated event rather than a wide-ranging critique of hypocrisy and an attempt to change the existing ideas about femininity, motherhood and honour.

The women's suffrage movement embraced every medium and field of popular culture. Images and texts were translated in different forms: songs were turned into tableaux;[27] short stories became recitations;[28] articles became plays.[29] Posters and cartoons were given equal status with the banners and plays of the movement. Art was seen in the broader context of culture, implying a democratising critique of the aesthetic. The relationship between value and gender was therefore presented as an issue: in several plays produced for the first time in 1911 the representation of woman as artist and as worker established the economic context of aesthetic judgements. The phenomenon of a woman winning a literary prize is the theme of Cicely Hamilton's *Jack and Jill and a friend.*[30] The play contrasts the different opportunities open to female and male writers and the impact which a woman's professional success (and consequently increased economic power) may have on her relationship with a man. Hamilton's critique of the aesthetic is characteristically grounded in an understanding of the economic inequalities faced by women. Similarly, Christopher St John's *The first actress* constructs the history of Margaret Hughes (d.1719), said to be the first actress on a commerical London stage, in order to establish a historical precedent for women's struggle to improve working conditions for women in the theatre.[31] St John presents Hughes as a 'forgotten pioneer' in a representatively male-dominated institution where professional judgements about performance are inextricably bound up with the politics of gender; Hughes's debut performance is subject to a wager on a woman's ability to act placed between two male rivals in the theatre. These plays demonstrate that aesthetic judgements are imbricated in a range of other values and beliefs and not independent of these. St John and Hamilton, as writers of such plays, regarded the ethics of aesthetic judgements as a major isssue for the women's suffrage movement.

The exclusionary practices of the aesthetic, condemned by several women's suffrage plays, have ironically marginalised women's suffrage drama both when it was produced and in recent years. Critics did not categorise these plays as 'women's suffrage drama'. They were considered to be 'propaganda' rather than art, a distinction endorsed by Rebecca West, whose condemnatory review of Florence Edgar Hobson's *A modern crusader* is unambiguous: 'The Pioneer Players and the AFL are perhaps the most shameless offenders in the way of producing degradations of the drama written by propagandists, whom nothing but the fire of Prometheus could make into artists.'[32] Presumably, Virginia Woolf agreed. The plays which marked this flourishing period of women's writing in Britain are absent from Woolf's landscape of women's endeavours.[33] Women's writing for the stage, as in other genres, has been subject to prejudiced judgements and although feminist critics have written widely to challenge such bias, drama has yet to receive the same attention given to the novel.[34]

Writing was perceived to be a political act for women involved in the women's suffrage movement and therefore its cultural as well as sexual politics were debated in newspapers. Edith Craig, for instance, claimed that 'one play is worth one hundred speeches',[35] but one dramatist, Madeleine Lucette Ryley, argued that dramatisation may trivialise women's suffrage issues and jeopardise the movement if it drew attention to an issue which could be solved without enfranchisement.[36] However, the comparison between the representation of women in culture and the representation of women in parliament was made explicit:

> Much of the misrepresentation of women is due to the playwright and the novelist of the past who have depicted women as concentrating on their emotions, and finding in erotic and domestic sensibilities the business of their lives. ... Those men who have had the power of speech have declared that they would represent [women]. But they have not done so, and the misrepresentation has been not so much on the part of the electorate as on that of their representatives.[37]

Women were reclaiming the power of speech. In the act of writing, or acting, women were challenging the common anti-suffrage arguments, such as the proposition that men should occupy a separate sphere. The representation of woman as writer (or public speaker or performer on stage) exposed the limits of this separate-spheres ideology by making women heard and seen in the public sphere.

In Cicely Hamilton and Christopher St John's *The pot and the kettle* the ideological challenge to the social order posed by a woman's involvement in political organisations and meetings is demonstrated, ironically, by an anti-suffragist. Marjorie Brewster's attendance at an anti-suffrage meeting ends with her not merely speaking in public, but assaulting the 'suffragette' who heckles.[38] A similar, ironic strategy is employed in H. M. Paull's *An anti-suffragist or the other side: a monologue in one act.* That the anti-suffrage arguments are wrong, illogical and misguided is demonstrated by Miss De Lacey, Secretary of Little Pendleton Anti-Suffragist Society in her report of the organisation's activities. The irony of the anti-suffragist position is reinforced when Miss De Lacey reports that 'Miss Prideaux wouldn't stand up to speak because she thought it unladylike to be so obtrusive'.[39]

The representation of women as workers also challenged separate-spheres ideology and is a common feature of plays of the movement. Some plays looked beyond middle-class occupations. Margaret Wynne Nevinson's *In the workhouse* exposes the invisibility of the woman worker, in law a married woman was her husband's property and would follow him to the workhouse if he became desti- tute, even if she was working. The subject of Edith Lyttelton's The thumbscrew is the sweated working conditions of women and children employed in sewing hooks and eyes to cards, a task allied to the clothing industry from which mid- dle-class women benefitted.[40] The complicity of women in the oppression of oth- ers is represented in The thumbscrew by Mrs Muggle, the Jewish middlewoman who increases the quota for piecework. The racial stereotype used to demonise the female oppressor detracts from the class conflict which divides women as well as men. Unionisation is not contemplated.[41] The ending of the play provides no solution to the social problem it has identified, but it does forge an alliance between mother and daughter (the latter decides against marriage and emigra- tion to Canada). Like Dorynne's The surprise of his life, The thumbscrew ends with the reinforcement of bonds between women across generations even while it exposes the complicity of other female characters in the oppression of women.

Many plays which were written and performed during the women's suffrage movement were not concerned with presenting 'positive' images of women.[42] Their scope was broader and attentive to the difficulties of bringing about change, social and economic. The representation of disagreement between women indicates the acknowledgement of diverse opinions. In order to abandon rivalry and competition women needed to accept differences. There was also a need to reject the anti-suffrage perspective associated with the Womanly Woman/mother. This is not achieved in Before sunrise,[43] but, like many of the plays of the movement, this emphasised the need for change even if it did not represent the process of that change in any developed or extended way.

Women are the agents of change in many of these plays, even though the political objectives of the movement could only be granted by a male parliament. This is perhaps most apparent in How the vote was won, which stages a women's strike as the motivating force to transform the anti-suffrage male. It does, how- ever, emphasise the need to involve and persuade men such as Horace Cole, who is an opponent, that women's enfranchisement will benefit them.[44] Similarly, A woman's influence shows that social change may be brought about indirectly, if therefore dishonourably, by women.[45] The devious Womanly Woman in this play is exposed as self-serving and willing to ignore the oppression of other women if their liberation will affect her financial investments.

The phenomenon of class conflict was explored by dramatists even though they were unable to develop a means of fully acknowledging differences other than those of sex. Racial and sexual identities were often positioned, or implied, as the 'other' against which the white, heterosexual, middle-class woman defined her new self.[46] John Austin's How one woman did it counters the 'physical force' argument against women's suffrage to the effect that women were disqualified from full citizenship because they lacked the strength to fight.[47] A fight between

two servants leads to the revelation that Wilson, one of the presumed male servants, is in fact a woman; Wilson's sex has been undetected for the six weeks of
her employment in the household. Wilson's employer Lady Petersfield and her
sister Flora Allington, hold differing views on women's suffrage. Although Wilson
shares Lady Petersfield's antipathy to women's suffrage politics she differs in her
method of expressing this. Wilson's decision to cross-dress has seemingly been
motivated by the desire for employment which is well paid; she presents a forceful argument which exposes the narrow upper-class perspectives of the other
women who she maintains are 'different' from herself.[48]

The question which is left unanswered by the play is whether the 'difference' identified signifies more than that of class. The significance of Wilson's
cross-dressing for her sexual identity is, and perhaps for its time has to be, left
implicit. For contemporary suffrage audiences, Wilson's arguments would allude
to the cross-dressing female warriors in A pageant of great women, for whom
masculine clothing opened up a world of occupational opportunities.[49] Wilson's
individualist argument for securing masculine privileges by any means fascinates
the pro-suffrage Flora, who is unable to counter it, but is left to ponder: 'I wonder if clothes do make all that difference'.[50] Plays produced in favour of women's
suffrage often demonstrated the difficulties of bringing about change in relationships between women, in relationships across social classes, and in relationships between women and men. The unresolved conflicts and uneasy
tensions in the plays symbolise the problems which could not yet be fully articulated. The endings of many of the plays are open, intimating the wider social
determinants of women's voteless status beyond the drawing-rooms and par-
lours presented on stage, like the more radical examples of naturalism associated with Ibsen.[51]

Women's suffrage drama changed with the movement in its diversity and
complexity.[52] Some plays which could be included in the category of women's suffrage drama are not immediately recognisable as such, demanding familiarity with
the history of women's suffrage, its arguments and campaign issues. For instance,
the Pioneer Players' early plays included Christopher St John's Macrena.[53] This
reclaims the history of Irena Macrena, a Polish nun who fought against the imposition of the Russian Orthodox religion in 1840 and whose actions 'stemmed the
tide of apostasy in Poland'.[54] Other plays performed at women's suffrage events
were male-authored and appropriated by suffragists, such as Ibsen's The doll's
house,[55] Herman Heijermans's The good hope reviewed as a 'suffragist play by
accident',[56] and Ellen Terry's lecture on Shakespeare's 'Triumphant Women,'
reviewed under the title 'Shakespeare as Suffragist'.[57]

Suffragists were questioning what theatre was by redefining what constituted the theatrical space. Theatres were sometimes used, but plays in support of
women's suffrage were more often performed in other spaces to which women
had better access: in public halls, in restaurants or in private homes. Since the

Lord Chamberlain's regulatory powers over public performances did not apply to privately produced plays, it was not necessary to submit copies of the plays for licence; they are therefore not held in the British Library, which means that they are now hard to find. The main bibliographical source for plays performed in London during this period only features those that were performed in theatres.[58] The use of public halls meant that the size of the audience could exceed the capacity of many theatres; some 2,000 attended the Sunderland production of *A pageant of great women*.[59] It also provided a degree of freedom in that the hall could be hired for a specific event and there would have been little interference in the details of production of the play. A further advantage of producing plays outside theatres in hired halls was the relative freedom from the constraints of the Lord Chamberlain. Edith Craig publicly acknowledged that the King's Hall in the National Sporting Club was chosen as a venue for a Pioneer Players' production in order that 'there may be no fuss about any possible censoring'.[60] In this respect, an alliance was possible between those campaigning for women's suffrage and those who were against the censorship of the stage represented by the Lord Chamberlain. It is in this context that Laurence Housman's *Pains and penalties* was produced by the Pioneer Players.[61] On some occasions plays produced for women's suffrage were submitted to, and granted a licence by, the Lord Chamberlain prior to performance.[62] Some plays castigated by the press for their advocacy of women's suffrage had already been endorsed by the Lord Chamberlain.[63]

The availability of plays, like suffrage newspapers, was crucial to sustain interest, to educate and persuade. Many plays were published by individuals[64] and by organisations such as the AFL.[65] The marketing of the plays for suffrage activists was predictable. Their wider availability – some were advertised in a major trade catalogue – indicates the level of interest in the production of plays and the commercial aspects of play publication, from which women's suffrage drama is not exempt.[66]

Women who worked in the theatre were interested in writing plays both to promote women's suffrage and to provide themselves with an income. These motives were sometimes in conflict and this reveals the tensions inevitably at work in the relationship between cultural production and political activism. One performance in Liverpool of *A pageant of great women* was not sanctioned by Hamilton and was probably produced by Craig.[67] Beatrice Harraden wrote for advice regarding the royalties for performances of her play.[68] Craig publicly encouraged women to write for the 'cause': 'All Suffrage writers ought to write Suffrage plays as hard as they can. It's a great work.'[69] Even a 'great work' can become a product. Craig personally owned the rights to performance of many authors' works,[70] and apparently competed for rights to George Bernard Shaw's *Press cuttings*.[71] The women's suffrage movement gave rise to changing relationships between producer and consumer, creating the opportunity both for collaborative work and the potential for exploitation.

The need to find new cultural strategies to sustain women's interest in the political campaign prompted Charlotte Despard to warn Edith Craig that 'bazaars are played out'.[72] The types of play produced therefore changed with the movement and responded to topical issues. At a time when the imposition of force-feeding was putting an intolerable strain on many activists *A pageant of great women* provided a morale boost. During this phase of the movement the representation of great historical figures was therefore a strategic response.[73] At other moments, different issues proved to be of more concern; prostitution, whether chosen or enforced, concerned suffragists and gave rise to plays such as *The daughters of Ishmael*.[74]

This exploration of the phenomenon of 'women's suffrage drama' may make us wary of the tendency to homogenise women's writings. This chapter has focused on the diversity of the plays produced and the various organisations involved in the British women's suffrage movement. The means whereby drama related to women's suffrage was produced and performed provides some insight into the tensions and conflicts to which this period of turbulent social change gave rise. The plays discussed here bear witness to the difficulty of representing women as independent or the relationships between women and men as egalitarian. In these plays the inter-related and deeply embedded inequalities in British society before the First World War are apparent; these are most poignant in the troubling repetition of motifs staging differences between women. A middle-class woman discusses women's suffrage with a servant; the working-class woman emerges as visible and vocal, becoming audible if not yet entirely intelligible to her middle-class sisters. An older woman provides advice or an opinion to a younger woman; their disagreement is represented but remains unresolved. Where the plays do not offer closure, they provide an uneasy exploration of problems, and expose the phenomenon of disagreement. Women's suffrage drama has been associated with a fairly straightforward dramatisation of polemical arguments, but this description applies to very few of the plays discussed here. Instead they engage with complex issues and attempt to acknowledge (if not accommodate) differences between women, an idea endorsed by Cicely Hamilton: 'We have got to allow for the difference of opinion, and to encourage it' and to accept that women 'see things very differently from the way our mothers saw them'.[75]

NOTES

I would like to acknowledge the National Trust for allowing me to quote from material held in the Edith Craig Archive, Ellen Terry Memorial Museum, Kent.

1 See J. Holledge, *Innocent flowers: women in the Edwardian theatre* (London, Virago, 1981); D. Spender and C. Hayman (eds), *How the vote was won and other suffragette plays* (London, Methuen, 1985); V. Gardner (ed.), *Sketches from the Actresses' Franchise League* (Nottingham, Nottingham Play Texts, 1985).
2 R. Williams, *Culture* (London, Fontana, 1981), p. 171.

3 M. Nevinson, *In the workhouse* (London, International Suffrage Shop, 1911); M. Nevinson, *Life's fitful fever: a volume of memories* (London, A and C Black, 1926), p. 234.

4 A. J. R. (ed.), *The suffrage annual and women's who's who* (London, Stanley Paul, 1913).

5 E. Robins, 'Votes for women', in Spender and Hayman (eds), *How the vote was won*, pp. 41–87.

6 C. Hirschfield, 'The Actresses' Franchise League and the campaign for women's suffrage 1908–1914', *Theatre Research International*, 10, 2, pp. 129–53.

7 C. Hamilton, 'Foreword', *A pageant of great women* (London, Marian Lawson, 1948), p. 7.

8 L. Tickner, *The spectacle of women: imagery of the suffrage campaign 1907–1914* (London, Chatto and Windus, 1987) p. 66.

9 R. Hennessy, *Materialist feminism and the politics of discourse* (London, Routledge, 1993), p. 105.

10 C. Battersby, *Gender and genius: towards a feminist aesthetics* (London, Women's Press, 1989), p. 3.

11 Edith Craig (1869–1947) actress, costumier, musician and theatre director; see N. Auerbach, *Ellen Terry: player in her time* (London, Phoenix House, 1987); K. Cockin, 'New light on Edith Craig', *Theatre Notebook*, 45, 3, 1991, pp. 132–43; K. Cockin, *Edith Craig: dramatic lives* (London, Cassell, 1997); J. Melville, *Ellen and Edy* (London, Pandora Press, 1987).

12 Tickner, *Spectacle of women*, p. 24.

13 See K. Cockin, 'The Pioneer Players (1911–25): a cultural history', Ph.D. thesis, Leicester University, 1994; K. Cockin, 'The Pioneer Players: plays of/with ideas', in G. Griffin (ed.), *Difference in view: women in modernism*, (London, Taylor and Francis, 1994), pp. 142–54; L. Wolf, 'Suffragettes of the Edwardian theatre: Edith Craig and the Pioneer Players', Ph.D. thesis, University of California, Los Angeles, 1989; Holledge, *Innocent flowers*; and for a discussion of the Pioneer Players' first production in the context of the New Woman, see C. Dymkowski, 'Edy Craig and the Pioneer Players', in V. Gardner and S. Rutherford (eds), *The new woman and her sisters: feminism and theatre 1850–1914*, (Hemel Hempstead, Harvester Wheatsheaf, 1992), pp. 221–33.

14 See documents relating to the nationwide productions of this play (1909–10) held in the Edith Craig Archive (ECD) at the National Trust's Ellen Terry Memorial Museum, Kent (ETMM).

15 *Votes for Women*, 15 April 1910, p. 455.

16 *The Vote*, 12 March 1910, p. 232.

17 Hamilton, 'Foreword', *A Pageant*, pp. 3, 7.

18 C. Hamilton and C. St John, *The pot and the kettle* (n.d.) and C. Hamilton and C. St John, 'How the vote was won' in Spender and Hayman (eds), *How the vote was won*, pp. 23–33.

19 *The Vote*, 7 May 1910, pp. 16–17.

20 Rosabel Watson conducted this orchestra in performing Mr J. M. Capel's arrangement of music to accompany *A pageant of great women* at its debut (play programme; ECD).

21 Pioneer Players' play programme, 30 November 1913 (ECD).

22 See I. Zangwill, 'Actress versus suffragette', *The Vote*, 18 November 1909, p. 44; and 'Underpaid Actresses', *The Vote*, 12 February 1910, p. 188.

23 J. Dorynne, 'The surprise of his life, ' typescript, n.d., pp. 15–16 (ECD).

24 *Ibid.*, p. 17.

25 *Ibid.*

26 Holledge, *Innocent flowers*, p. 129.

27 Ella Wheeler Wilcox's song 'Awakening' was interpreted by a tableau by the AFL on 27 October 1911, Lyceum Theatre (play programme; ECD; *The Vote*, 14 October 1911, p. 131).

28 O. Schreiner's 'Three dreams in a desert' was adapted as 'Two dreams in the desert' and given as a recitation by Nellie Sargent on 8 February 1911 at the Royal Albert Institute (play programme; ECD).

29 See Sue Thomas, 'Cicely Hamilton on theatre: a preliminary bibliography', *Theatre Notebook*, 49, 2, 1995, p. 100.

30 C. Hamilton, *Jack and Jill and a friend* (London, Lacy's Acting Ediction, 1911).

31 C. St John, *The first actress* (London, Utopia Press, n.d.).

32 R. West, 'A modern crusader', *The Freewoman*, 2, 27, 23 May 1912, p. 8.

33 V. Woolf, *A room of one's own* (Harmondsworth, Penguin Books, 1993).

34 A notable exception is M. Humm, *Border traffic: strategies of contemporary women writers* (Manchester, Manchester University Press, 1991), p. 166.

35 Cited by Holledge, *Innocent flowers*, p. 121.

36 *The Vote*, 26 March 1910, p. 257.

37 M. O. Kennedy, 'Woman articulate', *The Vote*, 28 January 1911, p. 166.

38 The play was inspired by 'an incident which occurred at a Meeting held by the Anti-suffrage League at Queen's Hall, London, in March 1909' (play programme; ECD).

39 H. M. Paull, 'The anti-suffragist or the other side: a monologue in one act', in Gardner (ed.), *Sketches*, p. 7.

40 E. Lyttelton, 'The thumbscrew', *Nineteenth Century*, May 1911, pp. 938–60.

41 *Daily Herald*, 17 December 1912, p. 5.

42 Holledge, *Innocent flowers*, p. 86.

43 Bessie Hatton, 'Before sunrise', in Gardner (ed.), *Sketches*, pp. 59–64.

44 I am grateful to members of the MA Women's Studies seminar on women's suffrage drama at Nene College for this point.

45 G. Jennings, 'A woman's influence', in Gardner (ed.), *Sketches*, pp. 67–74.

46 Hennessy, *Materialist feminism*, p. 94.

47 J. Austin, *How one woman did it* (London, Utopia Press, n.d.); ECD. Details of production are not known.

48 Austin, *How one woman did it*, p. 15.

49 In *A pageant of great women*, the 'warriors', Christian Davies (1667–1739) acted by Cicely Hamilton and Hannah Snell (1723–92) acted by Christopher St John, have been the subject of recent feminist criticism; see J. Wheelwright, *Amazons and military maids* (London, Pandora Press, 1989); see photographs reproduced in Gardner (ed.), *Sketches*, pp. 49–50.

50 Austin, *How one woman did it*, p. 23.

51 R. Williams, 'Social environment and theatrical environment: the case of English naturalism', in M. Axton and R. Williams (eds), *English drama: forms and development: essays in honour of Muriel C. Bradbrook* (Cambridge, Cambridge University Press, 1977), pp. 203–23.

52 Holledge, *Innocent flowers*, p. 86.

53 Author's Note, Christopher St John, 'Macrena,' typescript, n.d. (ECD).

54 *Ibid.* The Catholic Women's Suffrage Society invited St John to produce the play in June 1912 (CSWW records, Fawcett Library).

55 Scenes from Act 1 and Act 3 were performed on 27 October 1911 by the AFL at the Lyceum Theatre (play programme; ECD; *The Vote*, 14 October 1911).

56 *The Vote*, 8 November 1912.

57 *Ibid.*, 29 July 1911, p. 180.

58 J. P. Wearing, *The London stage 1910–19: a calendar of plays and players* (Metuchen and London, The Scarecrow Press, 1982). In addition the AFL acknowledged that it did not record all of its productions because they were so numerous (AFL Records, Fawcett).

59 *The Vote*, 22 October 1910.

60 *Pall Mall Gazette*, 13 April 1912, p. 5.

61 Queen Caroline's exile and exclusion from the coronation of her husband George IV is taken to be emblematic of all women whose unenfranchised state excludes them from Westminster.

62 This includes *Jack and Jill and a friend*, ADD LCP 1911/14, British Library (BL), *In the workhouse*, ADD LCP 1911/12, BL, *The first actress*, ADD LCP 1911/14, BL.

63 See M. Nevinson, 'A bewildered playwright', *The Vote*, 3 June 1911, p. 68.

64 Edith Craig organised the private printing of B. Hatton, *Before sunrise* and Hamilton and St John, *How the vote was won*.

65 The Utopia Press (printers of the *Clarion* newspaper) printed *The first actress*, the International Suffrage Shop printed *In the workhouse* and the AFL printed *A woman's influence*

and *An anti-suffragist*.

66 Hamilton, *Jack and Jill and a friend* and Countess von Arnim's *Priscilla runs away* were advertised in *French's alphabetical list of principal plays 1912–13* (ECD).

67 L. Whitelaw, *The life and rebellious times of Cicely Hamilton* (London, Women's Press, 1990), p. 126.

68 Unpublished letter from Beatrice Harraden to Edith Craig, 29 May [?]; 3.321, Edith Craig Correspondence File, ETMM (ECCF). B. Harraden, 'Lady Geraldine's speech', in Gardner (ed.), *Sketches*, pp. 51–8.

69 *Votes for Women*, 15 April 1910, p. 455.

70 Charlotte Perkins Gilman, *Three women* was produced by Edith Craig on Wednesday 13 and Friday 15 November [1912] at the 'Entertainment Hall' (prompt copy; props list; programme fragment; ECD). For a list of other plays to which Craig owned performance rights see Cockin, 'New light', p. 142.

71 Holledge, *Innocent flowers*, p. 69.

72 Unpublished letter from Charlotte Despard to Edith Craig, 30 March 1910; 3.191, ECCF.

73 Holledge, *Innocent flowers*, p. 86.

74 The production in 1914 of *The daughters of Ishmael*, adapted from Reginald Wright Kauffman's novel, coincided with the 'Piccadilly Flat' court case of Queenie Gerald for living off immoral earnings (*Common Cause*, 6 March 1914).

75 'The spirit of the movement', *The Vote*, 14 January 1911, pp. 140–1.

10

'A better world for both': men, cultural transformation and the suffragettes

WHETHER or not bell hooks is correct in arguing that bourgeois white feminists have reinforced sexist ideology by insisting that the contemporary feminist movement be 'women only', this was not the case in the women's movement at the turn of the century.[1] At that time white feminists certainly could conceptualise the bonds that develop between women and men during liberation struggle, since they had many positive experiences of working with men politically. Separatism was then, as now, seen by some feminists as essential to women's gaining self-confidence and to the development of solidarity between women, but it was a strategy not an ultimate goal. Like women, men are socialised to accept sexist ideology, but they are not *inevitably* sexist. We celebrate the men who worked to eliminate male supremacy by changing the British constitution, and who did this in partnership with women: John Stuart Mill, Henry Fawcett, Richard Pankhurst, Keir Hardie, George Lansbury and Frederick Pethick-Lawrence.[2] But the struggle to change the culture, to eliminate misogyny from the reproduction of gender ideology, was no less important. Certain plays which raised feminist consciousness at the turn of the century – plays like Ibsen's *The doll's house*, Shaw's *Mrs Warren's profession* and Granville Barker's *The Madras house* – even now have the power to shock us into recognition of the results of sex inequality. Dramatic representation is still one of the main vehicles for transmitting social values and for challenging them. I intend here to outline some of the ways in which men associated with the theatre supported women's use of theatre to create an alternative culture, a culture that was woman-centred and more feminine: caring, angry, funny and graceful, which foregrounded women as autonomous, responsible agents rather than sexual commodities.

The men I have chosen to discuss had different positions of power in relation to the dominant structures that awarded prestige to English, heterosexual, upper-class manhood. They were also personally related in different ways to women who were active in the women's suffrage movement. They are not the only men I could have selected, but their diversity should help to demystify the idea of an essential male opposition to women's equality. The five figures are Harley Granville Barker (1877–1946), Johnston Forbes-Robertson (1853–1937), George Bernard Shaw (1856–1950), Laurence Housman (1865-1959) and Henry Woodd Nevinson (1856–1941). The first three were married to prominent suffragists, and Forbes-Robertson was also brought up by a suffragist mother in a feminist household. Housman's elder sister, with whom he lived, was the suffragette artist Clemence Housman. Nevinson's first wife, Margaret Wynne Nevinson, was a suffrage activist who wrote an important feminist play, *In the workhouse*; in 1936 he married Evelyn Sharp, another member of the Women Writers Suffrage League, who left an account of her life as a suffragette in *An unfinished adventure* (1933). All these men worked energetically for the suffrage cause in the years leading up to 1918. I am going to discuss the combined assaults that they made on British culture, and the various aspects of the theatre by which they assisted women to be protagonists in their own struggle. From their splashes in London, results rippled out across Britain and helped support the sister movement in North America.

In June 1906 the actress Gertrude Kingston commissioned Elizabeth Robins to write a play for her to star in. Robins was herself a former actress who, having retired from the stage at the age of 40, had achieved popular success as a novelist. She was not, however, known as a dramatist. She had in fact been instrumental in introducing Ibsen to the English theatre, having aided William Archer in his translations, and both co-produced and starred in the first English productions between 1891 and 1896. In her own right she had written several plays which had never reached the stage: *The mirkwater* and *The silver lotus* in the 1890s, and in 1900 *Benvenuto Cellini*, a melodrama on which Herbert Beerbohm Tree kept an option for a year without finally taking it up. She had also collaborated with Lady Florence Bell in the writing of *Alan's wife*, a one-act play based on a short story by the Swedish writer, Elin Ameen. This was staged privately in 1893, by the Independent Theatre Society. Highly controversial, being about infanticide, it was produced and published anonymously.[3]

In response to Kingston's commission, by 30 August Robins had settled for her topic on the great issue of the day: women's suffrage. On Saturday, 13 October 1906, she was writing a letter to Florence Bell from a bench in Hyde Park 'near the crowd round a red Banner "Votes For Women"' and reporting some of the responses from passers-by.[4] This was one of many suffrage events she attended to gain first-hand knowledge, and it was, as Angela John points out, the process of researching the play which 'turned Elizabeth from being one more woman in broad agreement with women's suffrage into a committed suffragette publicly identified with the cause'.[5] In October she observed the results of a lobby protest at the House of Commons; eleven very respectable women, including Anne Cobden Sanderson, were arrested, and when Robins tried to attend their court-hearing the next day she was deliberately prevented by the police from acting as a witness. This flagrant breach of justice and the grossly distorted press accounts of the incidents, which labelled the women a vulgar and hysterical mob, led her to speak impromptu at a women's conference on the following day, where she met Millicent Fawcett for the first time.[6] These direct experiences prompted her into a strong personal commitment not only to the issues in the play, but to the political action advocated by the militant suffragettes.

At first Kingston had pressed for urgent completion of the script, and Robins, anxious to have the play produced to coincide with the major London suffrage demonstration of February 1907, tried to meet a December deadline. However, their negotiations faltered, as theatrical managements refused, on political grounds, to mount the play for Kingston.[7] On 1 November, Robins wrote to Millicent Fawcett that she was already adapting the play into a novel, since, on the one hand, regular theatre managers considered it too partisan, and, on the other, it had just been returned by Harley Granville Barker and J. E. Vedrenne at the Court Theatre, as they were unable to cancel other plans in order to produce it before the autumn.[8] Besides soliciting criticism from Millicent Fawcett, Emmeline Pankhurst and J. M. Barrie, in early November Robins also sought the advice of Henry James, an old friend in whose play *The American* she had acted in 1891. They spent hours discussing the precise psychological significance of the movements of particular characters, and he followed this up with fifty pages of meticulous notes.[9] For her novel this may have eventually been helpful; for the play it was not. James's insistence that for 'its full interest' the play required the '(male) centrality' of Stonor MP, that 'his presence, interest and figure' be strong, since the intensity and value of the female roles depended on his importance, was completely at odds with the feminism that determined Robins's approach. He spoke as if her concentration on the female lead was merely to satisfy Gertrude Kingston's ego, ignoring the radical assault on Victorian theatrical practice which Robins intended by making the protagonist a feminist, who was to be presented as a heroine rather than as a figure of ridicule. James's very concentration on details of gesture and innuendo was reducing the play to a comedy of manners, evading the kind of help Robins actually needed, which was a discussion that recognised the political argument of the play and advised how best to structure a plot which would relate the political issues to a convincing narrative embodying them. In the event it was Shaw and Barker who provided that aid.

Unlike James, Shaw was firmly committed to women's suffrage. In an article in the *Tribune* in March 1906, Shaw had recommended women to have a revolution: 'they should shoot, kill, maim, destroy – until they are given the vote'.[10] Shaw and Robins had known each other for years, partly through their mutual friend William Archer. They encountered one another again at the banquet thrown by Millicent Fawcett at the Savoy Hotel on 11 December to celebrate the suffragettes' release from prison. Along with a number of MPs and other celebrities, including the playwright Israel Zangwill, they were lending their public support to the toast proposed by Robins: 'Success to the cause of Women's Suffrage.'[11] Shortly after this Shaw sent Robins a letter regarding the typescript of her play. He advised her to simplify and clarify the thrust of the final act, and to compress the first two acts into one by cutting out all the small talk and complications that had been the results of Henry James's labours: 'What you have here is Greek tragedy, not fashionable comedy.' Instead of substituting his own writing for hers as James had done, Shaw suggested she keep straight to the main points, which he identified, and she would then have 'something fine'.[12] Robins reported in a letter to Florence Bell, having had lunch with the Shaws on 1 January 1907, stating that he was 'very encouraging', had offered to come to rehearsals and greatly uplifted her spirits. In view of all the setbacks, the encouragement was probably as important to her as the practical suggestions. Bell, her oldest friend, was an anti-suffragist and strongly opposed to the whole project.[13] Years later, Robins was to write to Shaw recalling 'how immensely helpful as well as *stirring* you were in those turbulent days'.[14] She followed Shaw's advice in regard to Act 1, but by the time that he wrote with further ideas about the final act in mid-March it was too late.

In the meantime, it seems he had used his influence to persuade his close friend Barker to mount the play after all. Barker wrote to Robins again on 22 February and – as Gates puts it – 'within hours of severing negotiations with Kingston and Kingston's return of the script',[15] on 28 February 1907 Robins had secured a contract with Barker and Vedrenne to produce the play at the Court. They re-arranged their current programme in order to put on Robins's play towards the end of April – the only one by a woman which they produced over three years. The play received just twenty-four commercial performances in all: eight at the Court between 9 April and 3 May 1907, and sixteen performances at Wallack's in New York in March 1909.[16] However, its impact was out of all proportion to that small showing. The London production attracted full houses, the audiences including not only prominent suffragists but MPs, which obviously stimulated discussion, and it generated pages of reviews and articles in leading publications. One of the main aims of the new campaign led by the Women's Social and Political Union (WSPU) was to publicise the suffrage issue and keep its arguments before people's minds. Robins's play clearly helped achieve this aim. That it did so is greatly due to the care Barker paid to its staging.

Robins could not have done better. Barker's 1904–7 collaboration with J. E. Vedrenne at the Court is legendary. Their innovative management was unique in its aim of presenting seasons of important new plays as well as classic revivals, performed in repertory by an acting company that they built up, which 'was a glory in its day, and remains a landmark'.[17] Besides supplying his own original plays, Barker solicited established writers to provide material for a system that both encouraged new work and provided variety for a regular corps of actors.

Robins's play was mythically to rub shoulders with Shaw's *Major Barbara* and *Man and superman*, Galsworthy's *The silver box*, and a new translation of *Electra* by Gilbert Murray, as well as Barker's own *The Voysey inheritance*. Barker was one of the new directors who wished to impose coherent vision on a play. Having himself started out as an actor, he was firmly opposed to the practice of the actor-manager which had become established at the end of the nineteenth century, and which notoriously, as in the case of Henry Irving and Ellen Terry, sacrificed artistic integrity and female talent to the star status of the male lead. By moving away from Victorian spectacle and developing balanced ensemble acting, Barker aimed to use stage aesthetics to focus the audience's attention on the argument of the play, rather than to stimulate an indulgence in the aesthetic experience for its own sake or to idolise the male protagonist. Influenced by his collaborative work with Shaw, Barker's emphasis on the intelligence of the audience and the ideas of the play was ideal for Robins's political purposes.

But Barker was not only the most enterprising and creative producer in London at that time; in his letter to Robins accepting her play, he also declared himself to be 'strongly prejudiced in favour of the subject'.[18] He was later to speak on suffrage platforms and to endorse a statement issued by the Men's League for Woman's Suffrage supporting votes for women, but the practical support he offered Robins was his unique contribution to the Cause. After signing the contract, Robins took a rest-cure in Dresden. We have a record, in the five letters Barker wrote to her there during March 1907, of the ways in which he prepared and rehearsed the play. There is further material evidence of the kind of care that he took, in the prompt-book he made.[19] It is well known that the eventual title, *Votes for women!* (in place of Robins's cautious 'The friend of women') was Barker's inspiration, due to his wish to help Robins focus attention on the political aspect of the play as well as to attract audiences. This is indicative of Barker's head-on approach in contrast to the wariness of other managers. Some of the initial suggestions regarding the length of Act 1 and how best to compress it are similar to those in Shaw's March letter; probably they had discussed the play together. They were in agreement that no changes were needed to the second act, except to provide patter for the crowd. However, Barker made alterations to Act 3, cutting business, shortening the end and suggesting a slight emendation to the plot in the light of current WSPU policy and parliamentary practice.

The play is built around Act 2, which sets the theatre auditorium up as Trafalgar Square, and places the audience as part of the crowd at a WSPU meeting, watching the speakers on the plinth of Nelson's Column. It is a technique that echoes Shakespeare's *Julius Caesar* and Ibsen's *An enemy of the people*, but with more immediacy. The forceful impact of Barker's staging of the scene, which was admitted and commented on even in adverse reviews, did not depend on spectacle, the visual recreation of a recognisable London typical of late Victorian theatre, as has been suggested by Sheila Stowell,[20] especially since the square was only indicated by the boring grey of masculine public space, set off by the airy banners and women's dresses; the startling effect was achieved by the re-creation of an open-air political meeting through *sound*. Robins had based her representation of the various speeches and the heckling, on notes taken at actual meetings in Hyde Park – and the figure of Ernestine Blunt is closely modelled on Mary Gawthorpe[21] – but Barker carefully wrote in and rehearsed all the background banter from the crowd, which was to be played by permanent members of the company.

One of the things that makes it difficult for any unpopular political speaker to project arguments is a barrage of noise deliberately maintained against her or his voice.[22] The special difficulty that this created for a woman was not simply that it was unfeminine to raise her voice in public, but that she had to resist all her training in what was womanly in order to combat the aggression inherent in such harassment, and not break down in face of it. Barker helped to create the adverse environment against which the courage and determination of Vida Levering were to be tested as she took the platform for the first time. Speaking in close interaction with the crowd, rather than reading from a prepared speech, Blunt and 'the Working Woman' had already displayed how to deal with individual hecklers. That left the problem of how to maintain composure against the blanket of random, contradictory sound from the rest of the casual bystanders, and to grasp the crowd's attention. By showing Levering so nervous at first, Robins engages the audience's sympathy, but the dramatic conflict which Barker enhanced, between Levering and the indifferent or hostile crowd, excites the audience too. The position of the crowd, between Levering and the influential, upper-class people she most needs to convince – Stonor MP and his fiancée, Bea, who stand uncertainly at the front of the stage, representing members of the theatre audience – emphasises the social difficulty of her task: the fear that association with the common people might result in a loss of respect. It is still a nerve-racking scene to read. The climax of relief when Levering, gathering confidence, manages to articulate her ideas through to her appeal at the end, in the face of continuous hostility, supports the impact of Bea's decision to act for herself, disregard Stonor and join the Union. The theatrical effect achieved by Barker and Robins is that the stage suffragettes, in managing to command respect from and establish authority over the unruly stage crowd, also command respect from the real audience, which, however unwillingly, is involved in the tension of the scene and in the struggle for feminist ideas to be heard.

Robins's success illustrated the way in which women might intervene in the cultural reproduction of female stereotypes, and use theatre for propaganda purposes. An outcome of her example was the formation of two professional suffrage organisations: the Actresses' Franchise League (AFL), of which she became a Vice-President, and the Women Writers Suffrage League (WWSL), of which she was the first President.[23] The WWSL was founded by two other dramatists who had also been actresses, Cicely Hamilton and Bessie Hatton (Margaret Wynne Nevinson acted as Secretary after Bessie Hatton). Associated with the AFL from its inception was the Shakespearian actor–manager, Sir Johnston Forbes-Robertson, popular in his day particularly for his partnership with Mrs Patrick Campbell, for which Shaw wrote *Caesar and Cleopatra*. He was already one of the famous Hamlets of his time, and his performance was immortalised on early film in a production in which Adeline Bourne played Gertrude. In 1900 he married the actress Gertrude Elliott (younger sister of the more famous American actress Maxine Elliott, and twenty years his junior) and they toured together in his company around Britain and across the United States. Following Royal Command performances he was knighted for his services to the theatre in 1912. As far as I know, he did not perform in any suffrage play, or anything remotely feminist. However, whenever the opportunity presented itself, he spoke publicly in favour of women gaining the vote.

His most notable appearance in public to support votes for women was to take the chair at the memorable meeting at the Criterion Restaurant on 17 December 1908, when the AFL was inaugurated.[24] The AFL was set up to propagandise arguments in favour of the vote for women through entertainment, and to train suffrage speakers, and it kept up morale as well as raising funds, drawing publicity to the issue and making new converts. Like many other women suffrage organisations, it was run entirely by women, although sympathetic men participated in the entertainments and acted male roles. Members of Forbes-Robertson's theatre company are usually credited with originating the idea of such an organisation.[25] Adeline Bourne remained one of its leading organisers as the Honorary Secretary, and Gertrude Elliott, having been one of its first vice-presidents, became president when Mrs Kendal (Madge Robertson) stepped down after the first year. Like his brother Norman, Forbes-Robertson remained a patron of the League and addressed its public meetings. There is no doubt that his name and support lent considerable respectability and prestige both to the AFL and to the Cause.

Forbes-Robertson's theatre company toured Britain and the USA between 1908 and 1916, and wherever he performed he also spoke. He believed it was the duty of every man 'whatever his position in life might be, to declare himself in some way, either by signing some document or by standing on the public platform' in favour of suffrage reform.[26] There are records of his speaking in Dublin, London, Newcastle and Edinburgh, and in Washington, New York, San Francisco and Portland (Oregon). What he said was not always reported in detail, yet I have found accounts in *Votes for Women*, *The Era* (the theatrical weekly) and the American *Woman's Journal* (Boston) which make clear what an eloquent speaker he was: direct, knowledgable and concise, but recounting amusing anecdotes to drive his points home, and not afraid to voice profound feeling. One of his speeches is reported at length in *The Era*, when he spoke on a WSPU plat-

form in Edinburgh, condemning the 'iniquitous things' done to women in what
he termed the 'Martyrdom of Holloway'.[27] His venues were extensive. Apart from
speaking on WSPU platforms in Britain and at Equal Suffrage meetings in the
USA, he also spoke to luncheon meetings of businessmen, when opening
bazaars, at receptions, at the launching of the California Civic League and,
importantly, at a demonstration held by the National Political League at
Kingsway Hall in March 1913 to oppose the forcible feeding of imprisoned suffragettes. On that occasion he shared a platform with George Bernard Shaw, and
reiterated the denunciation he had already expressed in letters to the press, condemning the practice as involving 'torture', 'barbarities' and 'filthy practices'
which brutalised those who performed them.[28]

The argument of Forbes-Robertson's speeches in favour of women's suffrage appears usually to have followed the same line: that it was not physical
strength which now ruled the world, but intelligence, and women were at least
as intelligent as men. Women's brains had a great power for good which humanity could not afford to reject. He followed common practice in humorously recommending people who were not yet convinced of the rightness of votes for
women to attend an 'anti' meeting, because the hopeless, helpless counter-argu-
ments there would be bound to convert them to 'this great reform'. But he also
spoke out of his own insight into androcentricity. On 1 February 1909, he made
a very stirring speech to the WSPU, reproduced in *Votes for Women* as 'A Declaration of Faith'. In this he admitted that he was one of those men who found
it hard to 'give up his throne'.[29] When he addressed the Irish Woman's Franchise
League in Dublin later that same month, he apparently packed the Molesworth
Hall. He took the opportunity to recommend women to keep the leadership of
their movement entirely within their own control: 'You cannot trust even the best
of men to guide your movement.' Paradoxically, he said that even though he was
'heart and soul with you in this ... the greatest reform of modern times', he would
not even trust his own advice to them, for 'our view of things, men's view, is ever
unconsciously warped by self-interest'.[30]

Forbes-Robertson's autobiography gives us no clue as to why he never performed in any of the suffrage plays specially written for the AFL, when even Ellen
Terry appeared in *The pageant of great women*.[31] However, it was at his request
that Shaw wrote *Press cuttings* for one of the AFL's first West End matinées in
July 1909. This was a farce in which the Prime Minister and a general were converted to the suffrage movement by the antics of a couple of anti-suffragettes.
Shaw's notoriety and the controversy over the play certainly attracted attention to
the suffrage issue. The play was refused a licence by the official censor until the
names were changed, but it seems unlikely Shaw really thought Forbes-Robertson would take the role of 'Balsquith', designed for him, or of 'Michener' (Bal-
four/Asquith/Kitchener). Certainly, Shaw did not think that any of the female
roles would be suitable for Gertrude Elliott.[32] Agnes Thomas, the comic actress

who had played 'the Working Woman' in *Votes for women!*, took the leading role of War Office charwoman. In the event the play was put on at the Royal Court as part of two afternoons of mixed entertainment in aid of the London Suffrage Society, during which Robertson read from *The ancient mariner.* At the play's second major production, a benefit matinée by the AFL for the National Union of Women's Suffrage Societies (NUWSS) at the Kingsway Theatre in June 1910, when it was part of a programme including *How the vote was won* by Cicely Hamilton and Christopher St John, Maxine Elliott substituted for her brother-in-law and read some more appropriate poems by Charlotte Perkins Gilman. Perhaps, by maintaining his dignity, Sir Johnston Forbes-Robertson's patronage of the suffrage movement carried more weight – especially in America.

Another of the male stalwarts of the AFL was Laurence Housman, whose activities on behalf of women's suffrage were so numerous I can only begin to sketch them here. Originally trained as a graphic artist, failing eyesight forced him to change his profession to author. The phenomenal success of his *An Englishwoman's love letters* (1900) seems to have enabled him for a few years to finance less profitable activities, such as his co-authorship of *Prunella* with Barker for the Court's 1904–5 season. An active member of the Men's League for Women's Suffrage, and a delegate to the first congress of the Men's International Alliance for women's suffrage in 1912, as well as a leader in the revolt over the National Census, like his sister Clemence he subscribed to WSPU, having been converted to militancy by a speech given by Emmeline Pankhurst. Following his feminist polemic *Articles of faith in the freedom of women* (1910), he wrote a number of speeches and articles for *The Vote*, which were republished as pamphlets through the Women's Freedom League (WFL). Clemence, an active member of the Tax Resistance League, was one of the co-founders of the Suffrage Atelier in 1909, and her brother chaired its first public meeting.[33] He designed 'five or six banners' including one of the prominent silk banners carried at several big London suffrage marches, which announced 'From Prison to Citizenship'.[34] This led a contingent of 5,000 women from Kensington in the WSPU march on 21 June 1908, and was carried again as part of the West Procession, which he helped Edith Craig design for the spectacular WSPU/WFL demonstration in favour of the Conciliation Bill on 23 July 1910.[35]

Housman placed his writing and design skills at the service of the AFL for indoor theatrical productions too, the most notable of which was his one-act play *Alice in Ganderland*, first performed as part of a matinée of mixed entertainment at the Lyceum on 27 October 1911, with a prologue by Israel Zangwill. Playing on the frequent suffrage allusion to 'What is sauce for the goose ...', this was a skit on Lewis Carroll's Mad Hatter's Tea-Party, at which the Mad Hatter, representing the Liberal Party, the March Hare as the Labour Party, the Dormouse, in coronet and Garter robes over a hunting kit to represent the Conservatives, and a green Bill the Lizard standing for the Irish Nationalists, did their best to keep

Alice out. Alice, played by Eva Moore, was appalled at the wasteful, careless mess they had made of the tea-table and summoned up her supporters who appeared as a pageant of thirty-two women, symbolising various suffrage organisations and headed by pioneers of the 1860s, all singing (Ethel Smyth's and Cicely Hamilton's) *March of the women* with Smyth conducting. They were triumphant, the March Hare capitulating with shouts of 'Votes for women! And more of 'em!'[36] This idea of an allegorical play incorporating a pageant followed a model devised by Edith Craig and Cicely Hamilton for *The pageant of famous women* (first performed at the Scala Theatre in November 1909 for a joint AFL / WWSL matinée, with a prologue by Housman). The model was adapted again in February of the following year when the WWSL mounted a pageant of Shakespeare's heroines, to words selected by Beatrice Harraden and Bessie Hatton, in a production by Edith Craig. This had a prologue by Hamilton and ended with a tableau designed by Housman, symbolic of women's struggle for freedom.[37]

In 1910 Gertrude Kingston took over the management of the Little Theatre for herself, and commissioned a play from Housman. He recounts in his autobiography how he offered her *Pains and penalties*, about the forced divorce of Queen Caroline, which by 'sublime fatuity' was then refused a licence, and so could not be publicly performed.[38] The following year Craig produced it privately at the Savoy with her Pioneer Players, with Kingston starring as Queen Caroline. (The play acquired topical interest again in the 1990s with the divorce of Princess Diana from Prince Charles in 1996.) Instead, Housman rapidly prepared a free translation of Aristophanes' *Lysistrata*, and Kingston opened in that, starring as Lysistrata and also directing. Having regarded it as a 'play of feminist propaganda which offered lurid possibilities'[39] Housman had incorporated suffrage jokes which were much appreciated by the reviewers in *The Englishwoman* and *Votes for Women*.[40] In November a scene from the play was given by Kingston as part of an AFL/WWSL matinée at the Aldwych. In this production the *Votes for Women* reviewer was startled by 'carefully planned typical interruptions from the audience' – presumably based on the example of Robins's *Votes for women!*[41] The play was published by the Women's Press in 1911, but not copyrighted in the USA; thus freely available, scenes from it were occasionally performed by American suffrage groups.

Shaw's plays were also performed in the USA. After its initial showing at the Court in 1909, *Press cuttings* was performed at the Gaiety, Manchester, and was then put on at the end of the year by the AFL for the WFL in a Christmas gala at the Albert Hall in London. After that it stayed in the AFL repertory until 1914, being performed around the country. It was also included in seasons at the Birmingham and Liverpool Repertory Theatres in 1912–13 and was mounted by American theatres in Boston and New York. But the suffrage play of Shaw's that made the most impact both in Britain and the USA was *Fanny's first play*. Although it is not about votes for women, I call it a suffrage play because it was clearly identified as such at the time. Indeed, Shaw himself referred to it as a 'suffragette play'.[42] It was his longest running success, both in London, where from 1911 it ran to 624 performances at the Little Theatre under Lillah McCarthy's management, transferring to the Kingsway, and in New York where it ran for 256 nights at the Comedy from 1912. It was revived at the Kingsway in 1915, the Everyman in 1922, and the Court in 1931.

Originally put on anonymously, *Fanny's first play* is a play-within-a-play. The conceit is that the wealthy father of a Cambridge graduate, Fanny, pays to have her play performed in front of professional critics who are kept ignorant of the author's identity (as were the real original critics and audience). Fanny's play is a broad comedy satirising suburban respectability. A young woman, Margaret Knox, gets gloriously drunk on the night of the Oxford–Cambridge Boat Race, picks up a Frenchman, and is imprisoned for disorderly conduct, having knocked out a policeman's teeth. Her religious mother (played by Cicely Hamilton in London and on tour) is horrified. Framing this farce is a satire that parodied famous critics of the day who were unable to comment on the play without knowing who wrote it. Part of the joke for the audience is that the critics cannot guess the gender of the author. Part of the pleasure for women in the audience at the time was undoubtedly the idea that such an outrageous play is supposed to have been written by a woman – and a suffragette at that. Yet, although Fanny is a suffragette (she 'did a month with Lady Constance Lytton'), her play does not discuss or advocate votes for women. Nevertheless, despite the fact that Margaret Knox explicitly denies she has joined the suffragettes, she was identified as one by real critics and by, for example, *Illustrated Play Pictorial* (in 1911) which published a full page photo of Lillah McCarthy in the role of Margaret, entitled 'Suffragette'.[43] In *The Era* the reviewer of this first production was polite about McCarthy, who 'as the revolutionary Margaret gave a very acute and vigorous impersonation of the high-spirited, impetuous and fearless girl'.[44] However, by 1913 the WSPU had embarked on its arson campaign. That same year the play went on tour, Rignold and Macdona's Company taking it to country districts and McCarthy and Granville-Barker's Company staging it in suburban theatres such as the Coronet. The reviewer of the production at the Coronet called the play a 'delightful exposition of Shavian wit', yet in March he felt that Phyllis Ralph 'as the emotional outspoken, self-important and hysterical militant suffragette, Margaret Knox, acts remarkably well and charmingly withal, and quite gains undue sympathy for the ill-balanced virago depicted', while by November he was saying that Constance Little 'as the impulsive, hysterical, plain-speaking, swollen-headed militant suffragette, Margaret Knox, acts with due verve and intensity, and aptly portrays the neurotic nature of the girl'.[45] Clearly Shaw had grounds for satirising the critics and their inability to be impartial or objective.

The vitriol in such subjective misrepresentation of the play, perpetrated by critics and sanctioned by their editors, demonstrates the importance of cultural interpretation in influencing political opinion. This was well recognised by the suffrage journals, which all ran review sections and developed feminist criticism. Men were using their theatre skills in writing, producing, designing and speaking in support of women, but their critical skills were also called for. One man who responded to this need was Henry Woodd Nevinson.

A prominant journalist, Nevinson became chairman of the Men's Political Union for Women's Suffrage; the most radical of the men's organisations, this supported the WSPU, and several members were imprisoned for their activities. Nevinson was so incensed by press misrepresentation of the suffrage campaign that in 1909, together with Henry Noel Brailsford, he resigned his job with the *Daily News* over its editorial support for the government.[46] He published many articles justifying suffrage militancy, gave whole-hearted support to Sylvia Pankhurst, and spoke tirelessly on platforms. His autobiography also recalls his making a spectacle of himself, riding on horseback in the great suffrage parades.[47] Housman recollected being one of a group of men including Brailsford and Nevinson who advertised a suffrage meeting by wearing top hats and carrying sandwich-boards along the main London streets. He called it 'an awful ordeal' and looking back he thought the hardest thing in his campaigning was feeling foolish.[48] The risk of making a fool of himself in public was never taken by Forbes-Robertson, but Nevinson constantly faced ridicule for his beliefs.

He produced theatre criticism from early on, and was one of the first to acclaim Elizabeth Robins's *Votes for women!* He might, like other reviewers such as Max Beerbohm, have praised Barker's direction while commenting on the old-fashioned, melodramatic conventions of the plot. Yet, recognising the political significance of the play, he classified it as a drama that could not be criticised on the lines of ordinary plays. Like other critics he praised the production and the acting for being remarkably true to life. But he praised this accurate reproduction of reality for its revelation of the nature of that reality. Its power came from the political conviction of the speeches. Its emotional force came from its attempts to catch the conscience of guilty creatures sitting at a play: men. Earlier plays, written by men, such as Molière's *L'École des femmes* or Aristophanes' *Lysistrata*, had voiced women's aspirations. But, however indulgently they did this, it was only in order to mock women's ideals. Nevinson found Robins witty. She laughed, but she was not satirising women. Sarcastic himself at the 'generosity' of the earlier, 'manly' satires which ridiculed women, he found that 'it is the lion now that is painting the picture of the lionhunt, and man can hardly be expected to enjoy it much'. He had found men the object of Robins's humour, and he was honest enough to recognise her accuracy.[49]

After the split in the WSPU in 1912, Nevinson helped form the United Suffragists, and served on the executive with Laurence Housman, May Whitty, Evelyn Sharp and others. Sharp continued to edit *Votes for Women* and Nevinson contributed articles. Amongst these is a review of Barker's 1913 production of

Shaw's *Androcles and the lion*, an example of 'reading as a feminist' if ever there was one. 'Of course, it is a suffragette play', Nevinson begins, and proceeds to interpret it as such. The awning of the arena was apparently painted the famous purple, white and green, and from there onwards it was easy to see the Christians as suffragettes in their perfect friendship and confidence, and, when the audience cheered the allusions in the Emperor's speech about how easily prisoners could gain their freedom, to hear the applause as meaning 'Down with McKenna!'[50] Nevinson was following a newly created practice here, in interpreting plays with feminist issues as suffragette drama. By contrasting Nevinson's use of the term and his attitude to the 'beauty and dignity' of suffragettes, with the anonymous reviews of *Fanny's first play* in *The Era*, we can see plainly how the political aspirations of women were being contested through the very use of the term 'suffragette', especially in relation to drama. Refusing to feel the term as an insult was an essential tactic in women's resistance to men's attempts to humiliate them into submission. Nevinson's linking of Robins to such classical writers as Gorky, Ibsen and Shakespeare was to insist on the dignity not only of her art but of her claims. Similarly, in 1912 *Votes for Women* had highlighted *Iphigenia* as 'a suffragette drama'. Suffragettes were tragic heroines. And in 1910, Emmeline Pethick-Lawrence had called Lysistrata 'a suffragette 2,000 years ago', quoting from Lysistrata's speech, where she mimics her husband, saying 'stick to your stitching or I'll break your jaw!'[51]

But some men helped with the stitching, tailoring a new cultural fabric. Of course they were not above reproach in their personal lives, but they accepted responsibility for helping women achieve their rights. They yearned, as Zangwill's Prologue put it, to set women free and by 'joint work of men and women ... to make a better world for both'.[52] Seeing the need for cultural transformation they worked with other men and in fellowship with women to alter the misrepresentations of the women's suffrage campaign and to create new constructions of women's point of view. Such men as Barker, Forbes-Robertson, Housman, Nevinson and Shaw receive their appropriate epitaph in Elizabeth Robins's acknowledgement in a letter to Florence Bell about the script for *Votes for women!*: 'Certainly all the men I've shown this thing to have been immensely good about it and the *trouble* they take!'[53]

NOTES

1 bell hooks, 'Men: comrades in struggle', *Feminist theory: from margin to centre* (Boston, South End Press, 1984), pp. 67–9.
2 For a detailed discussion of the feminist politics of these men, see Sylvia Strauss, *'Traitors to the masculine cause': the men's campaign for women's rights* (London, Greenwood, 1982).
3 The first three of these plays were unpublished and now form part of the collection of Robins's papers at the Fales Library, New York University Library; see 'Introduction' by Joanne Gates (ed.) in Elizabeth Robins, *Votes for women!* (privately printed, Jacksonville,

1989) p. 14; Florence Bell and Elizabeth Robins, *Alan's wife* (London, Henry, 1893), reprinted in Linda Fitzsimmons and Viv Gardner (eds), *New woman plays* (London, Methuen 1991).

4 The heading of an autograph letter from Elizabeth Robins to Florence Bell, 13 October 1906, in the Fales.

5 A. V. John, *Elizabeth Robins: staging a life, 1862–1952* (London and New York, Routledge, 1995), p. 144.

6 These events are variously recounted in E. Sylvia Pankhurst, *The suffragette movement* (London, Longman, 1931) and Evelyn Sharp, *An unfinished adventure* (London, John Lane, 1933). They were reported in *The Times* (24 October 1906), p. 9 and (25 October 1906), p. 9, and *Kent and Sussex Courier* (26 October 1906), p. 9. Robins's letter to Millicent Fawcett concerning the events, dated 27 October 1906, is lodged in Manchester Public Library M/50 Box 9.

7 The correspondence between Gertrude Kingston and Elizabeth Robins is lodged in the Fales. It includes two letters from Robins, dated 17 January 1907 and 22 January 1907, and the autograph letter from Kingston dated 19 January 1907, in which she claims that 'the political bias of the play is the stumbling block to immediate production'.

8 The letter from Robins to Fawcett, dated 1 November 1906, is lodged in the Fawcett Library, London Guildhall University, London. The novel was the bestseller *The convert* (London, Methuen, 1907).

9 Some of the correspondence between Robins and Henry James was published in Elizabeth Robins, *Theatre and friendship* (London, Cape, 1932) ch. 15. The originals of these letters are in the Harry Ransom Humanities Research Center archives at the University of Texas at Austin. The detailed advice, from which I quote and which Robins did not republish in her book, is in the Robins Collection at the Fales and is included in an Appendix in Gates (ed.), *Votes for women!*. Presumably Robins had not read James's novel on the American Woman Suffrage Movement, *The Bostonians* (1886).

10 'G. B .S. and a suffragist', *Tribune* (12 March 1906) p. 3, reprinted in R. Weintraub (ed.), *Fabian feminist: Bernard Shaw and woman* (Pennsylvania, Penn State University Press, 1977). Shaw's feminism is defended by Michael Holroyd, 'G B S: women and the body politic', *Critical Inquiry*, autumn 1979, pp. 17–32. Its contradictory complexity is indicated by Julie Holledge, *Innocent flowers: women in the Edwardian theatre* (London, Virago, 1981), pp. 29–32.

11 The event was reported in *The Times* (12 December 1906), p. 12. Israel Zangwill (1864–1926) would merit further research. Another playwright, and a Jewish activist, he was married to Edith Ayrton Zangwill, the daughter of the scientist Hertha Ayrton, and the sister of the suffragette Barbara Ayrton Gould, who figured prominently in the London processions. Edith was a member of the WSPU and the Women Writers' Suffrage League, like their long-time family friend Bessie Hatton. Articles and other writings by Edith and by Israel appeared frequently in the WSPU journal, *Votes for Women*. He did not, however, write any suffrage plays. There are photographs of him in the HRHRC archives, and he is briefly discussed in Sylvia Strauss, 'Traitors', pp. 219–21. This has also been a useful source for some of my factual information about other male activists discussed here.

12 Shaw's letter to Robins, dated 29 December 1906, is in the HRHRC archive.

13 Robins's letter to Bell, dated 4 January 1907, and lodged in the Fales, is reprinted in Gates (ed.), *Votes for women!*. Apparently Robins received further 'radical help' in writing the play from Bell (ER to FB, 25 January 1907, Fales) following an outburst from Bell hinted at in a letter from ER to FB (1 December 1906, Fales). I surmise that this help enabled her to placate anti-suffragists like Bell by implying in the final act that it was only childless women who should be public activists. For a discussion of this issue, see Sheila Stowell, *A stage of their own: feminist playwrights of the suffrage era* (Manchester, Manchester University Press, 1992), pp. 33–4.

14 Undated letter from Robins to Shaw in the Fales collection, quoted by John, *Elizabeth Robins*, p. 82.

15 Gates (ed.), *Votes for women!*, p. 7.
16 A history of the Court productions at this time is given in Desmond MacCarthy, *The Court Theatre 1904–7* (London, Bullen, 1907). Allan Wade, an actor who was Barker's secretary at the Court, recalled that Robins's play was so successful it was put into the evening bill. A Wade, *Memories of the London theatre*, ed. A Andrews (London, Society for Theatre Research, 1983). However, I can find no evidence that there were more than eight performances, as indicated by the receipts in the correspondence between Vedrenne and Robins, and data recorded in J. P. Wearing, *The London stage, 1900–1909, a calendar of plays and players* (London, Scarecrow, 1981), despite John's assertion that there were thirteen performances; John, *Elizabeth Robins*, p. 148. This seems to be a misreading of Vedrenne's letter, in which he was hoping to transfer the play to another West End theatre when the Court lease ended; but he did not manage to get Harrison to accept it for the Haymarket as he had hoped. See correspondence JEV to ER, 25 April 1907 and 3 May 1907, in HRHRC. If I am wrong, then the play ran at the Court for eight matinées, plus another thirteen evenings and two matinées, making twenty-three London performances in all. (I cannot make sense of Stowell's mathematics: Stowell, *A stage*, p. 36.)
17 R. B. Marriott, 'The Royal Court Theatre', *Theatre Museum card no 55* (London, HMSO, 1978).
18 Letter HGB to ER, dated 22 February 1907 in HRHRC. Four other letters from HGB to ER, dated February and April 1907, as well as the five concerning the details of the production during rehearsal, are also in HRHRC.
19 The prompt-book of *Votes for women!* is the only one of Barker's that survives. It consists of the original typescript with handwritten emendations by Barker, with inserted interleaves on which he wrote his annotations, such as the words for the crowd members in Act 2. This has been very usefully reproduced by Gates in her edition of *Votes for women!* In an addenda she notes the major differences between this original and the later version published in London by Mills and Boon in 1909, which was used for the reprint in D. Spender and C. Hayman (eds), *How the vote was won and other suffragette plays* (London, Methuen, 1985).
20 Stowell, *A stage*, p. 27. A famous photograph of the scene, first published in *The Sketch* (London, 15 May 1907) is reproduced in D. Kennedy, *Granville Barker and the dream of theatre* (Cambridge, Cambridge University Press, 1985), p. 60. Both Kennedy and Stowell include quotes from the countless positive reviews concerning the verisimilitude of Act 2. A further selection of reviews, American as well as British, is discussed in Jane Marcus, *Elizabeth Robins* (Ph.D. dissertation, Northwestern University, 1973).
21 A typescript of detailed notes of a meeting in Hyde Park, dated 21 October 1906 and presumably taken for ER by a stenographer, is lodged in the Robins Collection at the Fales. From ER's published letters it is likely that she herself witnessed the early WSPU rally in Trafalgar Square on 19 May 1906, reported in *The Times*, 21 May 1906 p. 7 and recalled by E. Sylvia Pankhurst in *The suffragette* (London, Gay and Hancock, 1911), pp. 79–80, and *The suffragette movement*, p. 212, as 'the first great open air public meeting for Women's Suffrage ever held in London'. Mary Gawthorpe left an account of her suffrage activities in *Up the hill to Holloway* (Maine, Traversity Press, 1962).
22 H. W. Nevinson wrote of the difficulty of 'speaking against the tumult' created by vast and mainly hostile audiences at open-air meetings, and of his admiration for both Emmeline and Christabel Pankhurst under such circumstances, in *Fire of life* (London, Nisbet, 1935), pp. 251–3.
23 A history of the Actresses' Franchise League has been constructed in Holledge, *Innocent flowers*. There is, so far, no such detailed history of the Women Writers Suffrage League, although a brief account is given in Elaine Showalter, *A literature of their own: British women novelists from Brontë to Lessing* (London, Virago, 1978), pp. 218–20.
24 *The Stage* (24 December 1908) and *Votes for Women*, vol. 2 (24 December 1908), p. 211.
25 See *Stage Year Book*, 1910, p.19, which attributes the founding to Mrs Forbes-Robertson, Winifred Mayo, Sime Seruya and Adeline Bourne, an attribution corroborated by *The Green*

Room Book, 1909, p. 665, although news items in The Era in 1907–8 indicate that much preparatory work had been carried out by other actresses who were members of WSPU, such as Jeanette Steer, in connection with the great London suffrage parades. Correspondence in the HRHRC archive shows that ER acted as a go-between for Emmeline Pankhurst and Gertrude Elliott to facilitate a drawing-room meeting hosted by Elliott, at which Pankhurst spoke to recruit for AFL.

26 The Era (17 April 1909), p. 21.
27 Ibid.
28 Letter to The Times (24 June 1912), republished in Votes for Women, vol. 5 (28 June 1912) p. 632. His speech on 18 March 1913 was reported briefly in Votes for Women, vol. 6 (29 March 1913), p. 368.
29 'A Declaration of Faith', Votes for Women, vol. 2 (11 February 1909), p. 326.
30 JHC and ME Cousins, We two together (Madras, Ganesh, 1950), p.171.
31 Johnston Forbes-Robertson, A player under three reigns (London, Fisher Unwin, 1925). Ellen Terry played the actress Nance Oldfield, as The Times enthusiastically reported (13 November, 1909), p. 12. For Ellen Terry's suffrage appearance, see also J. Melville, Ellen and Edy: a biography of Ellen Terry and her daughter, Edith Craig, 1847–1947 (London, Pandora, 1987), p. 210.
32 See the letter from GBS to Bertha Newcombe, Secretary of the Civic and Dramatic Guild, 14 May 1909, in G. B. Shaw, Collected letters 1898–1910 ed. Dan H. Lawrence (London, Reinhardt, 1972), p. 843. (This indicates that the play was directed by Barker.) The vertical file on Shaw at HRHRC includes an original playbill for the second production of Press cuttings, which was first published in German, and later in Translations and tomfooleries (London, Constable, 1926). The play is discussed by Stowell, A stage, pp. 63–4, who follows Holledge, Innocent flowers, pp. 68–9, in her analysis. The part of the General was played by the actor/playwright Harold Chapin (1886–1915) at the AFL's benefit for the WFL on 8 July 1910. Chapin's mother, the actress Alice Chapin, was a member of AFL whose one-act suffrage play, At the gates, was performed by AFL for the WFL at Caxton Hall, 1 March 1910, with both Harold and Alice acting and his sister Elsie in the lead, The Vote (12 March 1910), p. 230. An abridged version of the play is published in The Vote (9 December 1909), p. 94. Harold himself did not write any suffrage plays.
33 Lisa Tickner, The spectacle of women: imagery of the suffrage campaign, 1907–14 (London, Chatto, 1987), pp. 20–4. Housman also wrote a couple of short, non-suffrage plays, for an AFL entertainment to raise funds for the SA.
34 L. Housman, The unexpected years (London, Cape, 1937), p. 275.
35 Tickner, The spectacle, pp. 94, 116–17; there is a photograph of it on p. 118, but it has apparently not survived.
36 L. Housman, Alice in Ganderland (London, Women's Press, 1913). The production was reviewed in The Era (4 November 1911), p. 11 and The Times (28 October 1911), p. 10, as well as Votes for Women, vol. 5, (3 November 1911), p. 70. Zangwill's 'Prologue' was printed in Votes for Women, vol 5, (5 January 1912), p. 221. The programme also included Act 2 of Votes for women!, produced by Harold Chapin, with Agnes Thomas as Working Woman, and Harold Chapin as Mr Pilcher.
37 Reviewed in The Era, 17 February 1912.
38 Housman, The unexpected, p. 244–8. Housman was the only man on the advisory committee of the Pioneer Players, see C. Dymkowski, 'Entertaining ideas: Edy Craig and the Pioneer Players', in The new woman and her sisters: feminism and the theatre 1850–1914 (Hemel Hempstead, Harvester, 1992), p. 231, fn. 4. Craig's production, at the Savoy Theatre, 26 November 1911, was reviewed in Votes for Women by Emily Wilding Davison (1 December 1911), p. 141, who claimed that the reason for the play's censorship was that it was 'too unanswerable and eloquent a case for the emancipation of women'.
39 Housman, Unexpected, p.247.
40 The Englishwoman, vol. 8 (1910); 'The Greek Suffragettes', Votes for Women, vol. 3 (17 March 1911), p. 386.

41 *Votes for Women*, vol. 3 (25 Novemebr 1910), p. 130.

42 Shaw, *Collected letters*, p. 280. Sonja Lorachs has pointed that it was 'his first great success', in one of the few (only?) critical studies of the play, *The unwomanly woman in Bernard Shaw's drama, and her social and political background* (Uppsala, 1973), ch. 4, p. 113.

43 *Illustrated Play Pictorial* (London, 1911) no page number. See B. Shaw, *Fanny's first play* (Harmondsworth, Penguin, 1987), pp. 182 and 140.

44 *The Era* (22 April 1911), p. 17.

45 *Ibid.*, (8 March 1913), p. 12; (19 November 1913), p. 20.

46 H. W. Nevinson, *Fire of life*, pp. 260–1.

47 *Ibid.*, p. 263.

48 Housman, *Unexpected*, p. 277–8.

49 Max Beerbohm, 'Miss Robins' "Tract"', *The Saturday Review*, (13 April 1907), p. 103ff. H. W. Nevinson, 'Votes for women', *Essays in freedom* (London, Duckworth, 1909) pp. 221–6.

50 *Votes for Women*, vol. 6 (5 September 1913), p. 700.

51 *Ibid.*, vol. 5 (29 March 1912), p. 409 and vol. 3 (21 October 1910), p. 38. The cultural contest over the *iconographic* representation of the suffragette has been traced in brilliant detail and related to the political arguments by Lisa Tickner in *Spectacle*.

52 Zangwill, 'Prologue'. See fn. 36.

53 Autograph letter, ER to FB, 17 January 1907, in the Fales.

11

Christabel Pankhurst and the Women's Social and Political Union

THE Women's Social and Political Union (WSPU) was founded on 10 October 1903 by Emmeline Pankhurst and her eldest daughter Christabel, to campaign for votes for women on the same terms as men.[1] Both women were members of the Independent Labour Party (ILP) and, tired of its failure to make women's enfranchisement a key policy issue, decided that a new organisation and approach was necessary. Thus, Emmeline Pankhurst discussed the situation on 9 October 1903 with a small group of other women ILP supporters whom she invited to a meeting at her house at 62 Nelson Street, Manchester, the following day. The resolve was, she recollected, that the WSPU would limit its membership exclusively to women, keep free from affiliation to any political party and be satisfied 'with nothing but action on our question. Deeds, not words, was to be our permanent motto'.[2] Emmeline Pankhurst, as head of the WSPU, and Christabel as the main policy maker,[3] the 'supreme tactician',[4] became well known and admired figures during their suffrage days.[4] Yet Christabel Pankhurst is mainly presented in the secondary sources as a ruthless, cold, ambitious, unscrupulous, autocratic, snobbish, calculating, selfish, right-wing and unco-operative opportunist, especially in the only full length biography published of her, David Mitchell's *Queen Christabel*.[5] My aim in this chapter is to build upon that minority of more sympathetic representations and to offer a reassessment of this 'much misunderstood' feminist.[6]

The WSPU during its early years, although not officially affiliated to the ILP, had close links with it, as noted earlier, through the joint membership of a number of its members, including Emmeline Pankhurst's other two daughters, Sylvia and Adela. Yet Christabel warned, on a number of occasions, that the interests of women would not necessarily be safe 'in the hands of the men's Labour party'.[7] Working men, she pointed out, 'are as unjust to women as are those of other classes'.[8] Such views about what she called the 'tyranny of sex' rather than of social class did not endear her to many socialists.[9] Both she and her mother

believed that the injustices which women experienced in society, including exclusion from the political franchise, could be attributed to the power of men, a
world-view that sharply differed from socialist feminists who emphasised social
class inequalities under capitalism, including class conflict between women.[10]
Furthermore, Christabel increasingly realised the limitations of the peaceful work
that the WSPU engaged in during these early years when speaking at trade
union gatherings, debating societies, in parks and fairgrounds and at street corners, and decided upon a more confrontational approach.[11]

   Christabel Pankhurst's great strength as a leader of the WSPU was her
political flair, claimed Frederick Pethick-Lawrence. 'What she loved', asserted
Henry Woodd Nevinson, 'was the political tactics, the conflict with realities, with
the tricks of statesmen and the evasions of party interest'.[12] Such qualities are
clearly evident in the new strategy she devised to ensure that the issue of
women's suffrage became newsworthy. Thus, after careful planning, Christabel
and Annie Kenney, a working-class recruit to the WSPU, interrupted a Liberal
Party meeting on 13 October 1905 by shouting out 'Will the Liberal Government
give votes to women?' As expected, both young women were dragged outside,
where Christabel deliberately committed the offence of 'spitting' at a policeman
in order to court arrest.[13] Rather than pay a fine, both chose imprisonment, a
decision which brought about the desired result of widespread publicity for the
women's cause. The 'unwomanly' tactic of heckling politicians was quickly
adopted as an effective political tool by other militants. Indeed, one present-day
writer claims that women who learnt from Christabel Pankhurst to interrupt
male political discourse and speak in their own voice, for their own cause, were
taking one of the most important steps in the history of women.[14] For Christabel, such assertive action brought dignity to women who for years had accepted
their subordinate status. She believed that in a man-made world, militancy in
women meant 'the putting off of the slave *spirit*',[15] a challenge to traditional
notions of femininity. As she told a journalist in 1908, women must banish the
idea that 'weakness is womanliness. Women must be self-reliant and strong'.[16]

   After graduating from Manchester University in July 1906, with a first-class
honours degree in law, Christabel moved to London where she took up the post
of chief WSPU organiser on a salary of £2 10s (£2.50) per week. By this time,
Emmeline Pethick-Lawrence, a wealthy woman with competent administrative
skills, had been appointed treasurer of the Union and Christabel lived with her
and her husband Frederick for the next six years. Surveying the London work,
Christabel decided it was too dependent for its demonstrations on ILP working-
class women in the East End, and she thus re-emphasised one of the key principles on which the WSPU had been founded, namely that it should be based
on 'no class distinctions' and should include 'women of all classes'.[17] An opportunity to reaffirm this policy was presented at the campaigning before the Cockermouth by-election on 3 August 1906, when Christabel announced that

henceforward the WSPU would oppose not only all Liberal and Tory parliamentary candidates, but also be independent of Labour men. While Emmeline Pankhust shared this view, Sylvia and Adela did not.[18] Neither did the Manchester and Salford Branch of the ILP, of which Christabel was a member. The call for her resignation, however, together with that of her fellow co-worker Teresa Billington-Greig, was not supported by the main Manchester branch.[19] Christabel had no regrets about her action, since women who would not have supported a Labour-affiliated organisation began to join the WSPU, which expanded by 28 February 1907 to forty-seven branches with nine paid organisers.[20] The process of her withdrawal from involvement with the ILP was completed in April 1907 when, after the annual ILP conference, both Christabel and Emmeline Pankhurst resigned their membership.

The rift between the pro-ILP WSPU women and those favouring an independent policy widened during the summer of 1907, with the former group suggesting that the Union conference planned for October, in accordance with the 1906 constitution, should debate the issue of democracy and the election of members to the central committee. While Emmeline Pankhurst was in the North of England, unaware of these problems, Christabel and Emmeline Pethick-Lawrence spent many 'sleepless nights' trying to sort out the 'pros and cons'; Christable 'never doubted' that the tactics she had evolved would succeed in winning the cause, and they both feared that control by the leaders over the direction of policy would be weakened if a democratic structure was introduced.[21] When Emmeline Pankhurst returned to WSPU headquarters at Clements Inn and was told of the crisis, she replied, 'I shall tear up the constitution'.[22] The next day she informed the central committee that she had decided to select a new committee, abandon the conference and abolish that part of the constitution relating to organisation; furthermore, all members would be required to sign a pledge endorsing the objects and methods of the Union, including an undertaking not to support the candidates of any political party at parliamentary elections until women had obtained the parliamentary vote.[23] Charlotte Despard, Teresa Billington-Greig, Edith How Martyn and Caroline Hodgson refused to accept the situation, and left to form another militant organisation, later called the Women's Freedom League (WFL).[24] A charismatic and gifted speaker, Emmeline Pankhurst spent most of the next five years travelling around the country, trying to convert the opposition to the women's cause and acting as an inspirational force for WSPU members. Although she was consulted on major policy matters, the day-to-day administration of the WSPU fell to Christabel and the Pethick-Lawrences. And it was Christabel in particular who played the 'pivotal role',[25] emerging as a strong, fearless and imaginative strategist.

She planned spectacular events that attracted media attention and demonstrated the collective power of women. In 1908, for example, she organised a Women's Parliament, held on 11, 12 and 13 February, and a mass meeting in

Hyde Park on Sunday, 21 June. Such events were organised partly in the belief that a women's enfranchisement measure would be successfully introduced that year, and partly in response to the statement of the Liberal MP Herbert Asquith, rumoured to become the next Prime Minister after Campbell-Bannerman, that he would withdraw his opposition to women's suffrage if it could be 'proved' that women desired the vote.[26] A raid on the House of Commons on 11 February, the day of the opening of the Women's Parliament, was especially imaginative and made Christabel Pankhurst's name a household word. While she was speaking to WSPU members at Caxton Hall, warning that women in the past had trusted too much to talk and too little to action, a pantechnicon van, borrowed from a furniture removers, drew up outside the Commons and about twenty to thirty women jumped out in an attempt to gain entrance. They were unsuccessful, as were two later deputations to the Commons that day, some fifty women in all being arrested and sent to prison.[27] The publicity given to the 'Trojan Horse', as it became known, gave Christabel a high public profile, especially since a poem about her, written by one of the women prisoners, was smuggled out for publication and sung to the tune of a well-known nursery rhyme:

Sing a song of Christabel's clever little plan
Four and twenty Suffragettes packed in a van
When the van was opened they to the Commons ran
Wasn't that a dainty dish for Campbell-Bannerman.[28]

Similarly, the description of the gathering of between 250,000–500,000 men and women on 21 June as 'magnificent', 'a beacon day in the women's movement', was echoed by many.[29] WSPU women wore white dresses with favours of purple or green (the Union's colours of white, purple and green represented purity, dignity and hope, respectively). As 700 banners on two-foot long poles fluttered, Christabel, speaking from one of twenty platforms, discarded her graduate gown and cap in the heat and handled the crowds well, as they shouted 'We want Chrissie'. 'She was born to command crowds', asserted the *Daily News*.[30] Cautiously, however, she had already warned that if the government still refused to act after this display of support, 'then we shall know that great meetings ... fail as a means of directly influencing the action of the Government. We shall then be obliged to rely more than ever on militant methods.'[31] On 30 June 1908, without the knowledge of the WSPU leaders, Mary Leigh and Edith New broke two of Prime Minister Asquith's windows.[32] Although Mary Leigh was reputed to have said when arrested; 'It will be bombs next time',[33] Christabel carefully ignored this comment in her public statement of support for the women. 'Everyone must admire the courage and devotion which prompted the act', she wrote in *Votes for Women*, edited by the Pethick-Lawrences as the newspaper of the WSPU, 'and recognise the surprising fact to be, not that the thing has been done now, but that it was not done before'.[34]

A clever, articulate woman, Christabel 'saturated her mind with politics',[35] reading diligently the daily papers and writings of key politicians. Part of the public fascination with her, claimed her sister Sylvia, lay in the fact that she was young, graceful, slender, 'with the flawless colouring of a briar rose', embellishments that softened the 'sterner features of her discourse'. But the real secret of Christabel's attraction, continued Sylvia, was her audacity and assurance.[36] In the autumn of 1908, when the government failed to place in its programme a women's suffrage bill that had earlier passed its second reading, Christabel responded by having printed in the Union's colours thousands of handbills inviting men and women to 'Help the Suffragettes to Rush the House of Commons' on Tuesday, 13 October at 7.30'. Summonses were issued against Emmeline Pankhurst, Flora Drummond and Christabel to appear at Bow Street Court, alleging that they were guilty of conduct likely to provoke a breach of the peace. The trial, which began on 14 October, had to go into recess so that Christabel, for the defence, could gather evidence. In a brilliant move, two Cabinet Ministers, Gladstone and Lloyd George, were subpoenaed as witnesses since both had been present at WSPU demonstrations on 13 and 11 October, respectively. In another audacious tactic, the twenty-eight-year-old Christabel herself acted as lawyer for the trio when court proceedings were resumed on 21 October. She had already been called 'Suffragette Portia',[37] and it was a title that remained during the trial, as, with her quick, legally trained mind, she stated her case, cross-examined the two Cabinet Ministers and teased out what the term 'rush' meant. Although the women were found guilty and, since they refused to be bound over to keep the peace, sent to prison, the Bow Street trial was a wonderful publicity stunt, 'like a suffrage meeting attended by millions'.[38] By the end of February 1909 the WSPU had tripled its income in comparison with the previous year; furthermore, there were now also eleven regional offices, thirty paid organisers and regular 'At Home' meetings in the Queen's Hall, London, attracting about a thousand people each week.[39]

Events took a different direction in June 1909 when Marion Wallace Dunlop, sentenced to one month's imprisonment, announced that she would no longer eat food until her request to be treated as a political prisoner and placed in the privileged First Division, as befitted a political offender, was granted. After fasting for ninety-one hours, she was released. The hunger strike was quickly adopted by other imprisoned suffragettes as a form of passive resistance against the government's policy. Although it had been initiated without the prior knowledge of the WSPU leaders, it was welcomed as yet another tool to force the government's hand. On 22 July a jubilant Christabel wrote to the Tory Arthur Balfour saying that the militants had learnt to starve themselves out of prison, a power they would continue to use – unless the government preferred to let them die, which she doubted.[40] Confident in the WSPU's legal advice that forcible feeding by the prison authorities would be illegal, Christabel also believed, erroneously, that it could not be carried out 'with any real effect if the prisoners make a resistance'.[41]

In September, when imprisoned militants in Birmingham's Winson Green Prison began hunger strikes, the government responded with forcible feeding. The act was accompanied by considerable force, as the prisoners were held down by wardresses and rubber tubes inserted into struggling bodies. Seen as symbolic rape by a powerful male state against defenceless women, forcible feeding created amongst the WSPU leadership and rank and file feelings of shock, indignation, burning anger and disgust while, at the same time, strengthening their resolve to fight for the women's cause. On 29 September the leaders decided to take legal action against the Home Secretary, the same day that their letter appeared in The Times accusing the government of a 'horrible outrage' that 'violated bodies'.[42] A number of male supporters also voiced concerns. A memorial condemning forcible feeding was signed by 116 doctors, and two well-known liberal journalists, Henry Woodd Nevinson and Henry Brailsford, resigned from the Daily News in protest against their editor's support for the action of the prison authorities.[43]

New Year's Day 1910 saw Christabel in defiant mood as she protested to the Home Secretary about the forcible feeding of two remand prisoners, Selina Martin and Leslie Hall, in Walton Gaol, Liverpool; furthermore, after being kept in chains at night, Selina Martin had been frogmarched, head bumping on each step as she was carried up a flight of stairs. 'At one time', Christabel chided Gladstone, 'it would not have been thought possible such things could happen in this country'.[44] Although the brutality of the incident was widely reported, public interest soon focused on the forthcoming general election which, initially, it seemed the Tories would win. However, they held only 273 seats, the Liberals 275, the Irish Nationalists 82 and Labour 40, and it was Asquith, not Balfour, who formed the new government, only too aware that the passing of any new legislation would be dependent on the support of MPs outside his own party.[46] Realising that the political situation might be useful to the women's cause, Brailsford set about forming an all-party Conciliation Committee for Women's Suffrage to which the WSPU leaders ultimately agreed. Christabel was hopeful that a settlement could be reach by 'entirely peaceful means' since she believed that mild militancy 'was more or less played out'.[46] Thus, on 31 January 1910, Emmeline Pankhurst announced the suspension of militant tactics for the present, a 'truce' with the government during which only peaceful and constitutional methods would be used.

Militancy remained suspended until 21 November 1911, apart from one week during November 1910. During 1910 the demonstration on Saturday, 18 June held a special significance for Christabel, since although it was organised by the WSPU and included members from twenty other suffrage groups, including the men's societies, it was an outward expression of women's solidarity, comradeship and bonding in a common cause. Believing that women's interests transcended those of social class, and that in a man-made world there was more that united than divided women, she wrote:

[T]he Procession will include women who are rich as well as those who are poor, and women of every social degree. Everything which separates will be forgotten, and only that which unites will be remembered ... it will be a festival at which we shall celebrate the sisterhood of women. According to the old tale of men's making, it is not in women to unite and to work with one another. Women have only now discovered the falsity of this, and they are rejoicing in their new-found sisterhood.[47]

Optimistically, she hoped that such a display would help to grant women their 'political birthright'.[48] However, although a second reading of the Conciliation Bill was passed in July, it was announced on 12 November that it would not be possible for the Commons to find time for a women's suffrage bill that year. Feeling betrayed, the WSPU leaders renewed their threat of militancy and held a demonstration, led by Emmeline Pankhurst, to the Commons on 18 November, the day of the opening of parliament. In their attempt to force the women back, the police committed a range of unprecedented physical and sexual assaults – kicking, punching, grabbing of breasts and thighs, twisting of arms, thrusting of knees between legs and throwing women to the ground. Some members of the Men's Political Union rushed to WSPU headquarters to tell Christabel, who was working in her office, what was happening on this 'Black Friday', as it became known. 'She went quite pale', recollected Jessie Kenney.[49] Conscious that she would need to rally the women after such brutality, the next day Christabel sent a letter to every demonstrator praising their courage and calling each to a meeting on 21 and 22 November to determine any necessary further action.[50] On 22 November, Asquith announced that the government would give facilities for a women's suffrage bill so framed 'as to admit of free amendment' not during the next session but during the next parliament.[51] The WSPU, in session at Caxton Hall, regarded this as so unsatisfactory that Emmeline Pankhurst announced a immediate deputation to 10 Downing Street. During the ensuing struggle with the police, windows were broken and 159 women arrested. The members of the Conciliation Committee, strongly disapproving of WSPU tactics, argued that conciliation and militancy could not go hand in hand. The Union suspended any further militancy although it did campaign against government candidates in fifty constituencies in the general election of December 1910.[52]

Although the same government was in office after the general election, with a distribution of seats in the new Commons being nearly the same as the old, 1911 began in much hope. The MP Sir George Kemp gained first place in the private members' ballot and promised to introduce a revised Conciliation Bill, the second reading of which was secured for 5 May. Christabel Pankhurst, as chief WSPU organiser, was busy arranging a number of large and small meetings for the year, the sixth year in which the WSPU had worked with 'constantly increasing intensity in an ascending campaign ... Tired in body we could be, but the enemy never knew it'.[53] 'If we don't get the thing settled this year more drastic measures will have to be employed', she confided to Elizabeth Robins, WSPU member and well-known actress. 'We simply will not stand any more trickery & dishonesty.'[54] The revised bill passed its second reading with a large majority, and Prime Minister Asquith repeated his 'promise' in regard to facilities.[55] However, many criticisms about the proposed measure were voiced, especially by Labour and Liberal MPs who feared that the women to be enfranchised, being of the propertied classes, would vote Conservative. Many Labour supporters favoured instead 'adult suffrage', a term that was somewhat ambiguous, since, as Holton notes, it could connote either universal suffrage with both property and sex disqualifications removed, or the extension of the existing sex-exclusive franchise to all adult men.[56] Christabel was unmoved by these criticisms since she knew that few 'adultists' formulated their demands in terms of both women and men and were suspected of being 'Anti-Suffragists in disguise'.[57] But, more importantly, her main concern was not the numbers of women to be enfranchised, nor their political leanings, but the removal of the discrimination that prevented women voting on equal terms with men.[58] When Asquith announced on 7 November that the government would introduce next session a Manhood Suffrage Bill that could be amended to include women, she angrily claimed that the 'whole crooked and discreditable' scheme to cheat women of the vote was inspired by Lloyd George,[59] and she appealed for a thousand women to march to Westminster on 21 November. While the demonstration was taking place on the appointed day, a smaller group, armed with bags of stones and hammers, broke windows of government offices and businesses. In all, 220 women and 3 men were arrested.[60] When Lloyd George claimed a few days later that the Conciliation Bill had been torpedoed by the WSPU, any hopes for its success vanished as Christabel assertively defended the 'broken windows' policy: 'Realising the great evils that arise from women's disenfranchisement, we say that the breaking of windows is a small price to pay for the abolition of such evils'.[61] Another militant, Emily Wilding Davison, was arrested on 15 December for attempting to set fire to a letter-box, something which she claimed she had already done to two other post-boxes earlier that day, acting entirely on her 'own responsibility'.[62] Over the next two years such acts of freelance militancy became common as the government refused to grant women's suffrage.

On the evening of 1 March 1912, the Union engaged in an unannounced skirmish: at 5.45p.m. sharp windows of well-known shops in the West End of London as well as government offices were smashed, at a cost of about £5,000. Nine women were arrested, including Emmeline Pankhurst.[63] Although the event was well planned, Christabel was protective of the offenders and professed to a journalist that she knew very little about it apart from the fact that it was arranged to have a window-smashing campaign. 'The fact that the miners are going to get legislation because they have made themselves a nuisance is a direct incitement to women to endeavour to obtain a similar privilege', she wryly commented. 'We are persuaded', she continued, 'that the Government will not do anything until they are forced'.[64] Further widespread window-smashing action took place on 4 March, with ninety-six arrests.[65] The following evening, the police invaded WSPU headquarters with a warrant for the arrest of the Pethick-Lawrences, Christabel and Emmeline Pankhurst, and Mabel Tuke (the latter two were already in prison) on charges of conspiracy. Christabel, however, no longer lived at Clement's Inn but at a flat nearby, and informed of the arrest of the Pethick-Lawrences, spent the night in hiding. Alone, facing a great problem, she decided that if she remained in England she, too, would be imprisoned. Fearful that the movement would be crushed, she fled to Paris knowing that a political offender was not liable to extradition. Before she left, Christabel wrote to Annie Kenney, telling her that if she failed to escape, Annie was to take control of the movement until she was set free.[66]

In Paris, Christabel attempted single-handedly to lead the WSPU and write copy for *Votes for Women* and, from October 1912, a new WSPU newspaper, the *Suffragette*. Annie and Jessie Kenney, as trusted couriers, travelled regularly to see her as did Emmeline Pankhurst, in between imprisonments. Living at a distance, Christabel often did not know what kind of deeds the militants would engage in, as when Mary Leigh and Gladys Evans were arrested in Dublin on 18 July for, amongst other things, setting fire to the Theatre Royal where Asquith was present. Nevertheless, like Emmeline Pankhurst, she determined to stand by such action, knowing that the rank and file would 'respect life and hurt no one', a golden rule of WSPU policy.[67] Such support for acts of arson, plus the escalating scale of violence, however, lead to disagreements with Emmeline and Frederick Pethick-Lawrence.

On their return in October from a visit to Canada, the Pethick-Lawrences were shattered to be told by Emmeline Pankhurst that she intended to sever their connection with the WSPU. Christabel decided to cross to England, thus risking detection, in order to convince them that she and her mother were united in the matter.[68] Privately, however, she had 'torn allegiance ... was unhappy, distressed', although 'Godfather' (Fred) had begun to 'push himself to the fore, take more and more part on the platform'.[69] Although many WSPU members were shocked by the way in which the Pethick-Lawrences were expelled from the Union, most seemed to have rallied behind the Pankhursts. As Emmeline Pankhurst, in a rousing speech, invited women to 'be militant each in your own way',[70] and Christabel urged that 'Now, if ever, self-respecting women are stirred to rebellion',[71] widespread destruction of mail in letter-boxes became common. The burning of letters, argued Christabel, was but a 'serious remedy for a far more serious disease', namely the inequalities that women, especially poor, underpaid, working-class women, experienced as a disenfranchised sex.[72] From now on, militancy was driven further underground. The old spectacular, large scale demonstrations of the past were, with the exception of Emily Wilding Davison's funeral in June 1913, no more, as the WSPU found it difficult to hold outdoor meetings.[73]

On 27 January 1913 the militants felt cheated again when the government withdrew the Franchise Bill and offered, instead, a pledge for a private member's bill, not that year, but the next.[74] That evening, Emmeline Pankhurst denounced the government's trickery and proclaimed to an enthusiastic audience: 'if we are to succeed we must use guerilla warfare ... we have to take the enemy unawares'.[75] Thus began an underground campaign of arson, cutting telegraph and telephone wires, pouring acid on golf courses and mass breaking of shop windows in London's West End. When some of these militants were asked in court whether Christabel Pankhurst was 'directing affairs', they declined to discuss the matter.[76] However, articles in the Suffragette powerfully announced her views. The attempt by the government to coerce the militants, she pointed out, had been a 'ghastly failure' because the spirit of women was stronger than all the material forces at the disposal of the state.[77] After a bomb exploded in Lloyd George's partly completed house in Surrey, wrecking five rooms, Christabel warned that, without violence, nothing was gained from rulers. 'We have all the money necessary for intensifying our propaganda', she boasted. Emmeline Pankhurst, who did not know about the bombing beforehand, nevertheless accepted 'full responsibility' for the deed.[78] On 24 February she was arrested on the charge of inciting to blow up Lloyd George's house.

The increasing acts of violence by the militants was now met with increasing attempts by the government to restrict Union activities by prohibiting meetings and raiding the central offices and the printer.[79] Christabel, however, despite the gravity of the situation, especially after the trusted Annie Kenney was arrested on 1 May, determined to keep things going, including getting copy to the press on time. Jessie Kenney recollected:

> Militants in Britain ... thought C and I had an easy time of it. But it wasn't so. The tension was terrific. C felt it terribly, though she never showed it much ... she seldom showed the strain she was under. For make no mistake, she kept the Movement together by sheer willpower. Her output for the Suffragette alone was tremendous : she covered pages and pages at tremendous speed in her almost illegible scrawl (how the printers coped I don't know), and then I would post the copy from near the Gare du Nord about midnight or early hours of morning.[80]

On 25 April 1913 royal assent was given to the Prisoners' Temporary Discharge for Ill-Health Act, which allowed prisoners who had damaged their health through their own conduct to be released into the community and then, once fit, to be re-arrested to continue their sentence. Christabel, like many others, saw the 'Cat and Mouse Act', as it became known, as a further act of repression against forcibly fed militants ('Mice') who could be released on a licence and 'clawed' back, at the pleasure of the state ('Cat'). Indeed, to her, the government and state came increasingly to represent male oppressive power and everything that was evil. The men who have vainly tried to break the spirit of the militants in prison by torture, she angrily pronounced, are at last driven to bear witness that it is a spirit unbreakable – 'in fighting against evil, the few are stronger than the many, women stronger than men'.[81] The themes of the double sexual standard, prostitution and VD became more prominent in her writings.[82] She expounded how, in a male-ordered society, where women were kept in a subservient position and economic dependence, prostitution ('the Social Evil') was the chief fruit of women's slavery. As a result, the nation was poisoned morally and physically. 'The cure of the social evil', she explained, 'is to have stronger women and purer men. That cure will come with and through the vote. Admit women to citizenship and ... by altering their whole position you raise them in their own estimation and in that of men.' She also insisted that, because of white slavery, the human race was affected by the scourge of VD, and quoted from a doctor at a women's hospital who commented that most of the cases of VD that came before him were those of innocent women infected by their husbands.[83] Militancy was doing a work of 'purification' in the relationships between men and women and when this work was done, cleanness, respect and trust would arrive and 'perfect equality and justice' in the partnership between men and women.[84] Although most historians have labelled such views as prudish,[85] Jane Marcus suggests that Christabel was deliberately fanning the flames of sex hatred as a spur to revolutionary violence by women. Similarly, Margaret Jackson points out that for Christabel to demand an equal moral standard for men and women was a rational, political response to a system of male power which institutionalised female sexual slavery in its laws and practices, and justified it in terms of men's biological needs.[86]

The sentencing of Emmeline Pankhurst on 3 April 1913 to three years of penal servitude worried Union members and especially Christabel, the favourite daughter and close confidante, since there were fears she would die (she refused food, but was not force-fed). Her release on a license (which she promptly tore up) in a grave condition on 12 April was an occasion for Christabel to condemn bitterly the government's 'murderous' 'Cat and Mouse' policy which was proving to women 'how ludicrous and contemptible and undignified and cruel the other sex can be at their worst'.[87]

Criticisms of Christabel's residence in Paris were voiced in print, particularly from ex-WSPU member Dora Marsden, who noted that while Emmeline Pankhurst faced repeated arrests, 'her daughter settled as a quiet pamphleteering suffragist abroad'.[88] Indeed, Morley and Stanley suggest that Christabel's central role in the WSPU had changed to that of a 'removed and almost mythical "leader over the water"', seen by only the very few or the very pushy.[89] By the time a collection of her articles about the double sexual standard had appeared in book form with the title *The great scourge and how to end it*, in December 1913, there had been a marked decline in new subscriptions to the WSPU.[90] Yet Christabel remained convinced of the effectiveness of militancy, claiming that the vote would be won when the WSPU had created a difficulty so great as to be found 'intolerable' by politicians.[91]

In mid-January Sylvia Pankhurst travelled to Paris, where Christabel told her that her East London Federation must be separate from the WSPU, since it was allied with the socialist movement, contrary to Union policy. The refusal to compromise over matters of principle, even for a member of her family, should have come as no surprise, since many years earlier Emmeline Pankhurst had told her less favoured daughter 'Christabel is not like other women; not like you and me; she will never be led away by her affections!'.[92] Yet Sylvia was grieved by what she termed her sister's 'ruthlessness. Her glorification of autocracy seemed to me remote indeed from the struggle we were waging ... I thought of many others who had been cast aside for some minor difference'.[93]

The government in Britain had now introduced a Plural Voting Bill which dealt with men's franchise and which, the Labour Party believed, would give it some electoral advantage but without removing the sex disqualification against women. A bitter Christabel accused the Labour Party of betraying women[94] and then turned her attack on the Church − 'When women are insulted − assaulted − tortured in prison, the Church whitewash brush in hand, rushes to the rescue of the Government's reputation'.[95] The scale of vandalism began to rise as Mary Richardson, on 10 March 1914, slashed the *Rokeby Venus* as a protest against the re-arrest, amid police brutality, of Emmeline Pankhurst (still subject to a three-year prison sentence). Fourteen other pictures were slashed and nine women were arrested between March and July, some fifteen public galleries being closed at this time.[96]

The announcement on 9 March 1914 by Sir Edward Carson that he would not commit the Ulster Unionists to women's suffrage, since the Unionists were divided on the issue, aroused deep anger amongst WSPU women. Christabel's contempt for the British government and men's political parties was deeper than ever: 'No Tory Government could possibly be worse than the present Liberal Government', she thundered;[97] nor was there any difference between the official Labour Party and the Liberal Party since the cause of votes for women had not profited in the smallest degree from the presence of Labour members in the Commons. 'For Suffragists to put their faith in any men's party, whatever it may call itself, is recklessly to disregard the lessons of the past forty years ... The truth is that women must work out their own salvation. Men will not do it for them'.[98]

On 21 May a deputation to petition the King ended in disaster when the women were roughly handled, and forty of them, including Emmeline Pankhurst (who was openly defying the continuation of her prison sentence) were arrested.[99]

Two days later Christabel received a telephone call from WSPU headquarters saying they had been raided; two further raids were made in June.[100] Union plans were now made in great secrecy in private homes, many members travelled by night and if correspondence was used pseudonyms were common; Christabel became 'Amy Richards' or 'S.A.L.'.[101] The arrest and re-arrest of Emmeline Pankhurst on 9 and 16 July, respectively, in a severely weakened state, deeply distressed Christabel, especially since the whiff of 'negotiations' on unacceptable terms was in the air. One month earlier, the socialist George Lansbury and Sylvia Pankhurst had privately met Lloyd George, who, believing that a general election would be held before the next parliament, declared that he would refuse to join a new Liberal Cabinet unless a reform bill was introduced giving votes to women on broad, general lines, the issue to be decided by a free vote in the Commons. In return for his written guarantees of this, all militancy had to be suspended.[102] Christabel, deeply suspicious of the duplicity of politicians, took the same uncompromising view as her mother on this matter. 'There is no room for negotiations as to the terms upon which women demand the Vote ... They are – that women shall vote on the same terms as men'.[103]

On 1 August 1914, with the threat of a world war looming, Christabel left Paris for Brittany, where her mother had gone to recuperate. Twelve days later Emmeline Pankhurst issued a circular to all WSPU members announcing a 'temporary suspension of activities'.[104] The long years of militancy during which Christabel Pankhurst had been the key WSPU strategist were over, although some ex-Union members joined other groupings that continued to campaign for women's enfranchisement, such as the Suffragettes of the WSPU, the Independent WSPU, the WFL and the United Suffragists.[105] In 1918 a partial victory was won when women over the age of 30 were granted the vote if they were householders, occupiers of property of £5 or more annual value, or university graduates. Women were not enfranchised on equal terms with men until 1928, when the property qualification was removed.

In 1936, WFL member Alison Neilans claimed:

> Whatever may be thought about the militant methods, they certainly had the effect of rousing the whole country to a passionate and most controversial discussion of every aspect of the equality demands and of women's status in the community ... Not all women were suffragists, but the majority were affected by the propaganda and became more independent, more able to stand up for themselves, more self-respecting and respected.[106]

It is in this context, that Christabel Pankhurst, a strong, uncompromising, principled, feminist leader, made her greatest contribution to womankind.

NOTES

1 At this time in Britain, only about 59 per cent of men could vote, since enfranchisement was based on the ownership or occupation of property of a minimum value. In addition to this qualification based on class divisions, there was also sex discrimination since no women could vote – see S. S. Holton, *Feminism and democracy: women's suffrage and reform politics in Britain 1900–1918* (Cambridge, Cambridge University Press, 1986), p. 53.

2 E. Pankhurst, *My own story* (London, Eveleigh Nash, 1914), p. 38. A common term for the WSPU was the 'Union', which I shall frequently use in this chapter.

3 A. Kenney, *Memories of a militant* (London, Edward Arnold, 1924), p. 193; Henry Nevinson, *More changes, more chances* (London, Nisbet and Co., 1925), p. 311.

4 A. Morley with L. Stanley, *The life and death of Emily Wilding Davison* (London, Women's Press, 1988), p. 176.

5 D. Mitchell, *Queen Christabel: a biography of Christabel Pankhurst* (London, MacDonald and Jane's, 1977) and also E. S. Pankhurst, *The suffragette movement* (London, Longmans, Green and Co., 1931); G. Dangerfield, *The strange death of liberal England* (London, MacGibbon and Kee, 1935); S. Rowbotham, *Hidden from history: 300 years of women's oppression and the fight against it* (London, Pluto Press, 1973); L. Garner, *Stepping stones to women's liberty* (London, Hutchinson Educational, 1984); M. Pugh, *Women and the women's movement in Britain 1914–1959* (London, Macmillan, 1992). For sympathetic accounts of Christabel see D. Spender, *Women of ideas and what men have done to them* (London, Routledge Kegan Paul, 1982), pp. 397–434; E. Sarah, 'Christabel Pankhurst: reclaiming her power', in D. Spender (ed.), *Feminist theorists: three centuries of women's intellectual traditions* (London, Women's Press, 1983), pp. 256–84; S. Kingsley Kent, *Sex and suffrage in Britain, 1860–1914* (New Jersey, Princeton University Press, 1987); J. Marcus, 'Introduction', in her edited *Suffrage and the Pankhursts*, (London, Routledge and Kegan Paul, 1987), pp. 1–17, and J. Purvis, 'A "pair of ... infernal queens"? A reassessment of the dominant representations of Emmeline and Christabel Pankhurst, first wave feminists in Edwardian Britain', *Women's History Review*, 5, 1996, pp. 259–80.

6 J. Marcus, 'Transatlantic sisterhood', *Signs*, 3, 1978, p. 745.

7 Letter to the Editor, *Labour Leader*, 13 March 1903.

8 C. Pankhurst, 'Women and the Independent Labour Party', *ILP News*, August 1903.

9 C. Pankhurst, *The parliamentary vote for women* (Manchester, Abel Heywood, n.d.), p. 16.

10 Purvis, 'A "pair of ... infernal queens"?, p. 268.

11 C. Pankhurst, *Unshackled: the story of how we won the vote* (London, Hutchinson, 1959), p. 44.

12 F. Pethick-Lawrence, 'Preface', in Pankhurst, *Unshackled*, p. 12; H. W. Nevinson, *Fire of life*, (London, James Nisbet and Co., 1935), p. 253. The Pethick-Lawrences did not hyphenate their names during the years they spent in the women's suffrage movement.

13 Pankhurst, *Unshackled*, p. 52, where Christabel states that it was 'not a real spit but only ... a "pout", a perfectly dry purse of the mouth'.

14 Marcus, 'Introduction', in her edited *Suffrage and the Pankhursts*, p. 9.

15 E. Pethick-Lawrence, *My part in a changing world* (London, Victor Gollancz, 1938), p. 151.

16 *Sunday Times*, 8 March 1908.

17 Pankhurst, *Unshackled*, p. 67.

18 *Ibid.*, p. 69.

19 Minute Book of the Manchester Central Branch of the ILP, entry for 4 September 1906, Manchester Public Library Archives.

20 A. Rosen, *Rise up women! The militant campaign of the Women's Social and Political Union 1903–1914* (London, Routledge and Kegan Paul, 1974), p. 83. It is impossible to give WSPU membership figures, since the records do not exist.

21 Pethick-Lawrence, *My part in a changing world*, pp. 175–6.

22 *Ibid.*, p. 176.

23 Rosen, *Rise up women!*, pp. 90–1.

24 See chapter 3 by Claire Eustance in this volume.

25 R. Pankhurst, 'Introduction', in Pankhurst, *Unshackled* (London, Cresset Women's Voices edn., 1987) n.p.n.
26 *Votes for Women*, January 1908, p. 54.
27 *The Times*, 12 February 1908; *Votes for Women*, 13 February 1908, Supplement, p. lxxiv.
28 Quoted in A. Raeburn, *The militant suffragettes* (London, Michael Joseph, 1973), p. 49. Raeburn suggest that Harry Pankhurst devised the scheme; however, Christabel was the strategist who put it into action.
29 *Daily News*, 22 June 1908; *The Times*, 22 June 1908.
30 *Ibid.* See also D. Atkinson *The suffragettes in pictures* (Stroud, Sutton Publishing, 1996), p. 11 and chapter 6 by Diane Atkinson in this volume.
31 *Votes for Women*, June 1908, p. 217.
32 *Daily Mirror* and *Daily Chronicle*, 1 July 1908. See chapter 12 by Michelle Myall in this volume.
33 *Daily Chronicle*, 2 July 1908.
34 *Votes for Women*, 9 July 1908, p. 297.
35 Pankhurst, *The suffragette movement*, p. 220.
36 *Ibid.*, p. 221.
37 *Evening News*, 14 October 1908.
38 Pethick-Lawrence, *My part in a changing world*, p. 205.
39 Rosen, *Rise up women!*, pp. 114–15.
40 Letter dated 22 July 1909 from C. Pankhurst to Mr Balfour, BL Balfour Papers, Ms Add 49793.
41 Letter dated 23 September 1909 from C. Pankhurst to Jennie Baines, quoted in S. Stanley Holton, *Suffrage days: stories from the women's suffrage movement* (London, Routledge and Kegan Paul, 1996), p. 146.
42 *The Times*, 29 September 1909, letter signed by Emmeline Pankhurst, Emmeline Pethick-Lawrence, Mabel Tuke and Christabel Pankhurst.
43 Cited in Rosen, *Rise up women!*, pp. 124–5.
44 Letter dated 1 January 1909 [1910] from C. Pankhurst to Dear Sir, Viscount Gladstone Papers, BL Ms Add 46066, f.211.
45 The figures are quoted in Rosen, *Rise up women!*, p. 130.
46 Letter dated 9 February 1910 from C. Pankhurst to J. King, MP, Fawcett Library Autograph Letter Collection, London Guildhall University. Pankhurst, *Unshackled*, p. 153.
47 *Votes for Women*, 20 May 1910, p. 55.
48 *Ibid.*, 22 April 1910, p. 478.
49 Raeburn, *The militant suffragettes*, p. 154.
50 Circular letter dated 19 November 1910 from C. Pankhurst to Dear Friend, Maud Arncliffe Sennet Collection, C121g1, vol. 12.
51 Rosen, *Rise up women!*, p. 143.
52 Quoted in *ibid.*, p. 144.
53 Pankhurst, *Unshackled*, pp. 171–2.
54 Letter dated 10 February 1910 from C. Pankhurst to E. Robins, E. Robins Papers, Harry Ransom Humanities Research Center, University of Texas, Austin.
55 Letter dated 16 June 1911 from H. Asquith to Lord Lytton, as printed in *The Times*, 17 June 1911.
56 Holton, *Feminism and democracy*, p. 54. See note 1.
57 *Votes for Women*, 10 November 1911, p. 88.
58 Pankhurst, *Unshackled*, p. 186.
59 *Votes for Women*, 10 November 1911, p. 88.
60 *The Times*, 22 November 1911.
61 *Votes for Women*, 1 December 1911, front page and p. 142.
62 *Standard*, 15 December 1911.
63 *Pall Mall Gazette*, 2 March 1912.
64 *The Times*, 2 March 1912.
65 *Ibid.*, 5 March 1912.

66 Pankhurst, *Unshackled*, pp. 202–4.
67 *Ibid.*, p. 222.
68 Lord Pethick-Lawrence, *Fate has been kind* (London, Hutchinson, n.d. [1942]), p. 99.
69 Interview dated 2 July 1965 by David Mitchell with Jessie Kenney, David Mitchell Collection, Museum of London.
70 At the Royal Albert Hall on 17 October 1912, Pankhurst, *My own story*, p. 265.
71 *Suffragette*, 18 October 1912, p. 6.
72 *Ibid.*, 6 December 1912, p. 114.
73 B. Harrison, *Separate spheres: the opposition to women's suffrage in Britain* (London, Croom Helm, 1978), p. 188; M. Pugh, *Women's suffrage in Britain 1867–1928* (London, The Historical Association, 1980), p. 24; L. Tickner, *The spectacle of women: imagery of the suffrage campaign 1907–14* (London, Chatto and Windus, 1987), p. 205.
74 Pankhurst, *Unshackled*, pp. 236–7.
75 *Suffragette*, 31 January 1913, p. 240.
76 *Pall Mall Gazette*, 29 January 1913.
77 *Suffragette*, 14 February 1913, p. 274.
78 *Pall Mall Gazette*, 21 February 1913. The bomb had been placed by Emily Wilding Davison and others.
79 See Rosen, *Rise up women!*, pp. 193–5.
80 Interview on 23 March 1964 by David Mitchell with Jessie Kenney, David Mitchell Collection, Museum of London.
81 *Suffragette*, 28 March 1913, p. 384.
82 The articles in the *Suffragette* were reprinted before the end of the year as a book – C. Pankhurst, *The great scourge and how to end it* (London, E. Pankhurst, 1913).
83 *Suffragette*, 11 April 1913, p. 426.
84 *Ibid.*, 11 April 1913, p. 426 and 2 May 1911, p. 492.
85 See, for example, Mitchell, *Queen Christabel*, pp. 227–30; P. Ferris, *Sex and the British, a twentieth-century history* (London, Michael Joseph, 1993).
86 Marcus, 'Introduction', p. 14; M. Jackson, *The real facts of life: feminism and the politics of sexuality c.1850–1940* (London, Taylor and Francis, 1994), p. 49. See also S. Jeffreys, *The spinster and her enemies, feminism and sexuality 1880–1930* (London, Pandora Press, 1985).
87 *Suffragette*, 18 April 1913, p. 450.
88 *New Freewoman*, 15 June 1913, p. 3.
89 Morley and Stanley, *The life and death of Emily Wilding Davison*, p. 176.
90 Rosen, *Rise up women!*, p. 212.
91 *Suffragette*, 16 January 1914, front page.
92 Pankhurst, *The life of Emmeline Pankhurst*, p. 47.
93 Pankhurst, *The suffragette movement*, p. 517.
94 *Suffragette*, 6 February, 1914, p. 565.
95 *Suffragette*, 13 February, 1914, p. 389.
96 R. Fowler, 'Why did suffragettes attack works of art?' *Journal of Women's History*, 2, Winter 1991, p. 109; A. E. Metcalfe, *Women's effort, a chronicle of British women's fifty years' struggle for citizenship (1865–1914)* (Oxford, Blackwell, 1917), p. 323.
97 *Suffragette*, 27 March 1914, p. 542.
98 *Ibid.*, 17 April 1914, p. 10.
99 *Daily Mirror*, 22 Mary 1914.
100 Pankhurst, *Unshackled*, p. 274.
101 Rosen, *Rise up women!*, pp. 234–5.
102 Pankhurst, *The suffragette movement*, p. 582.
103 *Suffragette*, 24 July 1914, p. 260.
104 Circular dated 13 August 1914 from E. Pankhurst to Dear Friend, Private Papers of June Purvis.
105 For further discussion of these groupings see chapter 5 by Krista Cowman in this volume.
106 A. Neilans, 'Changes in sex morality', in R. Strachey (ed.), *Our freedom and its results by five women* (London, Hogarth Press, 1936), pp. 220–1.

'No surrender!': the militancy of Mary Leigh, a working-class suffragette

Many academic studies on women's suffrage make a number of questionable assumptions about the Women's Social and Political Union (WSPU), the most common being that it was essentially a middle-class organisation. Andrew Rosen, for example, presents the WSPU as a middle-class grouping, arguing that the split with Labour in 1907 marked the end of the involvement of working women, *en masse*, and any pretence that it was an organisation for working women.[1] Similarly, Constance Rover assumes that the suffragettes were middle-class. In her examination of the second phase of militancy, she states:

> At the start of this activity, the stones were usually wrapped in paper to avoid injuring anyone accidentally. Sometimes in addition, they were attached to string, the end of which was held by the thrower. It is difficult to imagine anyone but a middle-class Englishwoman resorting to such a procedure.[2]

Brian Harrison also presents the suffragettes as 'respectable Edwardian middle-class women'.[3]

Even writers of the 'new' feminist women's history in Britain and North America have assumed too readily that the WSPU was exclusively a middle-class organisation. In Britain, in particular, a prevailing tradition of socialist-feminism has meant that few feminists researching women's lives in the past have challenged the dominant historical assessments of the WSPU as an organisation made up exclusively of women from the middle classes. Jill Liddington and Jill Norris, in their account of the contribution of the radical suffragists in the North of England, *'One hand tied behind us': the rise of the women's suffrage movement*, identify the WSPU very largely with Emmeline Pankhurst and her daughter Christabel, and suggest that the break with the Independent Labour Party led to 'working-class women [feeling] increasingly out of place in the WSPU'.[5] This, combined with the autocratic running of the Union and the move towards more violent militant methods, they suggest, resulted in many working-class women withdrawing their support to join more democratic suffrage organisations such as the National Union of Women's Suffrage Societies (NUWSS) and the Women's Freedom League (WFL).

Although the WSPU did receive much of its of support from middle-class women, many working-class women continued to be involved with the Union well into the final phases of militancy, and, as June Purvis has described, were among those imprisoned for the 'cause'.[6] The assumption that only well-to-do women were involved in the militant campaign has led not only to misrepresentation of the WSPU's membership, but also to neglect of the significant contribution made by working-class women within it. In this chapter I attempt to recover some of this lost history by focusing on the militant actions of Mary Leigh, a working-class suffragette, active in the WSPU between 1906 and 1913.

Born in Manchester in 1885, Mary Brown had been a schoolteacher before her marriage to Mr Leigh, a builder. Few details are known about her personal life[7] and her marriage, in particular, although Sylvia Pankhurst notes that Mr Leigh was present at the trial of one of Mary's early acts of militancy.[8] As a 'freelance militant', acting often without the knowledge or consent of the leaders, she was imprisoned on more than nine occasions, and was among the first of the suffrage prisoners to be forcibly fed, in September 1909. A potted biography in *Votes for Women*, June 1908, revealed that since 1907, Mary Leigh had been active in the 'cause' for at least a year. She had already been involved in work at by-elections on behalf of the WSPU, and had suffered a term of imprisonment in Holloway in March 1907, following her arrest during a march on St Stephen's Hall.[9] She had been in charge of the women's stall at the Earl's Court Exhibition, and contributed to organising processions.

In May 1909 she demonstrated her militaristic tendencies as a mace bearer when she became drum major of the WSPU drum and fife band, which often accompanied Union processions and demonstrations. On this occasion in May, the band appeared in public for the first time, marching from Kingsway to Knightsbridge to advertise the Women's Exhibition at the Prince's Skating Rink.[10] Having undergone a course of drill under the instruction of military non-commissioned officers, and dressed in military uniforms in the Union colours of purple, white and green, the band created an impressive display. Mary, in particular, was noted for the way she swung 'her silver-mounted staff in a manner which would have done credit to the Guards'.[11] Being in the band required a great deal of commitment. Regular practice sessions and rehearsals were held in order to maintain the high standards of performance. The drum and fife band was important not only as part of the great 'spectacle' of women's suffrage, but also as a symbol of a new movement of women which was led and organised by women.

In recent years there has been much debate among historians as to the nature of suffragette militancy. Some mainstream historians have tended to trivialise it, dismissing it as the action of hysterical women. Moreover, militancy has been represented as the result of psychological imbalance, and those who carried out militant actions have been labelled as neurotic and irrational.[12] The more traditional historians have often been unable to reconcile militancy, particularly the use of violence, with the behaviour usually expected of women.[13] Feminist writers have set about redefining and reassessing militancy from a woman-centred perspective and have challenged the existing representations of suffragette militancy.[14] Sandra Stanley Holton, for example, in her work on the law-abiding suffragists in the NUWSS, has analysed the campaigning tactics of both militants and constitutionalists, and suggests that the distinction between them is not entirely clear-cut.[15] Similarly, Liz Stanley and Ann Morley have shown in their work on Emily Wilding Davison that militancy was often undertaken on the initiative of individual women, without the authorisation of the leaders.[16] Like Holton, they suggest that the WSPU was an organisation made up of women with differing opinions, some of whom did not always adhere to leadership dictates and who took action which they themselves deemed appropriate for the situation. Militancy may be understood, then, in relation to women's personal politics and in the context of their friendships, rather than as a response to official mandates.

There are three interlinked events which demonstrate an independent style of militancy on the part of Mary Leigh. Taking place over a four-year period, between 1908 and 1912, her actions reveal militancy to be a result of the continuous frustration felt by the government's refusal to grant women the franchise, and a response to the brutal treatment of suffragettes at the hands of the authorities. Furthermore, although freelance militancy may have been privately condemned by the leaders, some of these tactics were incorporated, at a later stage, into the WSPU campaign. This suggests that members of the rank and file were influential in the Union's policy-making and not simply following orders.

The first of these three incidents which demonstrate Mary Leigh's independent militancy occurred on 30 June 1908, when, accompanied by Edith New, Mary smashed the windows of the Prime Minister's residence in Downing Street, as a protest against the treatment that fellow suffragettes had endured at the hands of the police and public earlier that day as they attempted to lead a peaceful demonstration to the House of Commons. Women who had tried to speak from the steps of buildings were flung into the crowd by the police and a gang of roughs; they were also taunted by men who seemed to have come expressly for that purpose. As a result of their actions, both women were arrested and subsequently charged with committing wilful damage.[17] Upon their arrest, Mary Leigh told the policeman that 'it will be bombs next time, we are martyrs to the cause'.[18] When questioned further by the magistrate about her remark, as he sentenced both women to two months in the Third Division, without the option of a fine, Mary Leigh expressed no regret: 'We have no other course but to rebel against oppression, and if necessary, to resort to stronger measures. The fight is going on ... We quite realise that this is a serious position, and we hope the Government will also realise the serious position.'[19] In an interview with a journalist she stated categorically that smashing the Prime Minister's windows had not been an official instruction from WSPU headquarters, but independent action taken on the part of herself and Edith New. Both women saw their militancy in terms of their democratic rights as citizens to protest against perceived injustice:

> It was Miss New and myself who had the idea. We walked first of all from St. James's Park and there picked up some good big stones. Then we went to Charing Cross and took a taxi-cab, and told the driver to drive into Downing-Street ... This was just half past nine, and we jumped out of the cab and made a rush for the house. Both of us shouted 'We are rebels, and therefore we rebel,' and threw stones ... 'Is this Russia or England?,' I called as the police took us away.[20]

The action of Mary Leigh and Edith New represented the first act of damage against property committed by suffragettes using 'the political argument of the stone'.[21] In spite of the fact that their freelance militancy was condoned by Emmeline Pankhurst, window-smashing was not incorporated into WSPU policy on a large scale until 1913.

During 1908 Mary had taken part in a number of protests and endured more than six months imprisonment in Holloway. In October she had been one of the seventeen women arrested in connection with the attempt to 'rush' the House of Commons, for which she received a three-month sentence.[22] In January 1909, the WSPU held a public meeting at the Queen's Hall, London in honour of Emmeline Pankhurst and 'to express their respect for their brave comrade Mrs Leigh'.[23] However, as a modest woman who disliked such occasions, regarding them as unwarranted praise for the performance of her duty, she did not attend but instead sent a messsage of thanks.[24]

> Dear Comrades, – Many sincere thanks for your invitation. From the bottom of my heart ... I thank you for your presentation. It will always be a pleasure to me. ... My absence this evening is a grief it would be impossible to exaggerate. I wish success to the cause and happiness to you all. – Yours sincerely, MARIE LEIGH.[25]

A second event which illustrates Mary Leigh's independence of mind and action occurred on 17 September 1909, when she was arrested in Birmingham for throwing slates onto the roof of Bingley Hall, in which the Prime Minister, Asquith, was addressing a meeting. A month earlier, Mary had been charged with a similar incident in Liverpool when she conducted a roof-top protest at the Sun Hall, where the Secretary for War, Haldane, was speaking.[26] She received two months in the Second Division, but was released two days into her sentence; her health had became endangered as a result of hunger-striking whilst awaiting her trial, and which she continued in prison.

However, on 17 September the target for her militancy was the Prime Minister. With another suffragette, Charlotte Marsh, she climbed up onto the roof of a neighbouring factory and, with an axe, began to loosen the slates, which were thrown onto the roof of Bingley Hall and the Premier's car.[27] The police attempted to remove the two women by, among other methods, turning a hose-pipe on them and hurling stones; the women proved to be formidable opponents and were only brought down from the roof when three policemen managed to climb round the back of it and drag them to the ground. Keen to ensure that no one was injured the women had been careful not to hit either Asquith or his chauffeur. However, the two militants were not so fortunate as to escape unharmed themselves. Both had been hit by the missiles thrown by the police, and Charlotte Marsh sustained a deep wound to the head.[28] They were led away, wet, wounded and in their stockinged feet, their shoes having been lost during the struggle on the roof. Arrested and charged with assault and damage (bail was refused), both women were forced to remain in their damp garments for the entire night.

Press coverage of the Bingley Hall incident mainly took the side of the government, and offered little sympathy to the suffragettes. The majority of newspaper accounts presented the episode as one of premeditated violence, suggesting that it had been the intention of Mary Leigh and Charlotte Marsh to injure the Prime Minister and the police. Unable to reconcile women and militancy, particularly violent militancy, reports of the events made inferences about the women's morality and questioned the stability of their minds. The *Western Morning News*, for example, depicted the two women as 'furious feminists',[29] while the *Daily Graphic* suggested they were 'people whose minds were so warped that they think any violence excusable as a means of advancing political ends'.[30] While many of the newspapers reports devoted several paragraphs to the injuries sustained by the officers, little, if any, mention was made of those suffered by Mary Leigh and Charlotte Marsh as a result of the missiles thrown by the police.

Their case was brought before the magistrate on the following Wednesday; Mary Leigh was sentenced to three months hard labour for assault and one month (in default of a fine) for damages; Charlotte Marsh was sentenced to three months hard labour. Both expressed regret that their actions had brought them into conflict with the police and stated that their grievance was with the government which persisted in their refusal to grant women the same political privileges as men.[31]

On arriving at Winson Green Gaol, Birmingham, Mary broke the glass windows of her cell in protest against her treatment and the failure to be recognised as a political offender – a central objective of the militant campaigners was for recognition of the suffragettes as First Division political prisoners. As a result, she was taken to a punishment cell, consisting only of a plank bed, and was stripped and handcuffed with her hands behind her. She remained manacled at all times, even during meals, when her hands were brought to the front of her body; at night her palms were also placed together at the front.

The refusal to grant Mary Leigh political prisoner status prompted her to embark on her third hunger strike.[32] Hitherto, hunger-striking suffragettes had been released before any serious danger to the health occurred. However, on this occasion the authorities at Winson Green resorted to forcible feeding and she became one of the first suffragette prisoners to be artificially fed. When informed of the plan to feed her by force, Mary told the prison doctor that he would have to prove her insane as he was not permitted to perform legally an operation, which forcible feeding constituted, on a sane person without their consent: 'The feeding by mouth I describe as an operation, and the feeding by the tube as an outrage. ... I shall hold you responsible and shall take any measure in order to see whether your are justified in doing so.'[33] Rumours had circulated in the press of the intention of the prison authorities to forcibly feed the women at Winson Green and[34] the Home Secretary confirmed this during questions at the House of Commons.[35] Immediately, Emmeline and Christabel Pankhurst travelled to Birmingham, but were not permitted to see the prisoners and received no information as to the state of their health. As a result, legal proceedings were initiated against the Home Secretary, prison governor and doctor, on behalf of Mary Leigh and the other suffragette prisoners. To pay for the cost of the legal action a 'Mary Leigh Defence Fund' was opened.[36] Contributions from sympathisers began to pour in, and Emmeline Pethick-Lawrence, the WSPU treasurer, proclaimed the response as 'significant of the honour, admiration and gratitude which men and women of all classes feel for Mrs Leigh and for those she represents – those brave champions of human liberty who are standing up today against the forces of injustice, opposition and cruelty with almost incredible heroism'.[37]

However, when the case was eventually brought to trial, upon Mary's release in December 1909, the verdict went against her.[38] The jury upheld the defence's claim that forcible feeding had been necessary to preserve her life and that minimum force had been used. The outcome of this case had a number of important implications. Not only did it emphasise the relative powerlessness of suffragettes against the authorities ,but it also set a precedent for the forcible feeding of future suffrage prisoners who went on hunger strike. The horrors of forcible feeding were recounted in Votes for Women.[39] Articles and letters appeared in both the local and national press, some less sympathetic than others. An article in The Times, for example, suggested that attempts to whip up sympathy for the women were 'misguided' and went on to argue that their offence 'deserve[d] severer punishment than has been inflicted'.[40] Nonetheless, coverage of the subject in popular newspapers brought the issue into the public realm and gained a great deal of publicity for the suffrage campaign. Andrew Rosen estimates that between 1909 and 1910, 4,459 new paid-up members joined the WSPU.[41] Although these figures do not prove a direct correlation between objections to forcible feeding and increased membership, they do suggest that a link may be possible. At a time where chivalry was very much alive, even those who were vehemently opposed to women's suffrage were outraged by the women's treatment. Eminent medical opinion proclaiming the procedures as violent, brutal and tantamount to 'official cruelty'[42] provided expert confirmation that the practice should be prohibited. The publication by the WSPU of Mary Leigh's experiences of being forcibly fed attracted further condemnation:

> The sensation is most painful – the drums of the ears seem to be bursting, a horrible pain in the throat and breast. The tube is pushed down 20 inches. I have to lie on a bed, pinned down by wardresses, one doctor stands up on a chair holding the funnel at arm's length, so as to have the funnel end above the level, and then the other doctor, who is behind, forces the other end up the nostrils.
>
> The one holding the funnel end pours the liquid down; about a pint of milk, sometimes egg and milk are used. When the glass junction shows the fluid has gone down, a signal is given, a basin of warm water is put under my chin and the other doctor withdraws the tube and plunges the end into water. Before and after use, they test my heart and make a lot of examination. The after effects are a feeling of faintness, a sense of great pain in the diaphragm or breast bone, in the nose and in the ears. The tube must go below the breast bone, though I can't feel it below there.
>
> I was very sick on the first occasion after the tube was withdrawn. I have also suffered from bad indigestion. I am fed in this way very irregularly.
>
> I have used no violence, though having provocation in being fed by force. I resist and am overcome by weight of numbers. If the doctor doesn't think the fluid is going down sufficiently swiftly he pinches my nose with the tube in it and my throat, causing me increased pain.[43]

The treatment of Mary Leigh in Winson Green prompted a personal protest from Lady Constance Lytton.[44] Accompanied by Emily Wilding Davison, a close friend of Mary Leigh, and eleven other WSPU members, she was arrested in Newcastle for throwing a stone at the car in which Lloyd George was travelling and sentenced to one month in the Second Division. Although she went on hunger strike, Constance Lytton was not forcibly fed, and this was interpreted by the WSPU as a clear indication that more working-class women were fed by force than middle-class women. Constance Lytton later disguised herself as a working woman and, when arrested, was forcibly fed eight times with no checks made on her heart as they had been when she was previously imprisoned. 'When she realised that a working woman ... had been sentenced ... and was being tortured ... she magnificently resolved, as the daughter of a peer of the realm ... [to] challenge the Government to treat her as they have treated the body of her sister, a working woman.'[45]

Between her release from Winson Green, Birmingham at the end of 1909 and the incident in Ireland in 1912 to which I will next refer Mary Leigh remained active in the WSPU. During 1910 she was involved with by-election work in

Wales and in November was one of the women injured in violent scuffles with the police on Black Friday. On 21 November 1911 she was arrested during a deputation to the House of Commons from Caxton Hall and sentenced to two months hard labour for assaulting a policeman. She maintained that this had been in self-defence.

The third major incident on which I wish to concentrate, in order to illustrate Mary Leigh's independent activity as a militant, took place on 18 July 1912 in Dublin, Ireland. Along with Gladys Evans, Mabel Capper and Jennie Baines, she was arrested for setting fire to the curtains at the Theatre Royal, Dublin, throwing a flaming chair into the orchestra pit, and setting off small bombs.[46] Asquith was visiting the city, and the women seized this opportunity to protest about recent events, including the Conciliation Bill which had been torpedoed by Asquith some months earlier, only to be replaced by a bill for Manhood Suffrage. Earlier that day, Mary had approached the carriage in which Asquith and John Redmond, the Irish political leader, were travelling, and as a symbolic gesture placed into it a small hatchet, with the inscription 'Votes for Women'. However, it was alleged that she had thrown the implement, causing injury to Redmond's ear. She was charged with malicious damage for her arson attempt, with an additional charge of causing grievous bodily harm.[47]

The trial of the suffragettes took place on 6 August and while the other women were represented by counsel, Mary conducted her own defence.[48] In her speech, which was undoubtedly the focal point of the trial, she addressed the jury at considerable length on the history of the suffrage movement,[49] linking her motive for militancy with the failure of constitutional methods to bring about women's enfranchisement: 'Five years ago we found that constitutional means, although they have done a lot, although they have paved the way, had not won us reform ... something more must be done in order to establish the right to claim the independence and the emancipation of women.'[50] She also reiterated the importance of the vote for working women:

> There are five and a half million un-named workers in the labour market. They are earning their living some of them in a very hard and difficult way, and they have to work under conditions over which they have no control ... Some girls are working in a certain factory for 4s. 8d. [23p] a week, turning out every week thousands of men's shirts, all kinds ... and no matter how hard they work they could not earn more ... the women's economic problem will take its rightful place only when women are able to press these things forward through the medium of the vote.[51]

The outcome of the trial resulted in Gladys Evans receiving five years penal servitude and Jennie Baines seven months hard labour, although the case against Mabel Capper was dropped. The jury were unable to agree on a verdict for the charges against Mary Leigh, and so her trial continued the following day. She was found guilty and sentenced to five years penal servitude.[52] When sentence was pronounced, she informed the judge that 'it will have no deterrent effect upon us'. Imprisoned in Mountjoy Prison, Dublin, and denied political prisoner status, all the women went on hunger strike. Jennie Baines was released a few days into her sentence, as there was serious concern for her health. However, Mary Leigh and Gladys Evans were forcibly fed.[53]

The women's actions were viewed with great hostility in Ireland[54] but nonetheless the Irish Women's Franchise League (IWFL), at the risk of losing members, supported them. A petition organised by the Irish suffragists was sent to the Lord Lieutenant. Four IWFL women, who were serving terms of imprisonment and had full political status, entered upon a sympathetic hunger strike. But, as Margaret Ward suggests, feminist solidarity only went so far.[55]

The WSPU condemned the long sentences on their members. Christabel Pankhurst claimed that the verdict was the result of panic on the part of the government.[56] Later, she acknowledged that she had no prior knowledge of the specific acts that the women had intended to carry out in Dublin.[57] Tributes to the courage of Mary Leigh filled the pages of *Votes for Women*,[58] heralding her as a 'figure inspired by love for humanity'.[59] However, an article in *The Freewoman*, edited by former WSPU member, Dora Marsden, criticised the WSPU's hypocrisy. 'So swiftly does a daring deed ... turn an aforenamed traitor into an heroine.'[60] It was suggested that Mary Leigh knew she was disliked by the leaders, but refused to leave the WSPU, which she regarded as her Union, built up with her passion, and for which she had suffered enormous hardships.

On 20 September Mary was released on licence after a hunger strike of six weeks and in an emaciated condition, her weight having dropped to 5st. 4lb – a loss of more than 24lb.[61] She was released into the care of friends and was taken to the hospital, which she refused to enter. Although she was in an extremely weak state, she managed to utter her watchword 'No Surrender!'.[62] Following her release, Mary appeared in front of the magistrate on 11 February 1913 for failing to comply with the conditions of her licence.[63] No charges were brought, as the magistrate decided that the terms of the licence, which required her to inform the police of her address, had not been not made clear to her.

From 1913 Mary became increasingly involved with Sylvia Pankhurst's suffrage organisation in the East End of London: the East London Federation of the WSPU (ELF), which arose out of the WSPU campaign of 1912 to encourage larger numbers of working-class women to join the fight for the vote. The ELF continued to work as part of the WSPU until 1913 when a serious dispute between Christabel and Sylvia led to the latter breaking away from the Union and the rebuilding of the East End branches of the WSPU into an autonomous organisation. The ELF differed from the local and national organisations of the WSPU in that it advocated universal adult suffrage, its membership was entirely working class, it did not condone arson and both men and women were admitted as members. Sylvia's increasing involvement with socialism, her pursuit of policies which did not restrict the campaign to the vote and her welcoming of male members conflicted with the way in which both Christabel and Emmeline Pankhurst believed the WSPU should be organised. As a result, the ELF officially split from the WSPU in February 1914.

In October 1913 Mary joined Sylvia at a meeting at Bow Baths. Violent scuffles between the ELF and police took place, and in the mêlée, Mary was dragged from the platform and badly injured.[64] She was taken into custody but released without charge. Mary Leigh's gravitation towards the ELF can be seen as a result of the disillusionment she began to experience with the WSPU after her imprisonment in Mountjoy, Dublin. The failure of the WSPU to do anything tangible about her vindictive sentence inevitably led her to believe that she had been abandoned by the Union leaders. In an interview with David Mitchell in 1965, she told him of the change she had found in Christabel Pankhurst when she visited her in France, where she had fled in March 1912 after the police raid on the WSPU headquarters at Clement's Inn. In 1913 a heavily disguised Mary had crossed the Channel to inform Christabel of the existence to which some suffragettes had been reduced. She was concerned that 'some of our women were on the run with no money, no food, no shelter', but claimed that Christabel showed little interest, and said 'we were wasting our time'.[65]

Three points can be made about Mary Leigh's militancy between 1908 and 1912. First, it was reactive. Each incident in which she was involved was more daring and defiant than the previous one and each was a response to the government's initiatives on women's suffrage. The arson attempt in Dublin in 1912, for example, was partly a reaction against the defeat of the Conciliation Bill. Second, Mary Leigh's militancy has to be understood in the context of personal friendship, loyalty to her comrades, and as a response to what was happening to particular women at particular times. The stone-throwing incident of 1908 was motivated by concern for the way fellow suffragettes had been treated by the police – in 1909 Constance Lytton had linked her militancy at Newcastle to the vindictive sentence imposed upon Mary Leigh after her rooftop protest in Birmingham. Finally, a defining characteristic of Mary Leigh's militancy was that more often than not it was carried out independently of leadership orders. Mary had little time for officialdom and authority, and when she disagreed with their strategies she embarked on the action she deemed necessary for the situation. Her militancy reflected the qualities of a woman who was determined, unafraid to speak her mind and had firm beliefs in justice and freedom.

On 4 August 1914 it was announced that Britain was at war with Germany. Upon this declaration Emmeline Pankhurst immediately called a halt to militancy and demanded the release of all suffragette prisoners. At first the Home Secretary, Reginald McKenna refused to release the prisoners unless they signed an undertaking 'not to commit further crimes and outrages'.[66] However, on 10

August he reversed this decision and all suffragette prisoners were released unconditionally. On 13 August 1914 Emmeline Pankhurst issued a circular to all WSPU members announcing the cessation of all militant activity and appealing to women to rally to the country in this hour of need.[67] In September Christabel returned to London and both she and her mother became vehement supporters of the war effort.

However, Sylvia Pankhurst adopted an anti-war stance, and with the ELF and the constitutional suffrage societies persisted in her efforts to win the extension of the franchise. In the years following the end of the WSPU campaign Mary Leigh continued to assist Sylvia with her work in the East End and gradually became estranged from the former WSPU. In 1921 an article in the *Women's Dreadnought*, the official organ of the ELF, gave thanks to a number of people for their continued support, including George Lansbury, Edith Mansell-Moullin and Mary Leigh.[68] This severance of relations between Mary and the Union leaders was brought to a head on 28 October 1915 at a meeting at which Emmeline Pankhurst accused Mary of supporting the enemy (that is, Germany) when Mary attempted to ask her a question. Emmeline Pankhurst replied by saying 'that woman is a pro German and should leave the hall ... I denounce you as a pro German and I wish to forget that such a person ever existed.'[69] Such a public denouncement of an old comrade who had suffered greatly for the 'cause' troubled many ex-WSPU members, and Emmeline Pankhurst was asked to retract her statement and offer Mary a public apology at the next meeting. Many of those present at the Pavilion on this occasion recognised the potential damage of such an allegation; Mary Leigh was a working woman who earned her own living, and such slander could seriously damage her employment prospects.

In fact, during the war years Mary applied for war service but was rejected because of her reputation as a trouble-maker. Consequently, she reverted to her unmarried name of Brown, and eventually was put through a special course of instruction as an ambulance driver by the RAC. After the war she lived near Sunbury-on-Thames, was present at the first Aldermaston march and, as a committed socialist, regularly attended the Labour May Day processions at Hyde Park.[70] Mary Leigh's commitment to justice and loyalty to her comrades continued long after her days as a suffragette. In 1956 she wrote a poem in tribute to Helen Atkinson, a former suffragette, who had been knocked down and killed by a lorry in December 1955 on the way to visit her sister in hospital.[71] Every year following the death of Emily Wilding Davison in 1913, Mary made the pilgrimage to Morpeth, Northumberland to tend Emily's grave.[72] She was the founder of the Emily Wilding Davison Lodge and in 1921 was imprisoned for the last time for striking a policeman who attempted to prevent her chalking on the pavement details of a memorial service to be held in Hyde Park.[73]

The need to prevent women like Emily Wilding Davison from fading into obscurity was recognised also by other former suffrage workers. Consequently, in

1926 an organisation known as the Suffragette Fellowship was established for this purpose by former members of the WFL and WSPU. The aim of the Fellowship was 'to perpetuate the memory of the pioneers and outstanding events connected with women's emancipation and especially the militant campaign, 1905–1914, and thus keep alive the suffrage spirit'.[74] Although Mary Leigh agreed in principle with the aims of the Suffragette Fellowship, she found fault with the way in which it was organised and committee members selected, disliking in particular, the fact that Enid Goulden Bach, who Mary claimed was never in the movement, was elected as chair.[75] Mary felt that she had been cold-shouldered by the Fellowship, which refused to allow her access to the papers which had been collected in response to a questionnaire issued by Edith How Martyn, its secretary, requesting information on dates and details of suffragette imprisonments.

In spite of her disagreements Mary regularly attended commemorative celebrations organised by the Suffragette Fellowship. In 1955 she appeared as a speaker at the Golden Jubilee of the first suffrage imprisonments, held at Crosby Hall, London.[76] In 1967 she was one of many ex-WSPU members to pay tribute to Emmeline Pethick-Lawrence at a meeting to commemorate her centenary at the annual prisoners' reunion at the Royal Commonwealth League.[77] When David Mitchell interviewed Mary in 1965, he found her living impoverished and alone, but noted that she still recalled with pride her platform days as a member of the WSPU. In an article in the *Observer*, in the same year, she continued to stand by her actions as a suffragette and her convictions remained strong: 'If we condemn ourselves to prison, it is not a burden or an imprisonment. We had an obligation, we volunteered. I was in prison seven times, but I was arrested more than that.'[78]

In the past historians of many persuasions have represented the WSPU as a middle-class organisation and have underestimated the involvement of working women in the Union's militant campaign, particularly in the second stage when more violent methods were adopted. The three interconnected episodes in which Mary Leigh was involved illustrate the participation of one working woman in the militant campaign. This is not, of course, to suggest that all working-class women were able to partake in militancy on the same scale as Mary Leigh; a range of factors, including domestic and employment commitments, inevitably prevented many women from risking imprisonment. The task which lies before historians is to recover in full the experiences of working-class women and the contribution they made to the fight for the vote. For without this we are left with a distorted and incomplete history of the women's suffrage movement.

NOTES

1 Andrew Rosen, *Rise up women! The militant campaign of the Women's Social and Political Union* (London, Routledge and Kegan Paul, 1974), p. 77.
2 Constance Rover, *Women's suffrage and party politics in Britain 1866–1914* (London, Routledge and Kegan Paul, 1967), p. 81.
3 Brian Harrison, 'The act of militancy: violence and the suffragettes, 1904–1914', in his *Peaceable kingdom: stability and change in modern Britain* (Oxford, Oxford University Press, 1982), p. 27.
4 One exception is June Purvis, 'The experience of the suffragettes in Edwardian Britain', *Women's History Review*, 4, 1, 1995.
5 Jill Liddington and Jill Norris, *'One hand tied behind us': the rise of the women's suffrage movement* (London, Virago, 1978), p. 206.
6 Purvis, 'The experience of the suffragettes', pp. 116–118.
7 The Fawcett Library has a small archive containing personal documents on Mary Leigh and her daughter Helen Brown. As yet, the archive remains uncatalogued and until it has been itemised and indexed access is not permitted.
8 E. Sylvia Pankhurst, *The suffragette movement: an intimate account of persons and ideals* (London, Longman, 1931; repr. Virago, 1977) p. 286.
9 *Votes for Women*, 18 June 1908, p. 253.
10 *Ibid.*, 21 May 1909, p. 693.
11 Quoted in Lisa Tickner, *The spectacle of women: imagery of the suffrage campaign* (London, Chatto and Windus, 1987), p. 112.
12 See, for example, Roger Fulford, *Votes for Women* (London, Faber and Faber, 1957); David Mitchell, *The fighting Pankhursts: a study in tenacity* (London, Jonathan Cape, 1967).
13 See George Dangerfield, *The strange death of liberal England* (London, 1935; repr. Grenada, 1966), pp. 154-155.
14 Sandra Stanley Holton, *Feminism and democracy: women's suffrage and reform politics in Britain 1900–1918* (Cambridge, Cambridge University Press, 1986), pp. 29–52; Liz Stanley with Ann Morley *The life and death of Emily Wilding Davison* (London, Women's Press, 1988), ch. 5.
15 Holton, *Feminism and democracy* pp. 29–52.
16 Stanley with Morley, *The Life and death of Emily Wilding Davison*, p. xiii–xiv .
17 *Votes for Women*, 9 July 1908, p. 298.
18 'After the raid', *Daily Mail*, 2 July 1908, p. 7.
19 *Votes for Women*, 9 July 1908, p. 298.
20 'Raid on Downing Street, how we broke the Prime Minister's Windows', *Daily Mail*, 1 July 1908, p. 7.
21 This is the phrase used by Christabel Pankhurst to describe the actions of Mary Leigh and Edith New. Christabel Pankhurt, *Unshackled: the story of how we won the vote* (London, Hutchinson, 1959), p. 97.
22 'Seventeen suffragettes in gaol, glad to go to prison', *Daily Mail*, 23 October, 1908, p. 7.
23 'At the Queen's Hall', *Votes for Women*, 21 January 1909, p. 276.
24 References to Mary Leigh's modesty are made in an article in *Votes for Women*, August 1912, p. 749: 'She is an extremely modest woman, or since the word modest implies a certain degree of self-consciousness, we should rather say she is an extraordinarily impersonal woman. ... To tell the truth she is impersonal to a fault, and has more than once robbed her friends by her absence from some gathering held in her honour of the pleasure of applauding her courage and her service to the movement.':
25 *Votes for Women*, 21 January 1909, p. 277.
26 'All night on the roof, rain bedraggled suffragettes removed by police', *London Daily Chronicle*, 21 August 1909, p.1
27 'Mr. Asquith in Birmingham', *The Times*, 18 September 1909, p. 7.
28 'Mr. Asquith's visit to Birmingham', *Votes for Women*, 24 September 1909, p. 1206.
29 *Western Morning News*, 17 September 1909, p. 5.

30 *Daily Graphic*, 18 September, 1909, p. 6.
31 *Votes for Women*, 24 September 1909, p. 1210.
32 *Ibid.*, 1 October 1909, p. 1.
33 Mary Leigh, 'Fed by force: how the government treats political opponents in prison': statement of Mrs Mary Leigh (who is still in Birmingham Gaol). (London, the National Women's Social and Political Union, n.d; c. October 1909).
34 *The Times*, 25 September 1909, p. 8; 27 September 1909, p. 7.
35 *The Times*, 28 September 1909, p. 5.
36 *Votes for Women*, 12 November 1909, p. 105.
37 *Ibid.*
38 'Mrs Leigh's action against the Home Secretary', *ibid.*, 17 December 1909, pp. 185–6.
39 See for example, *ibid.*, 1 October 1909, p. 1.
40 *The Times*, 29 September 1909, p. 9.
41 Rosen, *Rise up women!*, p. 211.
42 *Votes for Women*, 1 October 1909, p. 2.
43 Leigh, 'Fed by force'.
44 *Votes for Women*, 15 October 1909, p. 36.
45 *Ibid.*
46 *Ibid.*, 26 July 1912, pp. 696–9.
47 *Ibid.*
48 A separate trial for the hatchet incident was held in December. Mary Leigh pleaded 'not guilty' to the charge of throwing the hatchet, but 'admitted that she was the woman who 'put' the implement into the carriage. She did not throw it. Therefore, it was impossible that Mr Redmond's injuries were received by her hand. The case was dropped for lack of evidence.
49 'Trial of the militant suffragettes in Dublin', *Votes for Women*, 9 August 1912, pp. 728–30.
50 'Trial of the suffragettes in Dublin', *Votes for Women*, 16 August 1912, p. 744.
51 *Ibid.*
52 *Daily Herald*, 8 August 1912, p. 15.
53 When Mary Leigh was first imprisoned, rumours circulated that attempts were made to commit her to an asylum. Grace Roe had been sent to Ireland to look after the interests of the women and expressed her concern with the way the Secretary of State suggested that Mary Leigh was mad. See *Votes for Women*, 6 September 1912, p. 784.
54 See, for example, *Irish Catholic*, 10 August 1912, p. 4.
55 Margaret Ward, 'Conflicting interests: the British and Irish suffrage movements', *Feminist Review*, 50, summer 1995, pp. 134–5.
56 *Votes for Women*, 16 August 1912, p. 728.
57 Pankhurst, *Unshackled*, p. 222.
58 Laurence Housman dedicated a verse 'To Mary Leigh, August 9 September 20', *Votes for Women*, 27 September 1912, p. 827.
59 *Ibid.*, 16 August 1912, p. 749.
60 *The Freewoman*, 22 August 1912, pp. 263–264.
61 After her release on licence, she was closely watched by the police, who considered her a 'murderous' and dangerous character who posed a threat to the life of government Ministers. See Home Office Registered Documents 144/1223/227166. Public Records Office, Kew.
62 'Release of Mrs Leigh', *Votes for Women*, 27 September 1912, p. 828.
63 *Ibid.*, 14 February 1913, p. 828.
64 'Attempted arrest of Miss Sylvia Pankhurst', *The Times*, 14 October 1913, p. 4.
65 Interview with Mary Leigh, David Mitchell Collection, The Museum of London.
66 E. S. Pankhurst, *The suffragette movement*, p. 591.
67 Circular letter, 13 August 1914, Suffragette Fellowship Collection, Museum of London.
68 *Women's Dreadnought*, March 1921.
69 'Particulars of slander on Mary Leigh uttered by Mrs Pankhurst at the pavilion on October 28th 1915', British Library, c121g1, Maud Arncliffe Sennett Collection, vol. 26.

70 Interview with Mary Leigh, 1965, David Mitchell Collection.
71 *Calling all Women* (Newsletter of the Suffragette Fellowship), February 1956, pp. 8–9.
72 *Ibid.*, February 1964, p. 6.
73 'Echo of the Suffragettes', *The Times*, 7 June 1921.
74 For a more detailed discussion of the Suffragette Fellowship, see Laura E. Nym Mayhall, 'Creating the "suffragette spirit": British feminism and the historical imagination', *Women's History Review*, 4, 3, 1995 pp. 319–44.
75 See interview with Mary Leigh, David Mitchell Collection.
76 See *Calling all Women*, February 1956, p. 3.
77 *Ibid.*, February 1968, p. 7.
78 John Gale, '50 years later the suffragettes remember', *Observer Colour Magazine*, 7 February 1965.

13

Suffrage, sex and science

THERE is a pervasive belief that the science of sex which developed in the last decade of the nineteenth and at the beginning of the twentieth century was a pernicious male construct to which feminists of the period were (or ought to have been) hostile, 'reject[ing] the work of male sexual radicals like Havelock Ellis and Edward Carpenter'.[1] In fact, questioning accepted conventions of sex had a long history in British feminism, even before the Contagious Diseases (CD) Acts in the 1860s aroused women's outrage by their assumptions about men, women and sex. As far back as Mary Wollstonecraft or before there were critiques of the assumptions about 'female nature' upon which social arrangements rested. Victorian women campaigned vigorously around marital and child custody issues, and concern with rescuing 'fallen women' predated opposition to the CD Acts. The relationship between the new sexual science and the suffrage movement was thus rather more complex than sometimes depicted.

Sexology was very far from being accepted orthodoxy throughout the first half of the twentieth century. A key text, Havelock Ellis's multi-volume *Studies in the psychology of sex*, was not and never has been published in its entirety in the UK, following the 1898 conviction for obscenity of *Sexual inversion*. The work was expensive and hard to obtain, with booksellers demanding a 'signed certificate from a doctor or lawyer'. Lady Rhondda, who read it at the International Women's Suffrage Club, found that Ellis 'opened up a whole new world of thought', though she was 'far from accepting it all'.[2] Emmeline Pethick-Lawrence wrote to Ellis that 'the issues that you live for are ... closely connected with the spirit' of the suffrage struggle.[3]

In Britain at the turn of century the double standard of sexual morality was alive and well. It may not have been assumed that a young man's first dose of clap was his passage into manhood,[4] but the belief that men had sexual needs for which prostitution was an essential, if deplorable, outlet, was pervasive.[5] The Divorce Law of 1857, not altered until 1923 in spite of the Royal Commission of 1909–12 and its recommendations, made a wife's single act of adultery grounds for divorce, whereas a woman could only divorce her husband for adultery plus another matrimonial offence. Women did seek and manage to obtain divorces, suggesting truly appalling matrimonial conditions[6] Venereal diseases were wide-spread, and frequently communicated to unsuspecting wives – doctors were reluctant to disturb marital harmony by indicating the nature of their malaise. Many women entered marriage entirely ignorant about the sexual relationship, and many husbands were not much better informed. Maternal and infant mortality rates were high. The use of contraception, though increasing, was sporadic, methods employed unreliable and the most widely practised reliant on male co-operation. The sale of abortifacients was a profitable business, and the failure of these spurious remedies led to self- or back-street abortion.

Celibacy was hardly an agreeable alternative. There was still social disapproval towards women who remained unmarried, and few could earn a living equivalent to what they might expect in marriage. An unmarried woman who associated socially with members of the opposite sex was likely to endanger her reputation, affecting such essential matters as keeping a roof over her head or retaining her job. Rebecca West remarked that single working women, under-paid and inadequately fed, were required to sacrifice personal liberty for a respectable roof over their heads.[7] Stella Browne argued that women who were 'unwilling to accept either marriage – under present laws – or prostitution', but 'refuse[d] to limit [their] sexual life to auto-erotic manifestations' and wished to enjoy intimate friendships or sexual relations with 'congenial men', had to 'struggle against the whole social order ... for [their] most precious personal right'. Many 'count[ed] the cost worthwhile', but risked 'the most painful experiences, and spend[ing] an incalculable amount of time and energy on things that should be matters of course'. Women of 'strong passions and fine brains' were, Browne claimed, under 'huge, persistent, indirect pressure ... to find an emotional outlet with other women' – not subject to the same social stigma, at least if conventional models of respectable feminine appearance and behaviour were adhered to.[8]

Prostitution was not illegal, but prostitutes were subjected to routine police harassment and repeatedly arrested for 'annoying' men by solicitation, even in the absence of actual complaints. Prostitutes who lived together for companionship and mutual protection could be charged with brothel-keeping, as could those who let accommodation to them. They were also denied male protection: men friends could be penalised for procuration and living on immoral earnings. The whole tendency of these laws was to isolate prostitutes. Women who were not prostitutes found police unsympathetic to complaints about men persistently annoying them, and women obliged to go out at night might be pestered by the police under the assumption that they had to be prostitutes.

Women involved in the wider emancipation struggle thought it vital to destroy the conspiracy of silence around sexual issues, in order to make all women aware of the ravages of venereal disease, of male immorality, of the inequality of the marriage laws and of the constraints upon women's lives. Recent historiography on the late nineteenth- and earlier twentieth-century women's movement has tended to assume a dichotomy between 'social purity' and 'sex reform'. In practice this was less than absolute, and in looking at the suffragists' considerations of sexual problems, it can be misleading to think in terms of two beleaguered opposing camps, rather than voices opposing contemporary conventional assumptions about sex and gender from a variety of individual and collective positions.

The social purity lobby was very aware of the sexual dangers that existed for women, and aimed to control sexual manifestations for the safety and protection of women and, of course, children. However, it attracted not only women who were interested in making the world safer for women, but men (and, indeed, some women) who wanted to ensure the general moral health of society by policing women, harassing prostitutes, vigorous censorship and persecuting male homosexuals. Josephine Butler and many of her supporters quit the National Vigilance Association to form the Association of Moral and Social Hygiene, because they did not see prostitutes themselves as a problem, but as victims of a broader social system, not ameliorated by further legal penalisation of women selling sexual services. The suffragist Elizabeth Wolstenholme Elmy commented: 'one of the unfortunate results of women's position of slavery [is] that so many seek rather power to coerce others than to free themselves'.[9]

The National Vigilance Association did seek such useful measures as female matrons in police stations and women court workers to support women and child victims in sexual assault trials. It promoted the prosecution of cases of indecent assault and abduction and also agitated for legislation against incest (an Act was passed in 1908), and it seems to have been well aware of the dangers of sexual abuse and harassment of women and children. By the early twentieth century social purity campaigners also demanded sex education, to warn children of dangers and counteract the 'gutter-smut' they might pick up. The movement was thus opposed to conventional conservative views on the immutability of human nature with the double standard reflecting innate differences, and the preservation of children's 'innocence'.

The social purity movement was more complex than sometimes depicted: for example, the Reverend James Marchant solicited and obtained volumes by Havelock Ellis, and Patrick Geddes and J. A. Thomson (biologist authors of *The evolution of sex*, 1889), for the National Council of Public Morals' New Tracts for the Times,[10] and by the 1920s social purity writers often cited sexologists' writings with approval.[11] In 1923 suffrage veteran Alison Neilans, of the Association for Moral and Social Hygiene (founded by Josephine Butler and continuing her feminist/civil libertarian approach), wrote to the penal reformer George Ives about homosexual law reform:

[T]his Association is to repeal laws and not to make them. Practically all the legislation which punishes people for breaches of public morality has a tendency to
do more harm than good, and I am always unhappy when this Association for-
wards any attempt to add to the number of crimes for which imprisonment and
punishment can follow.[12]

However, as a whole social purity was prescriptive, with a definite agenda of what
was right and needed to be done. Its model of the ideal society centred around
the monogamous family unit, in which both partners came to marriage chaste,
and practised a high degree of continence even within marriage. Differences
were largely tactical: could people be made virtuous by legislation, or were these
matters of individual conscience rather than law?

'Sex reform', however, had a higher respect for diversity. It attracted very
varied individuals, who might have very different ideas about the same phenomenon: for example, some who believed that homosexuality was an innate tendency and should thus be decriminalised, and others who saw it as the product
of social and educational practices, to be 'cleared up' by, for example, healthy-
minded co-educational schools. There was an activist aspect, but the major tendency was towards asserting the desirability of calmly discussing and considering
sexual phenomena – being 'a note of interrogation', as Laurence Housman put
it in his statement of the aims of the British Society for the Study of Sex Psychology. Sex reform was not predicated upon a belief that it knew 'the right way',
although it had many similar aims to social purity, for example the replacement
of the double standard by a higher, single, moral standard in sexual relations.
Sex reformers, however, had a rather more positive view about what sexual relations could be, freed from hypocrisy, ignorance and repressive social conventions.

Its roots lay in attempts during the 1880s among a few small, fairly informal groups of the relatively educated and articulate to discuss questions of sex,
stimulated by such public manifestations as Stead's 'Maiden Tribute of Modern
Babylon' articles in the *Pall Mall Gazette* and the subsequent passing of the
1885 Criminal Law Amendment Act. Wider progressive agendas of socialism
and feminism (also eugenics) were of considerable influence. Perhaps the most
well-known and most extensively written-up of these groups is the Men and
Women's Club of which Karl Pearson and Olive Schreiner were members. Other
groups were engaged in similar explorations, stimulated by the writings of Pearson himself as well as Edward Carpenter and, slightly later, Havelock Ellis. Young
provincial Fabians in the circle of John Bruce Glasier and Katherine Conway circulated a notebook of thoughts on 'free love, sexual emancipation, and the
possibility of socialist revolution'. Such thoughts during the 1890s drew on 'many
heterodox sources' to articulate sexual and emotional ideas and women's issues
in the context of social reform.[13] The Fellowship of the New Life in which Ellis
was a leading figure presumably discussed similar questions. Further evidence
for individuals and groups engaging in these explorations can be found in peri-

odicals such as Margaret Shurmer Sibthorp's *Shafts: A Paper for Women and the Working Class* (1892–9), and *The Adult*, the journal of the Legitimation League (which combined a programme of relieving the legal penalties of illegitimacy with broader sexual reform), and correspondence received by individuals such as Patrick Geddes and Edward Carpenter who wrote influential works on sexual issues.[14] Received ideas about sexuality and society were being queried within a context in which potential for deriving from their study a sound basis for social action was implicit.

Women were looking for ways of talking about sexual matters, and while, as Frank Mort pointed out in *Dangerous sexualities*, they were required to use the discourses available,[15] there were active attempts to adapt them, combine them with one another and create discourses which women could comfortably use to discuss their experiences. A significant model was Edward Carpenter, in particular *Love's coming of age* (1896), which combined utopian socialism, current scientific investigations and a theosophical mystical strain to create an eclectic brew which was extremely popular. Many feminists, in particular those for whom the emancipation of women was part of a wider vision of a reformed just society, responded to Carpenter's writings, and he had many women associates and correspondents, including such famous figures in the suffrage struggle as Charlotte Despard and Lady Constance Lytton.[16]

Shafts: A Paper for Women and the Working Class is a valuable source for uncovering 1890s feminist explorations of ideas around sex. In its columns questions were raised about, for example, the alleged greater degree of chastity manifested by women: was it an innate trait, thus nothing to be boasted about, or the result of real, therefore meritorious, struggle?[17] A reviewer of Edward Carpenter's *Sex – Love in a free society* had 'a fault to urge ... he writes with a masculine pen, he reasons with the masculine bias, he sees with the masculine dimness of vision'. The writings of 'a masculine pen on such subjects as these should be taken up and threshed out by women'; Carpenter was, however, conceded to be on the right track, and worth reading as a stimulus to further thought.[18] The editorial attitude towards 'scientific checks to undue and immoral reproduction' (birth control) was not sympathetic. Sibthorp's line was that 'Women must themselves be the controlling power, the arbiter and the authority' over reproduction, instead of 'enabl[ing] the husband to indulge himself without restraint'.[19] However, the columns were open to debate, and letters and articles put the Malthusian case, although Sibthorp carefully placed Jane Clapperton's 'Reform in domestic life' by commenting as editor, 'earnestly believing ourselves ... there is no justifiable remedy for overpopulation but self-restraint'.[20]

Shafts also reflected the growing concern about sex education for children. A Mrs Kapteyn of Hampstead's classes for this purpose were mentioned early in 1895.[21] Articles suggested that this was a good thing and that botany was an excellent way into a tricky subject, although a reviewer found *The human flower* by Ellis Ethelemer 'lacks somewhat ... delicacy and deep insight'.[22] A reader wrote that she had (after thought and prayer) 'made up my mind I would no longer be a coward, and shrink from my clear duty: so I too, by the aid of simple botany ... prepared their minds for the revelation, and then I talked of birds and their young, and animals'.[23] Edward Carpenter's correspondent Edith MacDuff apparently evolved a similar approach: feeling 'very strongly about the hollow and impure hypocrisy with which the conventional world surrounds the sacred and beautiful facts of physical life', she drew her children's attention 'to Nature's infinitely varied and beautiful schemes for the fertilisation of flowers'.[24]

The ideas being debated were not entirely self-generated by women, although they put new twists on them. Menstruation, for example, was argued in *Shafts* to be the pathological result of 'indiscriminate violation of ... sacred laws', establishing as '"habit" a morbid malady, unquestionably due to primeval man's uncontrollable depravity'.[25] Elizabeth Wolstenholme Elmy's husband Ben, in the poem *Woman free* published in 1893 under the pseudonym 'Ellis Ethelmer', depicted this 'heritage of woe' as 'unhealed ... scars of man's distempered greed'.[26] These theories elaborated upon that advanced in T. L. Nichols's widely circulated *Esoteric anthropology*, that sexual indulgence caused menstruation to degenerate into a 'real hemorrhage [sic] ... depraved in its character'.[27] Nichols presented this as a personal pathological consequence of overindulgence, but Elmy took a wider view. As women once more took control, 'purer phase of life' would release them from 'the wasting weariness'.[28] This was a reputable scientific position: F. H. A. Marshall's staid 1910 textbook *The physiology of sex* cited the physiologist Metchnikoff's suggestion that menstruation was 'essentially a "disharmony" of organisation ... brought about as the result of modifications acquired recently in the history of the species ... belonging to the borderland of pathology'.[29]

Some discussions of feminist writings on sex have failed to look at these wider contemporary debates, or indeed at the broader social context. Women writers certainly advocated sexual restraint within marriage, and intercourse only for procreation, but this was commonplace in Victorian writing on conjugal sex. Female writers did emphasise the woman's rather than the man's benefit (male Victorian advocates of conjugal continence tended to dwell on the dangers of reckless expenditure of semen). Women writers also tended to give significant weight to the importance of the woman's choice when to have children.

A recurrent question was whether women were superior to men. Opinions about the innate basis of female chastity varied. Elizabeth Wolstenholme Elmy wrote around 1897: 'I do not admit the superiority of women over men. Women have been repressed in every way while men's appetites have been equally encouraged.'[30] The extreme feminist and theosophist Frances Swiney, however, believed the sexes to be antithetical, the corrupt male hindering the higher evolution of the superior woman.[31] Nonetheless, she did allow that (male) scientists were 'doing the grandest, the most indispensable, work for the reformer, the metaphysician, and the philosopher'. Among those 'laying bare the foundations of the eternal temple' were Havelock Ellis, Patrick Geddes and J. A. Thomson. The latter two, in their volume *The evolution of sex*, had 'in a measure elucidated the mystery of sex'.[32] Swiney cited their theory of the catabolic nature of the male to confirm her own argument that 'the male element is invariably associated in all ages with destruction, disintegration, force, impurity, and evil'; contact with it rendered the female – the true source of creative energy – impure.[33]

Looking backwards to the debates of the late nineteenth and early twentieth centuries, we may be assuming dichotomies which were not present to the perceptions of the protagonists. Women alleged to have been in opposing camps in fact worked together in the struggle for suffrage and other women's rights: for example, within the Women's Freedom League Frances Swiney of the League of Isis, Mrs Drysdale of the Malthusian League, Alison Neilans of the Association for Moral and Social Hygiene, Marie Stopes (at that time a scientist of modest renown rather than a committed sex reformer), and Cicely Hamilton, the author of *Marriage as a trade*, all co-operated.[34] Few active suffrage campaigners were pursuing strict separatist strategies, and many were also to be found in organisations including, founded by or largely run by men. In fact, Swiney was put forward for election to the Council of the Eugenics Education Society, and was also associated with the Malthusian League.[35] Other women activists saw divorce law reform, amelioration of the illegitimacy laws and Malthusianism, as well as broader political commitments, as powerfully connected to the emancipation of women.

Debates on sexuality in most suffrage journals did tend to assume the primacy of chaste monogamous marriage – threatened by male vice and hypocrisy – and to depict female sexuality as predominantly maternal.[36] Given constraints on publication and distribution, editors may have felt they had enough problems. The controversial *The Freewoman*, 1911–13, certainly experienced censorship by retailers. It was allied with no organisation and saw suffrage as one branch of a wider feminist struggle which had been, it suggested, occluded by concentration on the suffrage and campaigning tactics. Under the editorship of Dora Marsden it provided a forum for the expression of views and airing of debate. It generated the Freewoman Discussion Circle which met to consider questions such as 'Sex Oppression', 'The Problems of Celibacy', 'Neo-Malthusianism', 'Prostitution', and divorce law reform, as well as the abolition of domestic drudgery.[37] There was considerable interest in, and support for, discussion of such topics, and for a space, printed and in terms of an actual group, which could provide a forum rather than laying down a programme.

Women were also actively involved in the British Society for the Study of Sex Psychology (BSSSP), inaugurated in 1914. This promoted 'reading of papers in agreement with the general objects of the Society', issued occasional pamphlets and hoped to collect data 'on matters within the scope of the society'.[38]

Membership and eligibility for office were 'open on precisely the same terms to women as to men', working 'together for a common understanding' upon 'matters which vitally concern both sexes'.[39] The first woman member was militant suffragist Cicely Hamilton, whose *Marriage as a trade* was a swingeing attack on marriage as it existed in contemporary society, and who clearly did not reject wholesale the teachings of Ellis and Carpenter.[40] There was an active policy of attracting woman members: Dr Alice Johnson and Mrs Mary Scharlieb were invited to join the committee. Scharlieb (one of the earliest British women to achieve medical qualifications and a leading light of social purity) attended one meeting but did not persist; possibly her concurrent duties with the Royal Commission on Venereal Disease proved too onerous.[41] Other 'Lady Doctors' were specifically approached, and one, Constance Long, soon joined the committee.[42] Far from women's voices being excluded, out of seven quarterly meetings, from autumn 1915 to spring 1917, four were addressed by women: Stella Browne (her famous paper on sexual variety and variability among women), Norah March on sex education, Edith Ellis (she was ill, and her paper on eugenics was read by Edward Carpenter) and Mrs Capel Dunne on intersexuality.[43] The committee included several women.[44]

The attitude of open-minded enquiry and a refusal to accept conventional dogma about sex and gender, which permeated the works of writers such as Ellis and Carpenter and the BSSSP, appears to have been highly congenial to women in revolt against conventional assumptions. Writers such as Carpenter could provide women already querying their own sexuality with a focus: one wrote to him that reading *The intermediate sex* 'made everything fall into place', another that 'it was like being given sight'. They were enabled to name and understand feelings which they had already had. As Liz Stanley has pointed out, sexology was not invented by sexologists and imposed upon women. The ideas sexologists advanced were often evolved in close contact with 'inverts' both male and female, and were perceived as benign and sympathetic by those endeavouring to make sense of feelings which did not fit the models of sexual emotion and identity offered by convention.[45]

Polarised camps of social purity and sex reform feminism have been read into *The Freewoman* debate over female chastity dominated by Kathlyn Oliver and Stella Browne early in 1912. An apostle of the practice of self-restraint in sex matters, Oliver argued that female celibacy was natural and desirable. Browne conceded that many women suffered from 'the unrestrained indulgence of married life with ignorant or brutal husbands', but, on the other hand, 'the health, the happiness, the social usefulness, and the mental capacity' of others had been 'seriously impaired and sometimes totally ruined' though unnatural restraint. Was there not, she argued, 'a middle path between total abstinence and excess'? Oliver riposted that 'in sex matters it is surely indisputable that we women are miles above and beyond men'. Browne responded that it was 'cruel stupidity' to enforce complete abstinence 'irrespective of temperament, circumstances, and point of view'. She argued that 'we should not endeavour *forcibly* to impose our own ideas and standards upon others'.

This debate has been rather misleadingly characterised by Margaret Jackson in *The real facts of life: feminism and the politics of sexuality c.1850–1940*, using pejorative terms such as 'patronising' and 'contempt' about Browne's tone, which could as readily apply to Oliver's. Jackson claims that eventually 'they no longer responded to one another's letters': they may well have been at one over Stella Browne's scathing comments on the Eugenics Education Society or pointed queries about the supposed virtues of regulated prostitution in Japan, and Oliver's contributions about the plight of the domestic worker. The 'mutual antagonism and personal animosity' Jackson suggests may not, in fact, have existed. It is almost certain that they were already acquainted via Morley College. Did Browne initially employ the pseudonym 'A New Subscriber' precisely to avoid personalising the argument? Could this debate have been less spontaneous, more orchestrated, than it appears? – a formal presentation of particular positions by protagonists who knew one another and were perhaps engaged in face-to-face explorations of the subject?

In 1917, Oliver, proposed by Browne and seconded by Laurence Housman, became a member of the BSSSP, which suggests that she had come round to some degree to Browne's plea for debate and tolerance.[46]

Mrs Frances Swiney, and her League of Isis, with its theories of women as innately superior to the male, and semen as a virulent poison, have been characterised by Sheila Jeffreys as wholly antithetical to sex reform, although, as previously mentioned, Swiney herself appears to have been prepared to work with the Eugenics Education Society.[47] (Stella Browne, often misleadingly described as a eugenicist, had a concept of being 'well-born', greatly at odds with the class-biased hereditarian determinism of this society, which she frequently attacked at this period.[48]) Geraldine Blair, organiser of the Eastbourne branch of the League of Isis, wrote to the BSSSP, which she had learnt of from Havelock Ellis himself: 'I was so delighted to hear yesterday ... that a society had already been started for promoting knowledge of what I consider one of the most vital questions of the day.' She was 'studying the problem of the Intermediate Sex' and had been reading Carpenter's books.[49]

Among other women associated with the BSSSP, of those erroneously identified as unlikely to be attracted by 'sex reform' were Alison Neilans of the Association of Moral and Social Hygiene and Cicely Hamilton, whose recent biographer seems to find difficulty in accounting for how she could have collaborated with Stella Browne and Dora Russell in the birth control movement.[50] Hamilton's attacks on the institution of marriage were quite logically associated with generally querying conversional attitudes to sexual matters, and she translated a German treatise on the 'Third Sex' (homosexuality) for the BSSSP.

Though (because?) a vigorous critic of marriage, Hamilton felt it appropriate to provide women with the means to improve their condition within it through birth control (she was an active member of the Malthusian League), and abortion law reform.

This generation of feminists was notable for empathy towards women who were in a different place from themselves, recognising that women's oppression in a male-dominated society took many forms. Campaigners for birth control might have a middle-class maternalism not always free from eugenic bias, but on the whole were concerned about women lacking access to knowledge which many middle-class feminists were able to take for granted. Stella Browne, a non-monogamous actively heterosexual woman who declared herself personally lacking in maternal instincts, condemned, besides the sufferings of the unwillingly fertile, the 'compulsory sterility' imposed upon unmarried women contrary to their maternal desires, even advocating that 'female inverts' should be enabled to gratify their often powerful desires for motherhood.[51] Passionate indignation at the system of prostitution was widespread, combined with sympathy towards actual prostitutes, exemplified in the vigorous protests against Regulation 40D under the Defence of the Realm Act in 1918, felt to be a reintroduction of the CD Acts under a new guise. Desire to discuss questions around sexuality – indeed to open rather than close a debate – even to engage in personal sexual experimentation – were not necessarily in practice dissociated from active campaigning on behalf of those without the time and leisure to indulge in debate.

Nor were such debates purely a middle-class pastime, though taboos among working-class women against discussing sexual questions may have been even more deeply seated. Initially shocked and offended by 'the woman on syphilis', the Richmond Branch of the Women's Cooperative Guild 'recanted their abuse', and asked Virginia Woolf to find a speaker on sex education.[52] A working-class woman wrote urging Marie Stopes to support marriage law reform, citing George Eliot's defiance of convention.[53] Mrs Layton of the Women's Cooperative Guild considered that marriage 'required a great deal of love to induce a thoughtful woman to give up so much'. In evidence on behalf of the Guild about relief to unmarried mothers, repudiating 'the statement that married women would be resentful', she argued 'every time a woman fell, a man fell also'.[54] The Guild also gave some of the most radical evidence and recommendations received by the Royal Commission on Marriage and Divorce in 1910.[55] The ferment of ideas about sex and a critique of established conventions was not merely a middle-class indulgence; it had immediate pertinence to many women's lives.

Women who engaged with sex reform were not simply succumbing to male-dominated ideology. Enquiry rather than dogma was the order of the day, and the works of male sexologists were seldom taken as holy writ, women being prepared to critique as well as supplement them. Stella Browne expressed certain reservations about elements in Havelock Ellis's works.[56] Can women determined to voice questions about women's actual sexual desires be accused of 'seeking male approval'? Social purity and sex reform may more helpfully be envisaged not as two embattled camps, but as elements within a spectrum of opposition to conventional assumptions of the day about sexual relations and the role of women, and individuals could and did shift about within this spectrum in a fluid, though not necessarily inconsistent, way. The women participating in these debates were not caryatids constantly supporting the weight of a single position, but welcomed the chance to ventilate opinions.

NOTES

1 F. Mort, 'Purity, feminism and the state: sexuality and moral politics, 1880–1914', in M. Langan and B. Schwartz (eds) *Crises in the British state, 1880–1930* (London, Hutchinson, 1985), pp. 209–25.

2 The Viscountess Rhondda, *This was my world* (London, Macmillan, 1933), pp. 126–7.

3 Emmeline Pethick-Lawrence to Havelock Ellis, 26 November [no year: by implication after the achievement of suffrage], Autograph Letters Collection, Fawcett Library, London Guildhall University.

4 W. Stekel, *Impotence in the male: the psychic disorders of sexual functions in the male*, tr. O. H. Boltz (New York, Liveright, 1927), vol. I, p. 170, and A. Flexner, *Prostitution in Europe* (London, Grant Richards Ltd, 1919), pp. 40–1, both mention this attitude as prevalent in Europe.

5 A. Marwick, *The deluge: British society and the First World War* (London, Bodley Head, 1965), p. 110; W. S. Hall, *Sexual knowledge: in plain and simple language ... [etc]* (London, T. Werner Laurie, [1926]), pp. 184–5, and N. March, *Towards racial health: a handbook for parents, teachers and social workers on the training of boys and girls* (London, George Routledge and Sons Ltd, 1920), p. 175, both warned respectable girls to avoid arousing their male friends' desires, thus thrusting them into the arms of prostitutes.

6 O. M. McGregor, *Divorce in England: a centenary history* (London, Heinemann, 1957); A. J. Hammerton, *Cruelty and companionship: conflict in nineteenth-century married life* (London, Routledge, 1992).

7 Rebecca West, 'A new woman's movement: the need for riotous living', *The Clarion*, 20 December 1912, reprinted in J. Marcus (ed.), *The young Rebecca: writings of Rebecca West 1911–1917* (London, Macmillan, 1982), pp. 130–5; similar views expressed in other articles by West collected therein.

8 F. W. S. Browne, 'Studies in feminine inversion', *Journey of Sexology and Psychoanalysis*, 1, 1923, pp. 51–8: based on paper given to the British Society for the Study of Sex Psychology, April 1918; and see L. Martindale, *A woman surgeon* (London, Gollancz, 1951), pp. 111, 228–36, on her relationship with a female barrister.

9 Mrs Elmy to Mrs McIlquham, 18 May 1898, British Library Department of Manuscripts, Additional Manuscripts 47451.

10 S. Hynes, *The Edwardian turn of mind* (Princeton, Princeton University Press, 1968), p. 288n; Sir Patrick Geddes papers at the University of Strathclyde, letters from Sir James Marchant, 13 June 1911, 4 December 1912, 8 February 1914, T-GED 9/1015, 1124, 1245.

11 See, e.g., The Revd A. H. Gray, *Men, women, and God. A discussion of sex questions from the Christian point of view* (London, Student Christian Movement, 1923).

12 British Sexology Society archives in the Harry Ransom Humanities Research Center, University of Texas at Austin: BSS 'Misc': letter from Allison Neilans to George Ives, 20 March 1923.

13 C. Steedman, *Childhood, culture and class in Britain: Margaret McMillan, 1860–1931* (Lon-

don, Virago, 1990), pp. 122–3; C. Dyhouse, *Feminism and the family in England 1880–1939* (Oxford, Basil Blackwell, 1989), pp. 157–66; J. R. Walkowitz, *City of dreadful delight: narratives of sexual danger in late-Victorian London* (London, Virago, 1992), ch. 5, 'The men and women's club', pp. 135–70; L. Bland, *Banishing the beast: English feminism and sexual morality* (London, Penguin, 1995), ch. 1, 'The Men and Women's Club', pp. 3–47. P. Grosskurth, *Havelock Ellis: a biography* (London, Allen Lane, 1980), R. First and A. Scott, *Olive Schreiner* (London, André Deutsch, 1980) and R. Brandon, *The new women and the old men: love, sex and the woman question* (London, Secker and Warburg, 1990), also discuss the club.

14 See correspondence in the Geddes papers at Strathclyde and the Edward Carpenter papers in Sheffield City Archives.

15 F. Mort, *Dangerous sexualities: medico-moral politics in England since 1830* (London, Routledge and Kegan Paul, 1987), pp. 112–19.

16 Carpenter papers, Sheffield City Archives: letters from Lady Constance Lytton MSS 386/164, 168, 170; from Charlotte Despard MSS 386/147, 148, 175; and many other women.

17 Debated in the November 1892 and June 1895 issues.

18 *Shafts*, July 1895.

19 *Ibid.*, 18 February 1893.

20 *Ibid*, July 1893.

21 *Ibid.*, January–February 1895.

22 *Ibid.*, June 1894.

23 *Ibid.*, April 1895.

24 Carpenter papers, Sheffield City Archives MSS 271/51.

25 *Shafts*, July 1896.

26 'Ellis Ethelmer' (Ben Elmy) *Woman free* (Congleton, The Woman's Emancipation Union, 1893); Bland, *Banishing the beast*, pp. 141–2.

27 T. L. Nichols, *Esoteric anthropology (The mysteries of man) ... [etc]* (London, Dr Nichols at the Hygienic Institute, [c.1873]), p. 109.

28 Ethelmer, *Woman free*.

29 F. H. A. Marshall, *The physiology of reproduction* (London, Longmans, Green and Co., 1910), p. 111.

30 Copy letter (n.d., c. 1897), in correspondence of Elizabeth Wolstenholme Elmy with Mrs McIlquham, vol. III: BL Add MSS 47451.

31 F. Swiney, *The cosmic processssion, or the feminine principle in evolution: essays of illumination* (London, Ernest Bell, 1906), p. 71n.

32 *Ibid.*, p. x.

33 *Ibid.*, p. 158n.

34 Women's Freedom League, *Annual Reports*, Fawcett Library.

35 Minutes of the Council and Executive Committee of the Eugenics Education Society, Committee Meeting of 22 February 1908: Eugenics Society archives in the Contemporary Medical Archives Centre at the Wellcome Institute for the History of Medicine: CMAC: SA/EUG/L.1: Bland, *Banishing the beast*, pp. 217–21.

36 L. Garner, *Stepping stones to women's liberty: feminist ideas in the women's suffrage movement* (London, Heinemann, 1984), pp. 21–2, 38–40.

37 *The Freewoman*, March–October 1912; V. Glendinning, *Rebecca West: a life* (London: Weidenfeld and Nicolson, 1987), pp. 37–9, mentions West as a 'lively presence' at these groups, which she herself described as 'too like being in church'; see also J. Lidderdale and M. Nicholson, *Dear Miss Weaver: Harriet Shaw Weaver 1876–1961* (London, Faber and Faber, 1970), pp. 48–9, 56.

38 BSS 'Misc': Minutes [1], 3rd meeting of committee, 3 November 1913.

39 F. W. S. Browne, 'A new psychological society', *International Journal of Ethics*, 28, 1917–18, pp. 266–9,

40 BSS 'Misc': Minutes [1], 3rd, 5th, 7th and 11th committee meetings, 3 November 1913, 10

January, 20 February and 8 June, 1914.

41 *Ibid.*, 5th and 10th meetings of committee, 10 January 1914, 19 May 1914.

41 *Ibid.*, 9th meeting, 20 April 1914, 10 meeting, 19 May 1914.

43 BSS 'Misc': Lecture lists.

44 For a more detailed study of the BSSSP, see L. Hall, 'Disinterested enthusiasm for sexual misconduct: the British Society for the Study of Sex Psychology, 1913–1947', *Journal of Contemporary History*, 30, 1995, pp. 665–86.

45 L. Stanley, 'Romantic friendship: some issues in researching lesbian history and biography', *Women's History Review*, 1, 1992, pp. 193–215; H. Oosterhuis, 'Richard Von Krafft-Ebing's "Stepchildren of Nature": pyschiatry and the making of homosexual identity', in V. Rosario (ed.), *Science and homosexualities* (London, Routledge, 1997), pp. 67–88.

46 M. Jackson, *The real facts of life: feminism and the politics of sexuality c.1850–1940* (London, Taylor and Francis, 1994), pp. 91–4; correspondence columns of *The Freewoman*, January–April 1912; BSS 'Misc': Minutes [1], 41st meeting, 12 September 1917, see also K. Oliver to Carpenter, 25 October 1915, Sheffield City Archives MSS 386/26.

47 S. Jeffreys, *The spinster and her enemies: feminism and sexuality, 1880–1930* (London, Pandora, 1985), pp. 35–9, 47; on Swiney and the Eugenics Education Society, see note 33 above.

48 See, e.g., letters to *The Freewoman*, 1 and 15 August 1912, pp. 217–18, 258, *The New Age*, 2 September 1915, p. 439, *The Clarion*, 3 September 1915, p. 5, review in *Plan*, 2/10, October 1935, p. 23.

49 BSS, 'Letters received': Geraldine Blair (?1914).

50 L. Whitelaw, *The life and rebellious times of Cicely Hamilton: actress, writer, suffragist* (London, Women's Press, 1990), pp. 203–6.

51 Browne, 'Studies in female inversion'.

52 A. O. Bell (ed.), *The diary of Virginia Woolf, Vol. 1: 1915–1919* (Harmondsworth, Penguin, 1979), p. 141: entry for Thursday, 18 April 1918.

53 Marie Stopes papers in the CMAC, WIHM: PP/MCS/A.246 Mrs. ECW.

54 M. Llewelyn Davies (ed.), *Life as we have known it, by cooperative working women* (London, Hogarth Press, 1931), pp. 32, 48, 51.

55 Gillian Scott, 'A "Trade union for married women": The Women's Co-operative Guild 1914–1920', in S. Oldfield (ed.), *This working day world: women's lives and culture(s) in Britain 1914–1945* (London, Taylor and Francis, 1994), pp. 18–28.

56 F. W. S. Browne, review of *The task of social hygiene*, *The English Review*, 13, 1912, p. 157; review of *Sexual inversion*, *International Journal of Ethics*, 27, 1916/17, pp. 114–15.

14

The old faith living and the old power there:[1]
the movement to extend women's suffrage

> It was said if the vote were given to young women they would invariably vote for the best looking candidate. 'Looking around this House,'said the Society's only woman MP, amid a burst of laughter, 'I cannot see that there is any need for honourable members to be worried.'[2]

THIS chapter concentrates on the inadequacies of the franchise legislation of 1918, the main events of the women's franchise extension campaign from 1918 to 1928 and successive government strategies for curtailing women's political demands. The partial enfranchisement of women in February 1918[3] did not mark the end of a fifty-year struggle, rather it signified the opening of a new chapter where 'the symbol must be made real'[4] through the expansion of the social, political and economic equality of women. The campaign for the franchise extension to embrace all women aged 21 and over (including those women over 30 who were still disqualified) consolidated a diverse women's movement during the 1920s. Finally achieved in July 1928, universal female suffrage is often viewed by historians as a legislative inevitability. However, as Millicent Fawcett, the veteran suffrage leader, observed, 'our future course at the time was not all quite such plain sailing as it may appear now to those who only look back upon it'.[5]

The Special Register Bill had been introduced in August 1916 to prevent the disenfranchisement of members of the armed forces and munition workers whose enforced absence from their permanent place of residence would otherwise have contravened the franchise residential qualification. Although Prime Minister Asquith had promised in 1913 that the next piece of franchise legislation would include women, the 1916 Bill contained no reference to female enfranchisement. The women's franchise campaign had been sustained through the early years of the war by such groups as the Actresses' Franchise League and the United Suffragists. Despite other wartime concerns, the campaign was reignited in response to the omission of women in the proposed Bill, and, after much contention, the incomplete inclusion of women in the 1918 legislation was secured.

The women's movement before the First World War had concentrated on the struggle for the vote, but once partial enfranchisement had been gained its net was spread wider.[6] Ray Strachey, an active suffragist, recorded the post-war transformation:

> The actual division of responsibilities among the societies was complicated and variable ... With the granting of the vote all the organisations of women became more or less feminist and political, and the doctrines of equal legislation and equal pay became, as it were, common form to them all. The war, too, had left a legacy of co-operation among them'.

With much work to be accomplished, the scale of the post-war propaganda required a network encompassing specialist groups, founded on a broad base of expertise, and able to employ common policy and strategies. This amalgamated strength was needed to mount mass actions at critical points during the campaign without impeding the progress of separate ventures. In the period from 1918 to 1922 a network of hundreds of political, party and non-party, industrial and professional, welfare and peace organisations was developed which embraced all aspects of women's interests and lives. The members of such organisations understood, as Winifred Holtby later wrote, that 'political emancipation is a condition of freedom; it is not freedom itself'.[8]

The rigours of war had left women exhausted and their organisations economically vulnerable. Many suffrage societies wound up their operations once the principle of women's suffrage had been achieved. Others reviewed their aims, methods, organisational structures and even their names The largest non-party political organisation, the National Union of Women's Suffrage Societies (NUWSS), revised its constitution to enable other women's group with the same aims to affiliate to it, and changed its name to the National Union of Societies for Equal Citizenship (NUSEC) at the annual meeting of its council in March 1919. This change ensured an expansion and consolidation of the women's movement and an opportunity to welcome more women from a broader spectrum of interests into the organised struggle.

Unlike the National Council of Women, solely a co-ordinating organisation,[9] the NUSEC aspired to act not only as a co-ordinating force but also as an originator of policy and campaigns. But there was an interconnecting web of affiliations between groups, both large and small, which highlighted their commitment to all strands of the post-war agenda. Smaller societies, such as the militant Women's Freedom League (WFL), which had broken away from the Women's Social and Political Union (WSPU) in 1907, had only fifty branches in England, Scotland and Wales. But many groups that were affiliated to the constitutionalist NUSEC also subscribed to the WFL. Overseeing co-operative efforts to represent industrial women's interests was the Standing Joint Committee of Industrial Women's Organisations, formed in 1916. The Consultative

Committee of Women's Organisations was initiated in 1921 by the first woman MP, Nancy Astor, in an attempt to maximise the movement's parliamentary profile and influence and co-ordinate the work of women in relation to parliament.

The Representation of the People Act of February 1918 enfranchised six million women, with five million added to the local government electorate. The basic features of the qualification were:

> The Parliamentary franchise is given to women of 30 or more who themselves have, or whose husbands have, a local government qualification; while the local government franchise is given to women of 21 or more who themselves have such qualification, and to women of 30 or more whose husbands have such qualification, where both reside together in qualifying premises.[10]

Both married and single women over the age of 30 could vote in their own right by virtue of their occupation of qualifying premises. This franchise applied to women in any one of five categories: owner, tenant, lodger, in service[11] or university graduate. The emphasis, in some cases, on the supply or ownership of furniture, led many women to complain that, as far as they were concerned, the vote had been reduced to the price of a husband or a vanload of furniture.

The disenfranchised women consisted of three million under the age of 30, with the remainder being over 30. These latter consisted of professional women in furnished lodgings, wives living in furnished rooms (their husbands could vote), women living in the same house as their employer, domestic workers and daughters or sisters who lived in their mother's or brother's house. The British wife of an alien could not vote, but the British husband of an alien could. A widow who gave up her home to live with her son had no vote and a recently widowed woman automatically lost her vote.[12]

There were also anomalies for women who did qualify. Male businessmen could vote in two constituencies if their domestic residence and their business premises were in two different counties; this did not, however, apply to women. The interpretation of 'joint occupation' meant that three single men sharing a house had a vote each; but in the case of three single women, 'joint occupation' only entitled two of them to vote.

Resistance to women having the vote at all was demonstrated in some instances of women over 30 being disenfranchised illegally. For example, before demobilisation was completed in 1922 some officials had claimed that women whose husbands were away on military service had lost their right to vote. There was no truth in this (except in cases in which the woman had given up the tenancy of the marital home), but the confusion did considerable damage to women's understanding of their legal entitlement.[13] Some electoral registration officers who insisted that women had to 'take their food' in their own furnished rooms before they would place them on the voting register were also acting illegally.[14] Wives of conscientious objectors, whose husbands were disqualified from voting for five years, were nevertheless entitled to vote. However, in practice, women whose husbands were in prison or absent from home were likely to experience difficulties in proving a husband's residency qualification and, hence, their own entitlement to vote.[15]

In view of the hostility expressed by many MPs to full female enfranchisement, the age limitation agreed in 1918 ensured that the male electorate was not 'swamped' by women voters; the prevalent fear seemed to be that if all women over the age of 21 had the vote they would outnumber the men by over two million, and institute some kind of 'unnatural' female rule. During parliamentary debates on the age limit for women, the ages proposed ranged from 40 to 21 years. The age of 30 was finally decided upon by the government as providing a ten to six million electoral ratio of men to women, deemed acceptable to the majority of men.[16]

Another justification for the age limit of 30 was that 'girls' of 21 were too irresponsible and ignorant for the exacting task of citizenship. It was hoped that by making marriage one of the means of entitlement, control of the women's vote would be exercised by their supposedly more emotionally stable male partners. Because married women over 30 were regarded as being more sensible than their younger, unmarried counterparts, 'erratic' behaviour at the ballot box by women might be minimised through a restricted female franchise. It was also possible that the linking of marriage and the vote was an inducement to return women to their domestic role after the war.

The age qualification particularly affected working women and made nonsense of the claim to be rewarding women for their war work. The WFL acknowledged: 'Women in the industrial world are more heavily handicapped than professional women by want of political power. The very great majority of women in industry are under 30 years of age and voteless'.[17] Ellen Wilkinson, the Labour MP and former NUWSS organiser, emphasised this point at a WFL meeting, explaining that an entire social class under 30 years old was powerless. She felt that her proposed lobbying in the Commons 'could only become effective if she knew that she had behind her the whole of the Woman's Movement'.[18]

During the 1917 debates on the inclusion of women in electoral reform, many MPs made it abundantly clear that they hoped the extension would not come for many years. Soon after the end of the 1914 war, the praise for women war workers rapidly gave way to a spirit of reaction.[19] Numerous articles exuding prejudice about, 'the modern woman' categorised young women under 30 pejoratively as 'flappers'. In magazines and newspapers, the pseudonym, 'A Mere Male' was frequently used in a spirit of mocking self-abasement and challenge.'What does the girl of today want?', by Gilbert Frankau was not untypical: 'That chain and that stick are still the prerogatives of us mere males, whom your Modern Girl affects to treat so lightly.' Frankau sustained the familiar male cry that 'we – and not she – possess the greater physical strength and the greater mental capacity'.[20] An article in similar style, 'Woman has failed! Why she is an outsider in public life', by a 'Truthful Man' concluded that by 1925 there was only a handful of women in public affairs because women did not possess the necessary skills and temperament, only being interested in love affairs.[21]

Such attitudes were pervasive outside the House, and were combined with opinions expressed within it by Unionist 'die-hards', such as Lord Hugh Cecil, who felt that the House had lost much of its dignity since women had been allowed in.[22] Lieutenant-Colonel Archer Shee remonstrated that handing over electoral power to women would 'make an election a joke'. Like many of his colleagues, he also argued that most women did not want the inconvenience of the vote.[23]

Even before the 1918 Bill was passed, the women's movement had attempted to secure an extension of the terms on offer. Although there had been a debate about resisting an age differential, some groups, such as the Suffragettes of the Women's Social and Political Union (SWSPU), a breakaway group formed in 1915, were prepared to accept whatever was awarded in order to get the sex barrier removed. As Millicent Fawcett put it, 'we preferred an imperfect Bill which could pass to the most perfect measure in the world which could not'.[24] However, acceptance did not preclude suffragists making their objections to the Bill's inadequacy clear. Discontent with the provisions of the 1918 franchise provision brought a recurrence of suffrage agitation in the run-up to the autumn general election. Unity derived from an awareness that 'the status of all women is lowered so long as the fact of being a woman entails the coming under different franchise laws to the fact of being a man ... [it] ... affects their value in the labour market and in the home'.[25]

The perennial optimism within the women's movement had been encouraged by an electoral statement signed in November 1918 by the Prime Minister, Lloyd George, and the Conservative Party leader, Bonar Law, as part of the Coalition government's manifesto, declaring that 'it will be the duty of the New Government to remove all existing inequalities of the law as between men and women'.[26] The WFL, for one, was not going to allow Lloyd George to forget this declaration, and, for many years, it was printed, banner-like, every month on the front cover of their paper, The Vote.

The Liberals and the Labour Party made similar manifesto promises. The first rebuff came when there was no mention of projected reforms in the King's Speech of 1919. However, in April 1919 there was a welcome surprise when the Labour Party introduced the Emancipation Bill, one of its provisions being to enfranchise all women under the age of 30. Despite opposition by Coalition Unionists, and the government's stated intention to amend the franchise clause, the Bill passed all stages and went to the Lords in July. Meanwhile, the women's societies had been taking part in deputations and propaganda work to ensure the passing of the Bill. On 30 June 1919 there was a colourful 'women under 30' procession in London, followed in July by a meeting jointly organised by the Standing Joint Committee of Industrial Women's Organisations and the NUSEC.[27] But on 22 July the government sabotaged the Emancipation Bill by introducing its own legislation which took precedence. Known as the Sex Disqualification (Removal) Bill, this would have allowed women entry to the legal professions and to the office of magistrate; it did not, however, extend the franchise: 'If this was the meaning of the Government's pledge then Mr Lloyd George's speech to the women electors should never have been delivered ... Is it any wonder that the old militancy stirs again?'[28] contended an article in *The Labour Woman*. Between 1918 and 1923, in the face of the often dire economic repercussions of the demobilisation of women war workers, a low-key franchise campaign was waged. There were deputations to Ministers and MPs and a reaffirmation of their policy on suffrage at the annual conferences of organisations such as the WFL, the London Society for Women's Service and the NUSEC.

For many years, the familiar campaigning pattern continued with the introduction of a private member's Franchise Bill, which was then boosted by the lobbying of supportive MPs, attempted deputations to the Prime Minister and publicity of a modest kind. Between 1919 and 1928 there were eight private member's bills: five from Labour, two Liberal and one from an Independent Conservative. The Six Point Group, established in 1921 by Margaret Haig, Lady Rhondda, a former suffragette, astutely analysed the futility and self-perpetuating nature of private member's bills and NUSEC's adherence to constitutional procedures:

> Private Bills are apt to absorb the energies of ardent reformers, to keep them happy and quiet and to distract them from what should be the main business of their lives ... making themselves apparent, and if need be so unpleasant, to the powers that be that they decide to give them what they ask.[29]

The National Union's approach contrasted with the Six Point Group's more urgent style, and threats to reintroduce militant methods reflected the strength of the ex-WSPU contingent in its membership. The Six Point Group believed that the only path likely to ensure success was to force the introduction of a government Bill.

The government prevaricated but 1923 marked a turning-point for the women's movement. A demonstration that had been postponed because of the election campaign took place in March at the Central Hall, Westminster. Organised by the NUSEC, it was attended by over fifty women's organisations, with the two women MPs, Nancy Astor and Margaret Wintringham, as speakers. Margaret Bondfield, representing Labour women, emphasised the importance of not allowing the government to foster the delusion that women were reconciled to the notion of this inequality'.[30]

The success of eight women candidates in the December 1923 general election, coupled with the election of the first Labour government, gave the women's cause high hopes that 1924 would bring success to their franchise claims. Labour women were confident that their party would fulfil its past promises, as was the NUSEC, whose close working relationships with the Labour Party since before the war gave them confidence in such an outcome. It also seemed in line with Labour's policy of using their Women's Sections to capture and consolidate women's allegiance through being seen as the party to give them the vote. Barely two weeks after Labour was asked to form a government, the WFL began to exert pressure in the first of three major rallies of the year. The women's movement still continued with its traditional strategies of lobbying, writing to MPs and the press, and holding meetings, demonstrations and rallies to keep the issue in the forefront of events. Yet only nine days after its initial rally, the WFL was relaying its misgivings about the Labour government's intentions.[31]

Events were moving rapidly; by 29 February 1924 a private member's bill was launched, proposed and seconded by Labour MPs W. M. Adamson and the former suffragette, Dorothy Jewson. Difficulties became apparent because of the additional citizenship implications in Adamson's Bill, dealing with parliamentary franchise for men (approximately 304,202 men still had no vote[32]) and the local government franchise. There were also two further interventions against the women's cause. Sir William Bull, Conservative (who had been a member of the 1916–17 Speaker's Conference), maintained that in 1918 leading women's societies had not only accepted the provisions of the Speaker's Conference, but had also agreed to cease suffrage agitation for a ten-year period. As a means of thwarting the extension, he declared that, consequently the House was now bound by nothing other than the women's 1918 undertaking.[33] This was the first debate in which raising the age limit to 25 had been put forward. Some MPs, such as Sir Martin Conway, Unionist, argued that 'A woman of between 21 and 25 years of age arrives at her flowering time ... I suggest that the young woman of that age ought to be paying attention to other matters than voting. She ought to have her eye upon ... the prospects of family, of man's devotion.'[34] This suggestion of an age limit, other than that of 21, introduced a fresh complication for the women's societies.

The Bill passed its second reading by 288 to 72 votes, and it was essential that the women's lobby sustained pressure on the government to give the Bill sufficient parliamentary time to pass through the requisite legislative stages. The women's fears about the complications which its additional proposals would engender were borne out when several amendments were tabled by Conservatives opposed to the whole Bill or to the 'contentious clauses'.[35] Singling out clauses for amendment was part of the containment strategy operated by parliament towards women. The device halted and prevented proposed legislation, and tied up future efforts of the women's movement on amendment issues.

Adamson's Bill passed its final Committee stage in June 1924, but, as a result of the amendments, ran out of parliamentary time.

That the Prime Minister Ramsay MacDonald and the Labour government had failed them came as a shock and was a bitter disappointment to the women's movement. Adamson's Bill had had a large degree of all-party support. The advantage to Labour's reputation of being the party which extended the franchise and the attendant gains at the ballot box would have been considerable. In retrospect, it is not difficult to understand why Labour disappointed, their brief spell in office having achieved little for anyone. As C. L. Mowat explained, 'Labour was unready. It was a minority government, in office, but not in power, shackled to the Liberals and pursuing a policy of moderation.'[36] The Cabinet was largely drawn from the upper and middle classes, with few traditional left-wingers or trade-unionists, in a country where Emmanuel Shinwell believed Macdonald's socialism was curbed because 'five out of every seven voters were anti-Socialist'.[37]

The campaign of political education instigated by suffrage societies in the spring of 1918 was aimed to increase political awareness among women voters and ensure that they were aware of their rights and responsibilities as citizens. As anti-suffragist MPs had anticipated, the campaigners intended to mobilise the political power of these six million women voters to press for an extension of this right. Towards the end of 1917 the National Union of Women Workers, the National Council of Women, with members from forty-nine affiliated societies, had formed a Women Citizens' Associations network throughout the country. Membership was open to all women over the age of 16 in order to encourage the study of political, social and economic questions, thereby providing an answer to the accusation that women were ignorant and irresponsible, used to justify the refusal of the franchise extension.[38]

After the first post-war election in the autumn of 1918, suffrage societies had prompted new women voters to take an active role as citizens. During the November 1924 election campaign, non-party women pressed the leaders of all the political parties for statements on their stand on the franchise issue. In November, the Conservative leader, Stanley Baldwin, published this pledge:

> The Unionist Party is in favour of equal political rights for men and women, and desire that the question of the extension of the franchise should, if possible, be settled by agreement ... they would, if returned to power, propose that the matter be referred to a Conference of all political parties.[39]

Such a timely declaration might be thought to trade on women's disillusionment with the Labour Party and increase the Tory vote among existing women voters.

Despite the Conservatives' 1924 landslide victory and Baldwin's pledge, the King's speech yet again contained no mention of a franchise extension. The Home Secretary, Joynson-Hicks, followed the well-worn path of excuse and promise, by explaining that the government could not introduce a Franchise Bill at such an early stage in its life, since this would necessitate an election and interrupt important government legislation. In mitigation, Joynson-Hicks insisted that the government intended to honour Baldwin's electoral pledge; but the 1925 conference that Baldwin had promised to examine the issues was postponed until 1926.[40] The idea of a conference was seen within the women's movement as a method of procrastination which stalled the implementation of the franchise extension without the Conservatives having to deny that they believed in it. The WFL pointed out that 'the suggested Conference is not only unnecessary but mischievous'.[41] The suggestion of raising the age limit for men from 21 was also regarded by the NUSEC and others as a further delaying tactic. The proposal by some Unionists that the age limit should be raised for men, as part of the franchise extension package, was a sure way of alarming Labour MPs who would not want a Franchise Bill for women which threatened to disenfranchise men, and reduce its party's support.

By February 1925 the *Daily Sketch* was commenting that the amount of lobbying and activity for votes for women at 21 was reminiscent of the early suffrage days, 'without however, the old danger'.[42] But by February 1926 the WFL realised that equal franchise had once more been betrayed, with the promise of a conference abandoned and no further parliamentary plans in hand.

A new determination in 1926 with a spring and summer offensive, aimed at arranging the maximum number of meetings, demonstrations and deputations to MPs on a national and regional level, culminated in a mass procession and rally on 3 July in London, originated by the Six Point Group and organised through an Equal Political Rights Demonstration Committee.[43] Decorated motorcades, bands, banners and pennants made an impressive sight, with the procession headed by young women in their various 'under 30s' groups, followed by political and suffrage societies from Britain and North America. Parliamentary candidates came next behind a red and black banner of Big Ben, the section completed by mayors and women magistrates. Veteran suffragettes wearing prison badges were part of the NUSEC's 'Old Gang' contingent, with Millicent Fawcett, Maude Royden and Margaret Ashton among them. Emmeline Pankhurst, welcomed back after her seven-year absence, with her old colleague, Flora Drummond, the WFL leader Charlotte Despard, and Dr Annie Besant, also walked the entire route from the Embankment to Hyde Park.[44] Meanwhile, more groups for women under 30 were formed, and the Equal Political Rights Demonstration Committee extended its life-span to co-ordinate action as the Equal Political Rights Campaign Committee. The year had been one of ceaseless activity – two hundred meetings held by the NUSEC groups alone, nationwide.[45]

With the third year of Baldwin's empty pledge, the campaign gathered momentum. In March 1927, for the first time since 1918, a Prime Minister agreed to receive a deputation. Introduced by Nancy Astor, the deputation was supported by fifty-six societies, although Baldwin permitted only twenty-four women to attend. Baldwin explained to the deputation how the General Strike, followed by the miners' lock-out and the war in China, had prevented the government from dealing with the women's franchise in the previous year, but he assured them that he would make a statement in the House before Easter.[46] With so many years of disappointment and broken promises behind them, it was unlikely that such an assurance would slow the pace of the women's campaign. On the contrary, women were determined to escalate the pressure, knowing as they did that most harm came from 'politicians outwardly friendly to the cause'.[47]

Their judgement was vindicated; no such statement was forthcoming from Baldwin, and in May a Labour Party Bill for the equalisation of the franchise due for its second reading had its parliamentary time appropriated for government business. In the face of such obdurate opposition, the women again took to the streets in a mass protest rally in Trafalgar Square. Arranged by the Equal Political Rights Campaign Committee and supported by forty-two organisations, the crowds were addressed by Charlotte Despard, Lady Rhondda and Emmeline Pethick-Lawrence.[48] The 1928 opening of parliament was preceded by a vociferous women's motorcade down Whitehall. Members of the Young Suffragist Society delivered a petition to Baldwin's home and attempted a break-in at Buckingham Palace to deliver a letter to the King.[49] Expectations were dashed when the anticipated statement failed to appear; but, in the evening debate, Baldwin announced the introduction of a Franchise Bill that session, with the necessary clause enabling all women to participate in the next election. The government's Representation of the People (Equal Franchise) Bill was introduced in March 1928 and enfranchised an additional 5,221,902 women.[50]

Why did successive governments of different political hue lack the political will to complete the enfranchisement of women until 1928? Traditional opposition to the very idea of women's enfranchisement, with its hypothesised reduction in male political power, was still ingrained among Conservatives and others after the war. This fear was articulated by many who believed that the historic concession to women over 30 was a sufficient beginning and that further enfranchisement should be resisted for as long as possible after that. Such attitudes were further entrenched by the severity of the post-war economic depression and the fears that men's social status had been undermined by women's employment in the war.

During his wartime premiership, Lloyd George had 'side-stepped much of the legislative power of parliament'[51] which resulted in the enhancement of the Prime Minister's power. This augmented power enabled succeeding Prime Ministers to operate with independence from the parliamentary machine and to determine policy unilaterally. Throughout the period from 1918 to 1928 the Conservative vote was decreasing in the face of Labour's ascent and the decline of the Liberal Party. During the early years of demobilisation industrial and civil unrest in many parts of the country fuelled Tory anxiety about the spread of communism. The Labour Party outstripped the Liberals in the 1922 election to become the largest party of opposition. The Conservatives opportunely blamed the women's vote for their 1923 defeat[52] and had deep misgivings about the radical political allegiance of women under 30. With the rise of the Labour Party, the Conservatives, as they reasoned, dare not risk further increasing the Labour vote by extending the women's franchise. Acknowledging the potential power of the combined women's vote, they tried to capitalise on class issues whilst using the 'waiting period' in the hope of stabilising the country and their own electoral following. Tory fears were confirmed when Labour was returned to government in the 1929 general election, their electoral pledges to world peace and disarmament offering an additional incentive for new women voters to vote Labour.

The dramatic nature of the suffrage campaign before the 1914 war has diverted attention from the post-war phase of the women's movement. As a result, our understanding of the narrative whereby women struggled to attain parliamentary power in Britain is still incomplete. Were there other, more effective tactics which they might have deployed to advance their case more rapidly? Explicit threats would have entrenched the government's position and been counter-productive. But a failure to pursue their cause robustly could indicate compliance and risked their demands being completely ignored. Women's trusting expectation of honourable conduct from political power-brokers disadvantaged them in anticipating outcomes and preparing alternative strategies. The lack of parliamentary experience of some of their Labour colleagues may also have been a handicap.

There was much at stake for the women's movement in the post-war period and placing women and their needs at the centre of the political agenda appeared to be fundamental. The goal of extending and utilising their role as citizens to emancipate, and thereby redefine, women's lives was in direct opposition – then as now – to traditional expectations of women's role in the private domain. Their aims contrasted with the government for whom the women's issue was simply an additional problem to be contained in the demanding post-war times. Women's organisations undoubtedly succeeded in using their influence and parliamentary support to keep the issue of equal enfranchisement on the parliamentary programme throughout the 1920s. The NUSEC attributed the eventual success of 1928 to its own strategies:

> There was always a section of opinion in the women's movement who said of further franchise reform, 'it will come of itself,' while another section said 'it is too soon to press for equal franchise yet.' If the National Union had yielded to either section in 1922, we should not have obtained from Mr Bonar Law ... his declaration of personal belief in equal franchise, which is said to have considerably influenced the present Government. If we had not again pressed the question on all three Parties at the General Election of 1924, we should not have obtained from the Prime Minister his now famous promise of 'equal political rights'.[53]

The Six Point Group had never put any faith in such pledges, and, had it been a larger organisation, might well have revived the militancy which still haunted parliament. Yet the women's movement made no use of this concern over militancy to advance the franchise extension more rapidly. Women's access to parliamentary power, with its attendant responsibilities, in some ways had constrained and limited their more adventurous campaigning options. Pertinently, Brian Harrison has dubbed the newly enfranchised women of the 1920s women's movement 'prudent revolutionaries'.[54]

In 1918, the ruling class had brought itself to concede the right to vote to women, and the threat they posed was now diminished by enclosure. Once inside the system, the power granted and the rights accorded to women were circumscribed by more intangible discriminations. Women's campaigners had the votes of six million voters to bargain with, but also the problem of delivering political education and instilling confidence into women, and the psychological difficulty of changing their self-identity from that of 'derided minority' to full citizen.[55] Inside the House, during the 1920s, the number of women MPs was in single figures. The bittterness, anger and frustration of the women's movement during this period is not to be underestimated, yet despite everything a relentless optimism was paramount.

In 1928 organisations began revising plans for outstanding campaigns in the light of their full citizenship, mindful that:

> To have won equal voting rights for women and men is a great victory, but it will be an infinitely greater achievement when we have succeeded in abolishing for ever the 'woman's sphere', 'woman's work', and a 'woman's wage'and have decided that the whole wide world and all its opportunities is just as much the sphere of woman as of man.[56]

NOTES

1 *The Woman Teacher*, 9 July 1926, p. 305.
2 *Evening News*, 20 February 1925, Ellen Wilkinson Newscuttings Collection, Labour Party Archive, TUC Library Collections, University of North London.
3 Partial in that the franchise only applied to women over the age of 30 who fulfilled certain property qualifications or were married to men who qualified.
4 *The Woman's Leader*, 6 February 1920, p. 7.
5 Millicent Garrett Fawcett, *The women's victory and after: personal reminiscences 1911–1918* (London, Sidgwick and Jackson, 1920), p. 134.
6 The term 'women's movement' as used in this chapter replicates that found in the literature of the women's organisations of the time as an inclusive, catholic term embracing the multifarious activities of organisations engaged in improving women's lives.
7 Ray Strachey, *The cause: a short history of the women's movement in Great Britain* (repr. London, Virago, 1978), p. 374.
8 Winifred Holtby, *Women and a changing civilisation* (London, John Lane, 1934), p. 34.
9 By 1928 the National Council of Women had 126 local branches and 142 affiliates, e.g. the Association for Moral and Social Hygiene (1915) and the Irish Women's Citizens and Local Government Association (1918).

10 Chrystal Macmillan, *And shall I have the parliamentary vote?* (London, NUWSS, 1918), p. 3.

11 *Ibid.*, p. 3, 'If she inhabits a dwelling-house or rooms as a dwelling-house by reason of her employment, unless her employer also lives in the same house. This is called the "Service Franchise."' For example, a school-mistress who has a house to live in as part of her salary would be qualified to vote, while a woman caretaker of an employer's dwelling-house would not.'

12 *The Vote*, 4 April 1924, front page, p. 106.

13 *The Labour Woman*, May 1918, p. 9; Macmillan, *And shall I have the parliamentary vote?*, pp. 6–7; *Home and Politics*, July 1922, p. 13.

14 *The Vote*, 27 May 1921, p. 485.

15 *The Labour Woman*, May 1918, pp. 9–10.

16 *Parliamentary Debates*, Commons, vol. 94, 22 May 1917, 2214.

17 *The Vote*, 21 January 21 1927, p. 20.

18 *Ibid.*, 22 January 1926, p. 29.

19 See Deirdre Beddoe, *Back to home and duty: women between the wars 1918–1939* (London, Pandora, 1989).

20 *Woman Magazine*, August 1924, pp. 399–401.

21 *Newcastle Chronicle*, 12 December 1925, Ellen Wilkinson Newscuttings Collection.

22 Henry W. Nevinson, 'Votes for women', *The New Leader*, 7 March 1924, p. 8.

23 *Parliamentary Debates*, Commons, vol. 163, April 23–May 1; April 25, p. 474.

24 Fawcett, *The women's victory and after*, p. 146.

25 'Equal political rights', *Time and Tide*, 29 January 1926, reprinted in Dale Spender, *Time and tide wait for no man* (London, Pandora Press, 1984), p. 167.

26 *The Vote*, 9 May 1919, front page.

27 NUSEC *Annual report*, 1919, p. 30.

28 *The Labour Woman*, August 1919, p. 94.

29 *Time and Tide*, 2 March 1923, pp. 242–243.

30 *The Vote*, 16 March 1923, p. 85.

31 *Ibid.*, 15 February 1924, p. 54.

32 Men who were neither property owners nor occupiers, i.e. tinkers, hawkers and caravan-dwellers, plus workhouse inmates, and those in receipt of Poor Law Relief. *Parliamentary Debates*, Commons, vol. 170, February 25–March 14 p. 892.

33 *Ibid.*, pp. 897–9.

34 *Ibid.*, 918–19.

35 *The Woman's Leader*, 23 May 1924, front page.

36 Charles Loch Mowat, *Britain between the wars 1918–1940* (London, Methuen, 1968), p. 174.

37 Emmanuel Shinwell, *The Labour story* (London, Macdonald, 1963), p. 118.

38 NCW, *Citizen's associations*, n.d, approx. 1917–18.

39 Note NUSEC *Annual report*, 1924, p. 9–10.

40 NUSEC, *Equal franchise 1918–28*, June 1927, p. 5.

41 WFL, *Annual report*, April 1924–5, p. 3.

42 *Daily Sketch*, 20 February 1925, Ellen Wilkinson Newscuttings Collection.

43 *The Vote*, 31 December 1926, p. 411.

44 *The Woman Teacher*, 9 July 1926, p. 305. There were 3,500 women, more than 40 societies, e.g. St Joan's Social and Political Alliance, Liverpool Dressmakers' Association, Electrical Society for Women, League of the Church Militant.

45 NUSEC *Annual report*, 1926, p. 20–8.

46 *The Vote*, 11 March 1927, p. 74.

47 *The Vote*, 3 June 1927, p. 172.

48 *The Woman Teacher*, 22 July 1927, front page and pp. 318–21.

49 *The Times*, 8 February 1928, p. 9.

50 Approximately 218 members absented themselves from the House for this momentuous

debate.
51 Charles, *Britain between the wars*, pp. 13–14.
52 *The Labour Magazine*, January 1924, p. 400.
53 NUSEC *Annual report*, 1928, p. 7.
54 Brian Harrison, *Prudent revolutionaries: portraits of British feminists between the wars* (Oxford, Clarenden Press, 1987).
55 Grace Hadow, former WSPU member, 'We shan't know ourselves in any other role than a derided minority', in Vera Brittain, *The women at Oxford* (London, Harrap, 1960), p. 146. Minority here refers to access to power and is not used numerically.
56 *The Vote*, 6 July 1928, p. 212.

DAVID DOUGHAN

Appendix

British suffrage repositories

The following is not intended to be an exhaustive list of repositories holding any sort of suffrage material, but only of those with a degree of major national significance. It will also be worth researchers' while to check local repositories (libraries, museums, galleries, record offices, etc.). In addition, other major university and public reference libraries are likely to hold some secondary, and possibly in some cases relevant primary material.

All the repositories listed here should be able to provide some degree of wheelchair access, but it is advisable to check with the individual institutions beforehand. Contact details are correct at the time of going to press.

LONDON LOCATIONS

British Library (St Pancras), 96 Euston Road, London NW1 2DB
Tel: 0171 412 7276
Fax: 0171 412 7736
Admission: by special permit, with at least one referee of good academic standing; not usually available to undergraduates. Apply to the Admissions Office.
Open Monday to Saturday.
In theory, the British Library should have a copy of every book, pamphlet, etc., published in the UK, and in practice it does indeed have a great deal, including much suffrage-related material. However, this is extremely difficult to identify as such, unless it is the publication of a specific suffrage society, or by an author known to have been involved in the campaign. In fact, most relevant material can be found more easily elsewhere, but in-depth researchers will still find it useful, partly to fill in gaps, and partly because of some of the special collections held there, for example Maud Arncliffe-Sennett's extensive collection of scrapbooks of suffrage ephemera and pamphlets. There are also some extremely important manuscript collections, such as the correspondence between Harriet McIlquham and Elizabeth Wolstenholme-Elmy – but special permission needs to be sought to gain access to the Manuscript Collections.

British Library Newspaper Library, Colindale Avenue, London NW9 5HE
Tel: 0171 412 7353
Fax: 0171 412 7379
Admission: free to researchers over 18 on production of suitable ID. If in doubt, it's best to check in advance. Note: turn up as early as possible; it is very heavily used, and you may find you have to wait a long time for a seat to become available. Also, although there are vending machines with basic sandwiches, hot drinks, etc., it is advisable to take a flask and sandwiches. Open Monday to Saturday 10.00–16.45.

This is useful not only for the newspapers of the time, but because it holds many weeklies, and even monthlies, relevant to the suffrage campaigns. Again, the major ones can usually be found elsewhere, but completists will want to check it. For most researchers, its main use is to see how the daily press dealt with a particular event on a given date.

The Fawcett Library, London Guildhall University, Old Castle Street, London E1 7NT
Tel: 0171 320 1189
Fax: 0171 320 1188
e-mail: fawcett@lgu.ac.uk
Admission: free to members of London Guildhall University and paid research staff at HEFC-funded institutions. Others pay as follows: full annual membership £30.00; non-member day fee £3.00; students and unwaged: membership £7.00, day fee £1.50.
Open in term: Monday 10.15–20.30, Wednesday 09.00–20.30. Thursday, Friday 09.00–17.00; in vacation: Monday, Wednesday, Thursday, Friday 09.00–17.00
This should usually be the first stop for anybody researching the British women's suffrage movement. It holds quantities of secondary books, pamphlets, etc., but the main attraction for most people is the original material – pamphlets and periodicals from all tendencies, pro and anti; papers of most national suffrage organisations (but not, alas, the WSPU); archives of individual women, and letters to and from a wide range of women involved in the movement. The documents from the Suffragette Fellowship Collection at the Museum of London are also available on film at the Fawcett Library. A suffrage reading list of secondary sources is available on request, or can be found at the Fawcett Library Website (http://www.lgu.ac.uk/phil/fawcett.htm).

Museum of London, 150 London Wall, London EC2Y 5HN
Tel: 0171 600 3699
Fax: 0171 600 1058
Admission: free during opening hours. Prior arrangement must be made to view the Suffragette Fellowship Collection.
Open Tuesday to Saturday 10.00–17.50, Sunday 12.00–17.50.
This holds the Suffragette Fellowship Collection of memorabilia – banners, sashes, badges, 'General' Drummond's cap, Mrs Despard's mantilla, etc. A selection of these is usually on public display. 'Behind-the-scenes' material includes many manuscript letters written by a wide range of militant suffragists, pamphlets, texts of lectures and articles, etc. To consult these, arrangements should be made with the appropriate curator well in advance. Note also that microfilm of the documents is held in the Fawcett Library.

LOCATIONS OUTSIDE LONDON

Bodleian Library, Oxford OX1 3BG
Tel: 01865 277000
Fax: 01865 277182
e-mail: bodley@vax.ox.ac.uk
Admission to non-members of Oxford University by prior application only, with academic references. Undergraduates of other universities are not usually admitted.
This is the Oxford University library; as with the British Library, it holds most material published in Britain, and much suffrage material is held there, but, again, may well be difficult to find unless the name of a relevant organisation or the author of a given work is known. One special collection that may be worth consulting is the John Johnson Collection of Ephemera (pamphlets, leaflets, hard-to-find periodicals, etc.). Otherwise it is probably better to use other sources when available.

The Cambridge University Library, West Road Cambridge, CB3 9DR
Tel: 01223 333000
Fax: 01223 333160
e-mail: library@ula.cam.ac.uk
Admission is free. Researchers will need a letter of introduction from someone of academic standing or a letter from a professional person – clergyman, doctor, solicitor, etc. – as evi-

dence of status. Undergraduates at British universities other than Cambridge are only usually admitted during the vacation. Applications should be made between 09.30 and 11.30
Monday to Saturday and 14.00 and 15.30 Monday to Friday.
Open Monday to Friday 09.30–19.15 (22.00 in Cambridge Easter full term). Saturday
09.00–13.00. Closed for one week in September.
This holds *The Vote, Votes for Women* and *The Suffragette*, but not *The Common Cause*, and is
excellent for anyone who wants to consult books and journals simultaneously. It is a deposit library
which should have one copy of all books published in Britain dating back to very early this century.
It also holds extensive newspapers and periodical collections including *The Victoria Magazine* and
many important nineteenth-century books and archives. There is a very good tea-room, and pho-
tocopying is inexpensive.

Ellen Terry Museum, Smallhythe Place, Smallhythe, Tenterden, Kent TN30 7NG
Tel: 01580 762334
Archival materials by prior arrangement with the Custodian only.
This theatre museum also holds papers of Ellen Terry's children, Edith (Edy) Craig and Gordon
Craig. The Edith Craig papers include much material relating to such suffrage organisations as the
Actresses' Franchise League and the Women Writers' Suffrage League. For specialist researchers
in these areas.

Girton College Library, Cambridge CB3 0JG
Tel: 01223 338897
Fax: 01223 338896
Admission by appointment with the Archivist.
An excellent source for the mid-nineteenth century; not only does it hold the papers of such pio-
neers as Barbara Bodichon and Emily Davies, but the Helen Blackburn book collection holds
interesting and useful material. Note: much of the Bodichon / Davies material is available on micro-
film at the Fawcett Library.

Glasgow City Libraries, Mitchell Library, North Street, Glasgow, Strathclyde G3 7DN
Tel: 0141 221 7030
Fax: 0141 204 4824
Admission free; make a prior appointment to consult archival material.
Open Monday to Saturday.
This is a very good starting point for researching women's suffrage in Scotland. In addition to the
Glasgow newspapers and *The Common Cause*, the Mitchell Library holds the Strathclyde Regional
Archives. These include papers of such suffrage-related organisations as the Scottish Women's
Hospitals and the Scottish Women's Temperance Association, as well as other collections con-
taining suffrage-related material, e.g. the papers of the Maxwell family of Pollok.

Manchester Central Library (Local Studies Unit), St Peter's Square, Manchester M2
5PD
Tel: 0161 234 1979/1980
Fax: 0161 234 1963
Admission by prior appointment only (Monday to Friday).
Holds organisational papers of the Manchester Society for Women's Suffrage, and a substantial
collection of papers of Millicent Garrett Fawcett.

People's Palace, Glasgow Green, Glasgow G40 1AT
Tel: 0141 554 0223
Fax: 0141 550 0892
Admission free.
Open all week.
This has a regular small but interesting display of women's suffrage artefacts, as well as women's
art work of the art nouveau period.

Index

Literary works may be found under authors' names. Page numbers in *italics* refer to illustrations.

Lightning Source UK Ltd.
Milton Keynes UK
UKOW04f1925021014

239566UK00003B/142/P